Justice Batted Last

Justice Behind Law

Justice Batted Last

Ernie Banks, Minnie Miñoso,
and the Unheralded Players
Who Integrated Chicago's
Major League Teams

DON ZMINDA

3 FIELDS BOOKS
An imprint of the University of Illinois Press

Library of Congress Cataloging-in-Publication Data
Names: Zminda, Don, author.
Title: Justice batted last : Ernie Banks, Minnie
    Miñoso, and the unheralded players who integrated
    Chicago's major league teams / Don Zminda.
Other titles: Ernie Banks, Minnie Miñoso, and the
    unheralded players who integrated Chicago's major
    league teams
Description: Urbana : 3 Fields Books, an imprint
    of University of Illinois Press, [2025] | Includes
    bibliographical references and index.
Identifiers: LCCN 2024039470 (print) | LCCN
    2024039471 (ebook) | ISBN 9780252046414
    (cloth) | ISBN 9780252088490 (paperback) | ISBN
    9780252047725 (ebook)
Subjects: LCSH: African American baseball players—
    Illinois—Chicago—History—20th century. | Hispanic
    American baseball players—Illinois—Chicago)—
    History—20th century. | Baseball players—Illinois—
    Chicago—History—20th century. | Chicago Cubs
    (Baseball team)—History—20th century. | Banks,
    Ernie, 1931–2015. | Miñoso, Minnie, 1922–2015. |
    Chicago White Sox (Baseball team)—History—20th
    century. | Minor league baseball—United States—
    History. | Discrimination in sports—United States. |
    Major League Baseball (Organization)
Classification: LCC GV863.I32 C4599 2025 (print) | LCC
    GV863.I32 (ebook) | DDC 796.35709773/11—dc22
LC record available at https://lccn.loc.gov/2024039470
LC ebook record available at https://lccn.loc.gov/2024039471

Contents

Photographs follow page 116

Acknowledgments

This book, which took well over three years to complete, would not have been possible without the help and encouragement of many, many people. I would like to recognize them here.

Finding the right publisher for a sports book that is a little more than just a sports book took a bit of time, but I am very pleased that it ended up in the hands of the University of Illinois Press. Many thanks to senior editor and project manager Tad Ringo, to acquisitions editor Martha Bayne, to associate acquisitions editor Mariah Schaefer, to cover designer Jennie Fisher, to content manager Kevin Cunningham, and to the many other people at the press who helped shepherd the project to completion. Special thanks go to copyeditor Jane Zanichkowsky for her meticulous, page-by-page review of the document.

I am extremely grateful to the people who agreed to sit for interviews, sharing personal and family stories as well as their knowledge of a subject.

- Former major league players Don Kaiser, Vern Law, and Ron Teasley and Hall of Famers Goose Gossage and Jim Kaat shared stories from their playing days that helped the book come alive. I am also deeply grateful to the late Hobie Landrith, the "personal catcher" for Sam Jones on three major league teams, for talking about his experiences with Toothpick Sam (unfortunately, not all of Hobie's wonderful stories made it into the book). Hobie is missed by all.
- In many ways the heart of the book is the information I received about early Black players for the Cubs and the White Sox (including minor league players) from friends and family members of these important baseball pioneers. Fabienne Anderson-Johnson shared a vast amount of information about both her father, Alvin

Spearman, and Alvin's lifelong friend Othello Strong. Shelley Arnold told many touching personal stories about her father, Billy Hart. Traci Carr was similarly helpful in discussing the life of her grandfather Charles Pope, the first Black player signed by the Cubs. Sarah Nicholson spoke to me about the life of her brother, Milton Bohannion Neeley (thanks also to Sarah's granddaughter, Jetaun Staley, for her help with setting up the interview). I learned most of what I know about the amazing life of Bob (Blood) Burns, an unforgettable character whose life merits a television series, through the help and generosity of his grandniece, Demica Williams. And Charlie Miñoso gave a son's valuable perspective about his Hall of Fame father.

- Much of the personal information about Paul Richards, the White Sox manager who was instrumental in the acquisition of Minnie Miñoso, came from interviews with his grandniece Michelle Foster and his son-in-law Bill McQuatters.

- Former UCLA basketball coach Gary Cunningham and former major league scout Artie Harris each provided a fan's perspective on Gene Baker, who was the Los Angeles Angels' shortstop when Gary and Artie were growing up.

- The story of Harvey Clark, who fought to rent an apartment in the all-white suburb of Cicero in the "Miñoso summer" of 1951 (and for many years afterward), is a key part of this book. Many thanks to *Chicago Tribune* columnist Laura Washington, who helped provide contact information for people who worked with Harvey's daughter Michele, and to Barry Hohlfelder, Joe Peyronnin, and Emmett Wilson for sharing their personal insights about working with Michele Clark at CBS.

- A number of writers and historians were generous enough to share their knowledge about people and subjects discussed in the book. These included Mark Armour, Marcos Bréton, Warren Corbett, Roberto González Echevarría, Gary Gillette, Leslie Heaphy, Thom Henninger, Bill Hoover, Sherman Jenkins, Bill Johnson, Rod Nelson, Scott Simkus, Dan Taylor, John Thorn, Doug Wilson, and Craig Wright. Ron Rapoport not only was very helpful with information about Ernie Banks, Phil Wrigley, and the Cubs of the 1940s and '50s; he also provided information about the papers of former Kansas City Monarchs owner Tom Baird. In addition to sitting down for a very helpful interview, Cubs historian Ed Hartig helped provide contact information for family members of several players discussed in the book. And Larry Lester's expertise on Black baseball is reflected throughout this volume.

White Sox vice president of communications Scott Reifert was extremely helpful with contact information for family members of Sox players—in particular, the Miñoso family.

A number of my fellow baseball writers and historians, all of them members of the Society for American Baseball Research (SABR), agreed to read chapters of the book and provide comments and suggestions. Many thanks to Alan Cohen, Gary Gillette, John Graf, Leslie Heaphy, Lee Lowenfish, Andy McCue, Dan Taylor, and Joe Wancho. Thanks as well to SABR, an organization that not only provides many tools that are invaluable to baseball historians and researchers (especially the SABR Bio Project) but also a vast membership of like-minded people who help one another in our work.

A major part of this book is the story of the early Black players in the minor league farm systems of the Cubs and the White Sox. I am extremely grateful to Gary Fink and Robert Schulz of SABR for their help with data about those players and for their invaluable help concerning the early years of baseball integration. And the writings of Brent Kelley, who has conducted more than 100 interviews with former Negro League players, have also been enormously helpful.

A book of this type requires extensive library research. Many thanks to the staffs of the National Baseball Hall of Fame, in particular, Cassidy Lent and Rachel Wells; the Chicago History Museum; the Chicago and Los Angeles Public Libraries; and the University of Kansas Library.

Throughout the long process of putting together this book, friends and family members provided wisdom, encouragement, and support. In particular, I would like to recognize John and Sharon Chornish, Coleman and Nadine Colla, Mitch and Donna Harrison, Brian Hayes and Deb Segal, Ron Klemp, Jack March, John and Jan McCarron, Terry and Emilie McIntyre, Rob Neyer, Meghan Sheehan, Bob Zaborowski and Anita Koch, and Phil and Peg Zminda.

And thanks as always to the "first team": my stepsons Steve and Mike, Mike's wife Nancy, our grandsons Matt and Sean, and most of all, my patient and ever-supportive wife Sharon. I could not do what I do without your constant love and support.

Justice Batted Last

1

The Comet . . . and the Riot

Frank Lane had done it again.

In his three-plus years as general manager of the Chicago White Sox, the 56-year-old Lane had earned nicknames such as "Frantic Frankie" and "Trader Lane" for the frequency—and sometimes the sheer impulsiveness—of his deals.[1] Earlier Lane transactions had resulted in the acquisition of second baseman Nellie Fox and pitcher Billy Pierce, both of whom would star for the White Sox for more than a decade, shortstop Chico Carrasquel, who would become the first Latin American–born player to start in the annual American–National League All-Star Game, and several other current and future major league All-Stars. But on April 30, 1951, Lane didn't simply make a trade; he made history. A little over four years after Jackie Robinson had become the first Black player for a formerly white major league team since 1884, the White Sox dealt for the man who was about to become their first Black player.

His name was Saturnino Orestes Armas Miñoso . . . "Orestes Miñoso" in most contemporary press accounts. He would soon become more popularly known as Minnie.

◆ ◆ ◆

Although he had played only 17 American League games since the Cleveland Indians had signed him in August 1948, Orestes Miñoso had already achieved a good deal of fame.

Born on November 29, 1923 (or possibly 1922 or 1925)[2] in El Perico, Cuba, Miñoso had been a local and then national baseball star in his native country before signing with the New York Cubans of the Negro National League in 1946. After two seasons as a Negro League All-Star, he was purchased by the Cleveland Indians late in the 1948 season. Sent to Dayton in the Class A Central League, Miñoso was an immediate sensation, hitting .525 in 46 at-bats before continuing to shine in the league playoffs. "Miñoso is not only good enough for the American League," raved Dayton manager (and former Indians star) Joe Vosmik. "If there were a higher league than the American, he'd be good enough for that."[3]

Cleveland's top brass seemed to agree that Miñoso was a special talent, but finding a spot for him in their starting lineup was a different story. After batting .400 in spring training in 1949, Orestes made the Indians' Opening Day roster. But after a brief 16 at-bat trial (with three hits, including a home run), he was optioned to Cleveland's Class AAA Pacific Coast League farm team in San Diego. Orestes played impressively for the Padres in '49, hitting .297 with 22 home runs. He was even better in 1950, hitting .339 with 20 home runs, 115 RBIs and 30 stolen bases. But despite those sensational numbers, the Indians kept Miñoso in San Diego for the entire 1950 season, not even bringing him up for a looksee in September.

To a degree, Miñoso was a victim of circumstances; until then he had primarily been a third baseman, and the Indians had an outstanding young third sacker in Al Rosen, who had hit 37 home runs in 1950, his first full major league season. The obvious alternative was to switch Orestes to the outfield, but as Mitch Angus wrote in the *San Diego Union*, "Cleveland has shown little desire to experiment with Miñoso as an outfielder. The general belief among the wigwam chiefs is that the Cuban is too unreliable to become a flyhawk." (Miñoso would later win several Gold Gloves as an outfielder with the White Sox.) Angus predicted that Orestes would be back with the Padres for a third season in 1951: "Although the Indians can't find a spot for Miñoso in their own lineup, they nevertheless regard him as too good to let go. . . . Cleveland, fearful lest it be embarrassed by Minoso's subsequent success, has pegged the price sky-high."[4]

The situation seemed made to order for Trader Lane, who had a well-known knack for working tirelessly to obtain a player he wanted. But for a while, Lane didn't seem all that interested in Orestes Miñoso—at least, not unless he could get him at a bargain-basement price.

♦ ♦ ♦

At the annual major league meetings in December 1950, Lane talked trade with Indians general manager Hank Greenberg, who was interested in acquiring one of Lane's left-handed starting pitchers, Billy Pierce or Bill Wight. During a three-hour session Greenberg made it clear that Miñoso was available as part of the deal. Acquiring Pierce, who was 23 years old and about to blossom into one of the American League's top pitchers, proved too difficult for Greenberg, so he turned his attention to Wight, who had gone 10-16 for the sixth-place White Sox but had an excellent 3.58 ERA. The teams could not agree on terms for a trade, however; after rejecting an offer of Wight for Miñoso and pitcher Steve Gromek, Lane instead dealt Wight to the Boston Red Sox. At that point, it appeared that Miñoso would not be going to Chicago.

But if Lane wasn't all that keen on acquiring Miñoso in December 1950, he would soon change his mind thanks to the new White Sox manager, Paul Richards. A light-hitting catcher (.227 lifetime) in a 523-game MLB career from 1932 to 1946—interrupted by several stints as a player-manager in the minor leagues—Richards was so highly regarded for his defensive ability and all-around smarts that he finished tenth in the American League Most Valuable Player voting in 1945, a year in which he had played in only 83 games for the World Series champion Detroit Tigers. When his MLB career ended after the 1946 season, Richards became a minor league manager. After leading the Tigers' top farm team, the Buffalo Bisons of the Class AAA International League, to the league championship in 1949 (Buffalo's first title since 1936), Richards became a prime candidate for a major league managerial position. Frank Lane was his hottest pursuer. But while Lane dearly wanted to hire Richards, the White Sox board of directors chose to stay with manager Jack Onslow, who still had a year left on his contract. So Richards accepted an offer to manage the Seattle Raniers of the Pacific Coast League for the 1950 season.

The PCL played a marathon two-hundred–game schedule, giving Richards plenty of chances to look at Orestes Miñoso. The more he saw of Miñoso, the more Richards wanted him on his team. "He had played just about every position for San Diego," Richards would recall. "I knew he could run and throw and hit. I think Cleveland was willing to trade him because they didn't think he could play a position." But when he pleaded with Frank Lane to trade for Miñoso at the 1950 winter meetings, Lane was lukewarm, sharing the Indians' doubts about Miñoso's defensive ability. Richards, who wanted to build a team based on speed and athleticism to play in Chicago's spacious Comiskey Park, persisted, insisting that he would find a position for Miñoso to play.[5] Eventually he wore Lane down. But there was one problem: Greenberg still wanted a good left-handed pitcher in a deal involving Miñoso, and, with Pierce unavailable, Lane did not have a pitcher who interested him.

It took several months for the pieces to fall into place. Miñoso had an outstanding spring for the Indians in 1951; sending him to the minors for another year in San Diego would have raised howls of protest. With rookie Harry Simpson, an African American outfielder who, like Miñoso, had had a big season with San Diego in 1950, also making Cleveland's Opening Day roster, the Indians began the season with four Black players: Simpson, Miñoso, Larry Doby, and first baseman Luke Easter. In baseball circles this was a potential problem. Four years after Jackie Robinson's debut with the Brooklyn Dodgers, there was talk about the danger in a team's having "too many Black players."

"The Indians can't keep Miñoso," an anonymous major league executive told *Cleveland Plain Dealer* sports editor Gordon Cobbledick. "They've got all the colored players they can handle. If we sit tight we've got a chance to get him at a bargain price." According to Cobbledick, the team that was most aggressive in trying to lowball the Indians in a deal for Miñoso was none other than the Chicago White Sox. "The offers came—notably from the White Sox, who make no secret of their anxiety to add one or two colored players to their roster—but the sums mentioned were a small fraction of Miñoso's value on the basis of his minor league performance," he wrote. "You and I agree, of course, that considerations of race and color are unworthy of the national pastime. But for the moment we aren't talking about things as they ought to be. We're talking about things as they are."[6]

Although Miñoso had been playing in either the Negro Leagues or in white baseball since 1946, he could do nothing to fight such treatment; baseball's infamous reserve clause essentially made him the property of the Cleveland Indians for as long as they chose. In terms of career choices, Miñoso could sit on the bench in Cleveland, spend another year in the minors, or go back to Cuba and work in the sugarcane fields. In the years before the Major League Baseball Players Association began to win expanded rights for its players under union president Marvin Miller, MLB teams had pretty much complete control over their players, including the freedom to discriminate against players of color like Miñoso. In his autobiography, Miller wrote about what he learned after becoming MLBPA president in 1966:

> The research I had done—and I had done a lot in the months preceding my first spring training trip—shocked me. Picture an industry where about a third of the players are black or Latino. And suppose from the time you began hiring those minorities (Jackie Robinson) to the time you finally hired one black manager (Frank Robinson), thirty-five years have elapsed. You might think that such an industry would have to have some kind of defense in the face of such shocking figures. Especially when one discrimination suit after another was being brought in other industries with similar violations. But in 1966, major league baseball was as lawless, in its own way, as Dodge City in 1876.[7]

In the spring of 1951 Miñoso's best hope was that Cleveland would trade him to the White Sox, the only other American League team at that time which was interested in adding Black players to its roster.

♦ ♦ ♦

In late April, Lane finally found a way to get Miñoso into a Sox uniform. After a marathon negotiating session, he worked out a three-team deal between the White Sox, the Indians, and the Philadelphia Athletics involving seven players. In the deal, the Sox sent starting outfielders Gus Zernial and Dave Philley to the A's, while getting outfielder Paul Lehner from Philadelphia. The Indians sent pitcher Sam Zoldak and catcher Ray Murray to the A's and got Lou Brissie, a left-handed pitcher greatly desired by Greenberg, from Philadelphia. And the Indians sent Miñoso to Chicago. According to Lane, he spent 36 hours on the phone in his hotel room consummating the deal, never getting out of his pajamas and stopping only to answer the door for room service.[8] But he finally had the man whom Paul Richards wanted.

Miñoso made his White Sox debut at Comiskey Park against the two-time defending World Series champion New York Yankees on Tuesday afternoon, May 1. Wendell Smith, the legendary Black sportswriter who was a key figure in helping Jackie Robinson make a successful debut with the Dodgers, introduced Orestes to Chicago fans that evening with part one of a three-part series called "Meet Miñoso" in the *Chicago Herald-American*. Writing in the same paper, Davis J. Walsh described "the formal presentation of a Negro playing major league baseball for Chicago IN Chicago for the first time" as a "quasi-historic event" and wrote of "the gifted Orestes" as "seemingly a man of almost mythical attainments."[9]

Meanwhile, Paul Richards was working to avoid any problems in the Sox clubhouse. At a clubhouse meeting prior to Miñoso's arrival, Richards told the team that the White Sox were going to have Black ballplayers and that Miñoso was going to help them. He said that anyone who did not want to play with Miñoso should raise his hand. No one did so, and Miñoso said that once he joined the club, he had no problems with his teammates. He became particularly friendly with Venezuelan shortstop Chico Carrasquel, one of the club's two other Latin players (the other was Cuban-born pitcher Luis Aloma). Miñoso credited Richards for the lack of disharmony after he joined the team.[10]

Richards put Miñoso at third base for the game, batting third in the Sox lineup against New York righthander Vic Raschi, one of the American League's best pitchers. In his first White Sox at-bat with a runner on in the bottom of the first, Miñoso blasted a 415-foot homer "high and far over Jackie Jensen's head to deep center field" to give Chicago a 2–0 lead. The homer electrified the crowd of 14,776, but the lead would not last. In the top of the second an error by Miñoso with two outs let the tying runs in, and the Yankees went on to an 8–3 win. A highlight for the Yankees came in the sixth inning, when rookie outfielder Mickey Mantle, playing in his 13th major league game, hit the first of his 536 career home runs, off Sox righty Randy Gumpert. Miñoso singled in the eighth to give him a 2-for-4 day; "the error," wrote Walsh, "was only mildly anticlimactic in view of Miñoso's startling premiere." Along with part two of Wendell Smith's Miñoso series, the evening *Herald American* included an interview with the legendary Satchel Paige, who raved about Miñoso's talents. "He's no rookie even if this is his first chance in the big leagues," said Paige. "He's the fastest there is, just like lightning. And he can hit that ball, too."[11]

The White Sox lost their first three games with Miñoso in the lineup, leaving them with a 6-7 record on the year. But then the Sox, who had posted a winning record only seven times in the 30 seasons from 1921 to 1950, began to click. Six wins in nine games from May 4 to May 13 (one of them a tie) lifted the team to third place with a 12-9 record. Beginning with a 9–7 win at Boston's Fenway Park, the White Sox won 14 straight games, the longest streak in club history since an American League record (since broken) 19 straight victories by the World Series champion 1906 club. Miñoso was the catalyst, scoring an astonishing 21 runs in the 14 games. Though he finished May ranking among the American League leaders in numerous categories, it was Miñoso's speed and daring on the bases that drew the most attention. Davis J. Walsh cited two examples of Miñoso's speed at Fenway Park during the win streak. Miñoso, on first base when Al Zarilla belted a long drive to left center during the first game of the winning streak, had passed second and was on his way to third when Boston center fielder Dom DiMaggio made a sensational catch. Miñoso had to turn back, retouch second base, and then race all the way back to first. Though DiMaggio made a strong throw in an attempt to double him up, Miñoso "still beat a very sharp relay with something to spare," wrote Walsh. "The chances are that not more than a dozen men in baseball history could have got away with that one." The next day, Miñoso startled the Fenway Park crowd—and Dom DiMaggio—again, this time tagging up from third on a flyout and beating "Dom's perfect, one-bounce throw from a mere 160 feet or so."[12]

White Sox coach Doc Cramer, who had frequently played against Negro Leaguers in barnstorming games, compared Miñoso to the greats of Black baseball. "He's out there hustling every minute," said Cramer. "And the guy's got his eyes open. He doesn't run just to be running, but he has an object to his scooting around the bases. He reminds me of some of those old time players like Martin Dihigo, Oscar Charleston and others. They were big league material."[13]

◆ ◆ ◆

Miñoso was not just the first Black player to take the field for the White Sox: he was the first Afro-Latino to play in the formerly white major leagues. Lighter-skinned Latin-born players had performed in the white majors since the 19th century and were often treated coldly, both because they spoke a foreign language and because many baseball executives, players, and fans suspected that they were less than 100 percent white. When the Cincinnati Reds signed Cuban-born players Almando Marsans and Rafael Almeda in 1911, the *Cincinnati Enquirer* assured its readers that the players were "two descendants of a noble Spanish race, with no ignoble African blood to place a blot or spot on their escutcheons. Permit me to introduce two of the purest bars of Castilian soap that ever floated on these shores."[14] The 1911 Reds were managed by Clark Griffith, who would sign a number of Latin-born players after becoming owner of the Washington Senators in 1920. It was a constant struggle for these players to win acceptance. Hall of Fame manager Bucky Harris, who had three stints totaling 18 seasons as manager of the Senators, summed up his view of Spanish-speaking players in 1940. "They're trash," Harris said. "They're doing no good and they aren't in place here. They don't fit. . . . If I have to put up with incompetents, they better at least speak English."[15]

The dark-skinned Miñoso was well-known among Latin American baseball fans, especially among Afro-Latinos, long before he made his White Sox debut. Future Hall of Famer Orlando Cepeda, a native of Puerto Rico, recalled listening to an All-Star game between Puerto Rico and Cuba in 1944, when Cepeda was seven years old. "He was so fast and played with such intensity that he had the old-timers talking in superlatives," wrote Cepeda about Miñoso. "Before the game began, they broadcast a foot race between Minnie and the great Puerto Rican speedster Luis Márquez. I don't remember who won the race, but I do remember becoming a devout Minnie Miñoso fan at the tender age of seven." Remembering the excitement created by Miñoso's 1951 debut with the White Sox and the continued brilliance of Minnie's career, he added,

> Believe me when I say that Minnie Miñoso is to Latin ballplayers what Jackie Robinson is to Black ballplayers. As much as I loved Roberto Clemente and cherish his memory. Minnie is the one who made it possible

for all us Latins. Before Roberto Clemente, before Vic Power, before Orlando Cepeda, there was Minnie Miñoso. Younger players should know this and offer their thanks. He was the first Latin player to become a superstar.[16]

Author and journalist Marcos Bretón, who has written extensively about Latin baseball, noted that Miñoso succeeded as a baseball pioneer while dealing with racial and language barriers. "I would put Minnie as one of the more significant players who've ever played major league baseball, both because of his Cuban background and because he was a Black man trying to make it in the United States in the 1940s and early '50s," said Bretón. "It was very racist; he experienced segregation and violence and hatred directed to him every day. And he had the added burden of having a language barrier because English was not his first language. . . . He was literally a foreigner in a foreign land."[17]

◆ ◆ ◆

The White Sox' 14-game streak finally ended with a 5–1 loss to the Athletics on June 2. After losing game one of a doubleheader to Boston the next day, the team ripped off six more wins in succession, leaving the Sox with a 32-11 record and a four-and-a-half game lead when the second-place Yankees came to town on June 8. Sox fans were so confident that the June 14 *Chicago Sun-Times* reported that the club had already received over 150 requests for World Series tickets.

When the Sox opened their four-game series against the Yankees with a night game on Friday, June 8, the attendance was a staggering 53,940. This was an all-time record for Comiskey Park, which had opened in 1910, and nearly 6,000 more than the park's listed seating capacity. Another 52,054 packed the park for a Sunday doubleheader two days later. By year's end the White Sox, who had never drawn a million fans to their home games in any season, had a total home attendance of 1,328,234, beating the club record by nearly 350,000. Among the 16 major league teams in existence in 1951, only the Yankees and the Indians, both of whom played in much bigger home parks, outdrew the White Sox in home attendance.

By this time, the White Sox had acquired a nickname that the team would carry through the 1950s: the "Go-Go Sox." From the time he was named White Sox manager, Richards had vowed to build a team centered around speed, defense, and pitching. With a lineup that included not only Miñoso but other speedsters like Jim Busby, Chico Carrasquel, Nellie Fox, and Bob Dillinger, Richards emphasized speed and daring on the bases. Miñoso led the way. "Miñoso's fast," commented Yankees manager Casey

Stengel. "He's safe on an error. He's safe on ground balls that should be double plays. He scores on short flies. He's safe going from first to home. All those things average up. All those things beat you."[18]

This was a daring style of play that had largely gone out of fashion in the American League. Unlike the National League, which now featured a bevy of speedy players, many of them Black, led by Jackie Robinson, the AL had become extremely pedestrian in the years since World War II. In 1950 no AL team stole more than 42 bases, and Boston's Dom DiMaggio led the league with just 15 steals—the fewest in American or National League history by a league leader. Paul Richards changed all that. The 1951 White Sox stole 99 bases, the most for any American League team since 1945; Miñoso led the league with 31 steals, with Busby ranking second with 26 and Carrasquel tied for fourth with 14. Comiskey Park fans would chant "Go-Go-Go" whenever a Sox speedster reached base, and the colorful team nickname was born.

Orestes Miñoso had also acquired a couple of soon-to-be familiar nicknames. One of them, "The Cuban Comet," had been used on occasion during his minor league days, but it now began to be used with increased frequency. Miñoso had also been called "Minnie" from time to time in the past, but by the end of the 1951 season he was almost always being referred to by that moniker. It took the *Chicago Tribune* some time to get with the program: For several weeks, the man causing all the excitement was "Minny" Miñoso to *Tribune* readers.

♦ ♦ ♦

It is sad, but not surprising, that as one of the American League's pioneering Black players, Miñoso often found himself being greeted with names that were much less pleasant. Minnie singled out the Philadelphia Athletics, who were managed in 1951 by Jimmy Dykes, the former White Sox manager (1934–46). "In those first years in the majors, some teams would call me names," he later wrote. "Jimmy Dykes . . . used to call me every name in the book: 'you black n___ so-and-so.' One or two of his players would go along with him."[19]

Dykes's Athletics attacked Miñoso with more than words. In a five-game series at Philadelphia June 15–17, Minnie recalled, "I was low-bridged a number of times. . . . I was nicked with pitches once in each game [of the June 17 doubleheader], but the aim of the A's pitchers was bad enough for me to get out of the way the rest of the day. I responded the best way I knew—I got 10 hits in 22 at-bats for the entire five-game series."[20]

While Miñoso was known for the fearless manner in which he crowded the plate, he, along with other prominent players of color during that era, was hit by pitches so frequently during his career that it is difficult not to conclude that race was a major factor. In the 11 seasons from 1951 through 1961, Miñoso led the American League in being hit by pitches 10 times; the exception was 1955, a year in which Minnie missed 15 games after being hit in the head by a pitch from the Yankees' Bob Grim (Miñoso ranked fourth in HBP that year). Black players also led, or tied for the AL lead, in HBP in 1949 and 1950. In the 20 seasons beginning with Jackie Robinson's debut with the Dodgers (1947–66), five of the top seven players in total hit by pitches were Black, with Miñoso (195) leading the way.

For the most part Miñoso responded to the frequent beanings by letting his bat do the talking, but sometimes it was too much even for the usually cheerful Minnie. After a pitch from the A's Carl Scheib on June 17 left Miñoso with a painful bruise beneath the left shoulder blade—necessitating a visit to a doctor—Miñoso lashed out. "You know, it's gotten so bad that I'm thinking of wearing a head guard even in bed," said Minnie. "Maybe somebody will throw at me when I sleep, too. I don't know what kind of baseball this is. Yes, you try to get a man out. You brush back. But you don't try to kill him. All I have sometimes is somebody yelling, 'Hit him right between the eyes.'"[21] A few weeks later, after being hit by pitches during both games of a July 4 doubleheader at Detroit, Miñoso asked White Sox trainer Mush Esler if he had any white paint in his medicine kit that he could douse himself with. He did so with a smile and everybody laughed, but as writer John C. Hoffman noted, "the implication was obvious."[22]

◆ ◆ ◆

Though their win pace had begun to slow, the White Sox entered the All-Star break with a 49-29 record, one game ahead of the second-place Boston Red Sox. The Yankees were two games back. Six White Sox players were selected for the American League All-Star team, including two starters: the double-play combination of shortstop Chico Carrasquel and second baseman Nellie Fox. Though he didn't make the starting lineup for the game, Miñoso was hardly being snubbed. With 1,261,394 votes in the fan balloting, Miñoso recorded the highest vote total of any nonstarter on either the American or the National League team. Unfortunately for Minnie, he was listed on the ballot as a left fielder, a position long ruled by Boston's Ted Williams.

While Miñoso and the White Sox were battling to hold onto first place in the American League pennant race, a different sort of fight was taking place in Cicero, a suburb less than 10 miles northwest of Comiskey Park. On June 8, the day the White Sox began their four-game series against the Yankees in front of record-breaking crowds, a Black man named Harvey

Clark Jr. and his family attempted to move into a $60-per-month apart-
ment at 6139 19th Street in Cicero. Clark, a 29-year old graduate of Fisk
University in Tennessee and World War II veteran who was working as
a bus driver for the Chicago Transit Authority, said that when he and
family—his 26-year-old wife Johnetta and their children Michele (8) and
Harvey III (6)—tried to move in, "they were kicked and beaten with night-
sticks and pistols by more than 50 policemen and 'told to move out of town
if they knew what was good for them.'"[23]

Clark responded by filing suit in federal district court, asking for
$200,000 in damages from the Town of Cicero. On June 26 Judge John P.
Barnes issued a temporary injunction against the town, warning it, "You
are going to treat these folks just like white people. See to it that they are
not molested." United States attorney (and future governor of Illinois)
Otto Kerner announced that he would look into "presenting the case to
a federal grand jury for violating the 1870 civil rights law, originally an
anti-Ku Klux Klan measure."[24]

As the National League was defeating the American League 8–3 in the
All-Star Game at Detroit's Briggs Stadium on the afternoon of July 10, the
Clarks, guarded by deputy sheriffs and Cicero police, succeeded in moving their furniture into the Cicero apartment. They then departed by car.
That night an angry crowd of about five hundred people gathered outside
the building. Cook County Sheriff John Babb, who arrived unescorted and
urged the crowd to disperse, was shouted down. When Babb drove away,
the mob easily overpowered the small number of Cicero police officers
who were on hand. They began throwing rocks and bricks, smashing the
windows of the Clarks' third-floor apartment. Two more nights of violence
followed, with Cicero police doing little to stop it as the mob grew to several thousand. Peace was finally restored after Illinois governor Adlai Stevenson summoned the Illinois National Guard, but not before the building
had been set on fire and the Clark family's furniture had been destroyed,
with damages estimated at more than $20,000. Many of the mob fought
with the troops. A total of 157 people were arraigned, and a Cook County
grand jury was formed to investigate.

Harvey Clark vowed to fight on. "If I should back out now, I would be
letting down the 13 million Negroes in this country," he said. "We can't
continue crowding, crowding, crowding into one small section. . . . Are we
to live in one room and watch our children grow up in slums? All we want
is to live quietly and raise our children right."[25]

Although the Supreme Court in 1948 had outlawed the restrictive cov-
enants that kept housing units segregated, what happened to the Clarks
was still a commonplace occurrence in the Chicago area (and across the

country). As for the all-white Bridgeport area close to the ballpark, the home base of five Chicago mayors, including future mayor Richard J. Daley and his family dynasty, Chicago-based journalist Natalie Y. Moore wrote:

> Black kids grew up intuitively knowing not to roam Bridgeport. If they crossed the invisible "no blacks allowed" sign at the border, someone might hiss "n___" at them. The White Sox baseball park offered the only safe place for Blacks to wander, because whites knew that Black spectators would return to their own neighborhoods after the ninth inning.[26]

When Minnie Miñoso arrived in Chicago after the trade from Cleveland, he was met at Union Station by a Black couple, Simon and Henrynne Lewis, who rented Miñoso a room in their South Side home at 6409 South Maryland; they accompanied Minnie, who did not know the way to Comiskey Park, to his first White Sox game via streetcar. The following year Miñoso would move to the Wedgewood Hotel, an 11-story building at 64th and Woodlawn that was partly owned by track and field legend Jesse Owens. Minnie was comfortable at the Wedgewood, which had long catered to such Black athletes and celebrities as boxing champion Joe Louis. Despite his enormous popularity in Chicago, Minnie likely would not have been welcomed at a hotel in a white area. When Larry Doby made his historic debut as the American League's first Black player in Chicago in July 1947, he had not been allowed to stay with his teammates at the stylish Hotel Del Prado at 5307 South Hyde Park Boulevard—at the time, an almost exclusively white area. "No coloreds allowed," he was told. The Indians had to scramble to find a "Black hotel" for Doby.[27] In the early 1950s Black players in the major leagues also had to deal with segregated hotels in Philadelphia and St. Louis, as well as in spring training in Florida and Arizona.

◆ ◆ ◆

When the White Sox resumed play after the All-Star break, their slump continued. From July 14 to the end of the month, the Sox lost 14 times in 18 games and dropped out of first place. During the tailspin catcher Gus Niarhos suffered a broken wrist, and the club recalled Negro League veteran Sam Hairston from its Class AAA Sacramento farm club. When Hairston pinch hit and stayed in the game to catch against the Washington Senators on July 21, he became the second Black player and first African American to play for the White Sox. A 31-year-old native of Crawford, Mississippi (at the time, his listed age was 28), Hairston had played for the Cincinnati-Indianapolis Clowns from 1944 to 1950. He was purchased by the White Sox on the recommendation of former Negro League star

John Donaldson, whom the club had signed as a scout in 1949. Hairston and another Negro League veteran who had been signed on Donaldson's recommendation, first baseman-outfielder Bob Boyd, had been with the Sox in spring training prior to the 1951 season before being farmed out. Hairston would stay with the 1951 White Sox for five weeks but get into only four games, with five official at-bats and two hits for a .400 average. Though he would have a long career in the White Sox farm system with impressive hitting stats wherever he performed, Hairston never played in the majors after 1951. However, he would continue to work for the White Sox for many years after his retirement, and he had two sons and two grandsons who played major league ball. Boyd became the team's third Black player when he joined the team in September (batting .167 in 12 games).

◆ ◆ ◆

The White Sox posted an 11-21 record in July, and by month's end the club had dropped to fourth place in the American League race behind the Yankees, the Indians, and the Red Sox. Chicago was basically a breakeven club in August and September (27-28), finishing the season in fourth place with an 81-73 record. While the finish was a little disappointing after the club's red-hot start, it was the greatest number of wins by a White Sox club in eight years. The Sox were clearly a team on the rise.

As the team struggled through the second half of the season, Harvey Clark was struggling in his battle for justice with the Town of Cicero. His family's case drew worldwide attention and sympathy. But when the Cook Country grand jury investigating the riots concluded its work in mid-September, five of the six indictments were issued to people who were trying to *help* the Clarks rent their Cicero apartment. The landlady of the building, her attorney, her real estate agent, an alleged "communist sympathizer" who was distributing pamphlets, and an NAACP lawyer representing the Clarks were charged with "conspiracy to damage property, deplete the value of neighboring real estate and incite a riot." The sixth indictment went to the Cicero chief of police for misconduct in office.[28]

Although there was some support for the indictments, there were also numerous protests of outrage across the country. "The wording of the indictments against those concerned in some way with the Clark rental indicated that the grand jury suffered from the same frame of mind that possessed the rioters," said the *Chicago Sun-Times* in an editorial.[29] Within 10 days United States Attorney General James Howard McGrath announced the formation of a federal grand jury to investigate the riots. In December federal indictments were issued against six Cicero officials; in the interim the Cook County grand jury indictments against those trying to help the Clarks were quietly dropped. As for the rioters themselves, a total of 59 people had their cases adjudicated in October. One of the rioters was issued a $25 fine, while another nine were fined $10 each. The remaining 49 defendants were found not guilty and dismissed.

The Clark family's legal battle would continue into 1952.

♦ ♦ ♦

Minnie Miñoso finished the 1951 season with a .326 batting average, second in the American League behind Ferris Fain of the Athletics (.344). He led the league in triples, stolen bases, and hit by pitches, while ranking in the league's top five in runs scored, doubles, on-base percentage, slugging percentage, and on-base plus slugging. White Sox fans celebrated his outstanding season by honoring him with Minnie Miñoso Day on Sunday, September 23. Among the gifts he received were a new automobile, a matched set of luggage, a movie camera, and $300 of equity in a housing apartment project (presumably not in Cicero). That night a dance held in his honor on the South Side drew a crowd of three thousand people. The crowd grew so large that it spilled out into the street and blocked traffic—a tribute to Miñoso's enormous popularity in Chicago. "The Cuban," wrote Chicago sportswriter Ed Burns, "is believed to be one of the greatest gate magnets the Sox have had in several decades."[30]

In a page one article in the September 19 issue of *Sporting News*, Edgar Munzel wrote that the Major League Rookie of the Year Awards, given annually by the Baseball Writers Association of America, were certain to go to Miñoso in the AL and Willie Mays of the New York Giants in the NL. "Even Joe Stalin couldn't be more certain of election in Russia than this brilliant pair of Negro stars is of topping the balloting on freshman honors," wrote Munzel. "They simply have run away from the field. And both are fast enough to do it!"[31] The publication, which issued its own rookie award based on a poll of sportswriters, gave its awards to Mays and Miñoso in the November 14 issue. While Mays easily won the National League vote in *Sporting News*, Miñoso, who received 122 votes from AL writers, was met with a strong challenge from Yankees infielder Gil McDougald, a white player, who received 100. According to *Chicago Tribune* sports editor Arch Ward, Yankees coach (and Louisiana native) Bill Dickey was conducting a one-man campaign for McDougald, whose numbers in most categories were dwarfed by Miñoso's. "Five years from now," Dickey complained, "a lot of people might not remember Miñoso. But five years from now McDougald will be the best infielder in the American League."[32]

When the AL Most Valuable Player Award voting was announced by the Baseball Writers Association of America on November 8, Miñoso finished fourth in the voting, which was won by Yankees catcher Yogi Berra. McDougald finished ninth. Yet when the organization announced its rookie awards a week later, McDougald was the choice, receiving 13 votes to Miñoso's 11 (Mays easily won the NL voting). Many were stunned, and the most vocal critic was Sox general manager Frank Lane. "McDougald is a good ball player. I don't want to take anything from him," he said. "However, his record doesn't compare with Miñoso's."[33] Lane noted that the rookie voting took place after the World Series and that McDougald had played a starring role in the Yankees' six-game triumph (currently all regular-season award voting is conducted before postseason play begins). He did not dismiss the idea that the voting had a racial element. "Could it be that some [of the voters] didn't know that Miñoso was a first-year rookie or were some of them prejudiced in other ways?"[34]

Was race a factor in the voting? The notion can't be entirely discounted. Unlike the National League, which was moving much more quickly to sign talented Black players and was honoring them frequently with MVP and Rookie of the Year Awards, the AL had only a handful of Black players in 1951. No Black player would win an American League MVP Award until 1963 (Elston Howard), and the first Black BBWAA Rookie of the Year in the AL was Tony Oliva in 1964. On the other hand, Miñoso *did* finish fourth in the MVP voting and would continue to rank high on MVP ballots for the next decade. Most likely the biggest factors in Miñoso's loss to McDougald were the facts that McDougald had played on a pennant-winner and then gone on to star in the World Series.

Whatever the reasons, Miñoso had been denied an honor he deserved, and he and the White Sox knew it. It was something that would happen to Minnie Miñoso a number of times over the rest of his life.

2

A Long and Winding Road

Long before Orestes Miñoso made his White Sox debut, Chicago was a major hub of Black baseball. African American amateur and semiprofessional teams in Chicago date back to the middle of the 19th century; the most notable of the early teams, the Chicago Blue Stockings, played and often beat white opponents during the 1870s, though they were denied admission to the state's Senior Amateur Championship tournament. The Chicago Unions, formed in the late 1880s by Frank Leland, played more than seven hundred games over the course of their 12-year existence and "dominated the amateur baseball scene in Chicago," according to author and historian Leslie Heaphy.[1] In 1895 they played a three-game series against the Dalys, one of Chicago's best white semipro teams and the Unions' fiercest rival. The Unions won two of the three games, taking the finale, 9–8, before a crowd of 3,600 at the South Side City League grounds.[2]

Frank Leland went on to organize the Chicago Union Giants in 1901 and the Leland Giants in 1905. Two years later one of the major stars of Black baseball, pitcher Andrew "Rube" Foster, became manager of the team as well as the club's booking agent. After winning the Chicago City League semipro championship in 1909, the Giants played a three-game series against the mighty Chicago Cubs, who had won three straight National League championships from 1906 to 1908 and then finished second in the NL in 1909 while winning 104 games. Although the Cubs won the first two games and were ahead, 1–0, when the third game was called owing to darkness after seven innings, the series was close and highly competitive.[3]

Though Leland and Foster were successful on the field, they soon became involved in a legal battle for control of the team. "Foster fought to get the team because he believed that Frank Leland was not treating his players appropriately," Heaphy said in an interview. "And most importantly, he didn't think that the players were getting their fair share of the money."[4] Leland was able to keep most of the team's players, but Foster won the right to keep the Leland Giants team name. He soon changed it to the Chicago American Giants—one of the iconic franchises in Black baseball for the next four decades. Leland's team, known as the Chicago Giants, continued after Leland died in 1914.

During the 1910s the Chicago American Giants were considered Black baseball's preeminent team. Taking on all levels of competition, the American Giants went 78-27 in 1911 and 112-30 in 1912. The club was so strong that in 1916, the *Chicago Defender* wrote that the American Giants "would make the White Sox look like a bunch of bush leaguers."[5]

The rise of the American Giants took place during a period of enormous growth in the Black population of Chicago and other northern cities as Black southerners moved north in search of a better life during the Great Migration. Between 1910 and 1920 Chicago's Black population grew by 148 percent. As it increased, so did racial tension, which erupted into violence on Sunday, July 27, 1919. It began when a makeshift raft, piloted in Lake Michigan by a group of Black teenagers, drifted near a South Side beach that was considered white only. Rocks were thrown at the group, and one of them hit 17-year-old Eugene Williams, who fell into the water and drowned. When police refused to arrest the man who allegedly had thrown the rock that hit Williams, the long-simmering hostilities between Black and white residents of the area turned into open warfare. When the Illinois state militia finally restored order after days and nights of brutal fighting, 38 people were dead and hundreds injured. Black businesses were destroyed in the rioting, and many Black residents lost their jobs, yet Black Chicagoans suffered most of the arrests and bore most of the blame for the unrest.[6]

For Rube Foster, whose American Giants had to postpone their return from a road trip as troops were bivouacking at their home field, Schorling Park, the 1919 riots were a spur to action. Historian Matt Kelly wrote:

> While Foster was enjoying considerable financial success with his American Giants, he remained frustrated by how fellow owners and players were being treated by booking agents. In 1919, he began writing a series of columns in the *Chicago Defender* in which he advocated the need for a Black professional baseball league that would "create a profession that would equal the earning capacity of any other profession . . . keep Colored baseball from the control of whites (and) do something concrete for the loyalty of the Race."[7]

"You have to understand it from an African American's point of view that sometimes white America says: 'These things will happen. Good things will happen, but you have to be patient. Let's wait,'" wrote Black baseball historian Larry Lester. "African Americans respond: 'I've waited long enough. I want it now. I want equal rights now.' And I think [Foster] had that type of attitude that said, 'I'm tired of waiting.'"[8]

In February 1920 Foster called a meeting of Black owners at a Kansas City YMCA, and the Negro National League was born. Foster became the league's first president. In order to help the new league achieve competitive balance, he permitted some of his players, most notably all-time great Oscar Charleston, to join other teams. Even so, the American Giants won the league's first two championships in 1920 and 1921. Physical and mental health problems necessitating commitment to an institution forced Foster to step down in 1926, and he was only 51 when he died in 1930.

With Foster's death, Chicago businessman (and future owner of the NFL Chicago Cardinals) Charles Bidwill took over the American Giants franchise. According to SABR historian John Bauer, "Bidwill seemed unsure what to do with his new asset"; several players left the team, and the franchise began the 1931 season as the Chicago Columbia Giants.[9] Midway through the season the team dropped out of the Negro National League, and the Columbia Giants finished the year as an independent team. The NNL disbanded after the season.

Though the Negro National League did not survive the Great Depression, other Negro leagues came into being, and the Chicago American Giants returned in 1932 and continued as a franchise into the 1950s. Over the course of the team's history, 13 players who wore an American Giants uniform were elected to a Hall of Fame, either in the United States or in Latin America.[10]

♦ ♦ ♦

Although 1931 was a disastrous year for both the Negro National League and the American Giants franchise, the year featured one event that would prove to be of great significance to Black baseball, especially in Chicago. On January 31, Ernest Banks, the second of 12 children born to Eddie Lee Banks and his wife Essie, was born in Dallas. Like all of the Banks children, Ernie was born at home; at that time, only one Dallas hospital—one not equipped to deliver children—would admit Blacks.[11]

As was the case for much of America during the Great Depression, life was a struggle for the Bankses, who had the added challenges faced by a large Black family living in the South. Finding enough food to feed everyone was a constant challenge. "We lived near a supermarket and we would go there and look in the trash can and get chicken, beef, ham hocks or whatever they threw away," Ernie recalled in 2004. "We would bring it to my mother, and she would fix it and make soup, make something out of it." When not taking care of things at home, Essie sometimes worked as a domestic for white families. Eddie washed cars, helped load trucks, shined shoes, and worked as a janitor, often leaving before sunrise and not returning until after it was dark. He also picked cotton, sometimes bringing his eldest son with him to help. "I understood work, and I picked cotton with my dad in the fall. I enjoyed that," Ernie recalled. "Whatever came up, I could adjust to it."[12]

Eddie and Essie Banks met at a baseball game, and the sport was Eddie's lifelong passion. He played catcher for a local semipro team, the Dallas Green Monarchs, and boasted about once catching the great Satchel Paige in a barnstorming game. Local fans thought Eddie was talented enough to play for a Negro League team, but he was in his mid-20s when Rube Foster founded the Negro National League and never got the chance. Eddie hoped that things would be different for his son. According to Ernie, Eddie would pay him a nickel to play catch with him and often brought Ernie along to be the batboy when he was playing in a game. "I didn't say anything to him," Ernie recalled. "You know, 'Why was I playing catch all the time with him and being the batboy for the team he played for?' I didn't ask him that, I just followed his guidelines. But he wanted me to be a baseball player. Later, I found that out."[13]

Two decades later, in Chicago, Ernie Banks would fulfill his father's dream.

♦ ♦ ♦

In addition to the success of the American Giants franchise, Chicago was the hub of Black baseball for an annual event that began in 1933 and continued for 30 years: the East-West All-Star Game. Usually played at Comiskey Park, also the site of the first American-National League All-Star Game in 1933, the game was played in front of crowds that grew to more than fifty thousand and often exceeded the attendance at the white All-Star contest. "It was an All-Star game and World Series all wrapped up in one spectacle," wrote Larry Lester.[14] Scouts and managers of white MLB team frequently attended the games, which featured many memorable contests. The 1941 game drew a crowd of 50,256 to Comiskey Park on a brutally hot day, with many more fans turned away at the gate. Two years later a record 51,723 were on hand as Paige started for the West against another future Hall of Famer, Leon Day. Ernie Banks of the Kansas City Monarchs was in the starting lineup in the 1953 East-West All-Star game at Comiskey Park. Although the estimated attendance for the game was a disappointing 10,000, scouts from many major league teams were on hand to watch Banks;[15] his contract was purchased by the Cubs a few days later.

Reflecting on his first East-West appearance in 1941, when he was 21, Monte Irvin remembered the excitement of being one of the centers of attention at the Grand Hotel at 5044 South Parkway, with the chance to see the likes of Count Basie, Ella Fitzgerald, and Billie Holiday at the local night spots. "You didn't go to Chicago to sleep," he recalled fondly. "But more than anything else, our games gave Black Americans hope all across the country. . . . They said, 'If these ball players can succeed under these very difficult conditions, then maybe we can too.'"[16]

◆ ◆ ◆

Negro League teams like the Chicago American Giants typically played more than two hundred games per year, only a third to a half of which were part of the official league schedule. The rest of the games were contests against a variety of competitors, white and Black, with the teams frequently playing games in two or three different ballparks in a single day. In the off-season, Black teams regularly defeated white major league teams and all-star squads; one study showed that of 438 recorded games between Black teams and white opposition over the years, the Black squads were victorious 309 times, a .705 winning percentage.[17] The success of Black teams against white MLB clubs became so common that baseball commissioner Kenesaw Mountain Landis finally limited the contests to games against white all-star clubs.

During the Great Depression, MLB stars such as Babe Ruth and Dizzy Dean formed barnstorming squads that often met Black opponents. During Dean's most famous barnstorming tour, which took place immediately after Dizzy and his brother Paul (also known as "Daffy") had led the St. Louis Cardinals to the 1934 World Series championship, the Dizzy & Daffy All-Stars played 14 games in 14 days against Black opponents. During the latter stages of the tour, the legendary Satchel Paige signed on to pitch for the Black teams. In one three-day stretch Paige pitched in all three games, hurling six perfect innings with 13 strikeouts in the first game and three two-hit innings with nine strikeouts the next day; he weakened on day three, yielding two runs in two innings, but Paige's team won all three games.[18]

◆ ◆ ◆

In the summer of 1939 Wendell Smith of the *Pittsburgh Courier* spoke with players and managers from each of the eight National League clubs, asking the question: What is your opinion of the Negro ball player? While the level of enthusiasm varied, representatives from every team voiced the opinion that the best Black players were capable of succeeding in the white major leagues. When Smith visited the Chicago Cubs—at the time, the defending National League champions—player-manager Gabby Hartnett told him: "There are any number of good Negro ball players around the country, and I'm sure that if we were given permission to use them, there would be a mad scramble between managers to sign them." Dizzy Dean, then a member of the Cubs with his career winding down, said: "If some of the colored players I've played against were given a chance to play in the majors they'd be stars as soon as they joined up. . . . Satchel Paige could make any team in the majors. I pitched against him in about six exhibition games and came out the loser in four or five of them." Other Cub players mentioned Josh Gibson and Mule Suttles as players who could be stars in the white major leagues.[19]

But the obvious caveat was "if we were given permission." In part one of his eight-part series, Smith wrote: "There is no written law which bars the Negro from playing in the big leagues. It is simply a 'gentleman's agreement' between club owners that the sepia player is not to be included. . . . Ford Frick, President of the National League, whom we interviewed not long ago, gave us the owner's side of this vital question when he stated that the complex social barometer of this country makes it impossible for the Negro player to crash the big leagues."[20] In other words, though Blacks might be qualified to play in the white major leagues, MLB players, many of them southern, wouldn't stand for it. Neither, the story went, would the fans.

Attitudes were beginning to change, however—albeit very slowly. Much of the shift was due to the relentless work of such Black sportswriters as Smith, Fay Young, Doc Young (no relation), Dan Burley, and Sam Lacy (who joined Fay Young on the staff of the *Chicago Defender* in 1940). Some white sportswriters were also speaking out: Smith mentioned Jimmy Powers, Lloyd Lewis, Shirley Povich, Bill Corum, and Dan Parker; in support were Bob Considine and Hy Turkin, and in Chicago, Warren Brown, Gene Kessler, and John Carmichael.

◆ ◆ ◆

One Black sportswriter willing to directly challenge baseball Jim Crow was Herman Hill, West Coast sports editor of the *Pittsburgh Courier*. In the spring of 1942 Hill accompanied two young Black players to Brookside Park in Pasadena, California, where the Chicago White Sox were working out. One of them was no stranger to that club. His name was Jackie Robinson.

Robinson, who was 23 years old in 1942, had grown up in Pasadena and attended Pasadena Junior College before moving to UCLA, where he became a nationally known multisport star. In 1938, while Robinson was still at PJC, his team played a spring training game against the White Sox. Robinson had two hits in the game and, even though he was nursing a sore leg, impressed the White Sox with his speed and athleticism. Sox manager Jimmy Dykes—the same Jimmy Dykes who would welcome Orestes Miñoso to the American League in 1951 with beanballs and racist taunts—raved about the young infielder, according to contemporary accounts. "The youngster is worth $50,000 of anybody's money," he was reported to have said about Robinson. After being told of the player's sore leg, Dykes commented that Robinson "stole everything but my infielder's gloves. I'd hate to have seen him with two good legs."[21]

By the spring of 1942 Robinson was far better known for his prowess at football, basketball, and track than for baseball. He was also about to enter the military. Nonetheless, Herman Hill wanted to see if the White Sox were willing to give Robinson a tryout. So he took Robinson and Nate Moreland, a former Pasadena Junior College pitcher, over to the White Sox camp. "Jimmy Dykes, manager of the White Sox, had once praised Robinson and said he was worth $50,000 of anybody's money," Hill recalled in 1970. "Dykes had even seen Jackie play semipro ball. But he blushed when [Robinson] came on the diamond. He refused to pose for pictures with Jackie and Nate. Several White Sox players hovered around menacingly with bats in their hands."[22]

Over the years, the chronology of Robinson's 1938 and 1942 experiences with the White Sox has become muddled, with Dykes's comment about Robinson being worth $50,000 usually portrayed as coming after his 1942 "tryout" with the Sox. However, the Pittsburgh Courier had reported the quotation by Dykes in 1940 (with Jackie being referred to as "Robertson") and 1941 (in an article written by Herman Hill). It is very doubtful that there was a tryout at all in 1942. Hill's article about the events in the March 21, 1942, Pittsburgh Courier is headlined, "Chi White Sox Reject Race Players: Jackie Robinson, Nate Moreland Barred at Camp," and the article states only that "the two players had asked for a trial with the White Sox team."[23]

Dykes's attitude toward the Black players has also been misrepresented. Hill's 1942 Courier article quotes Dykes as saying, "Personally, I would welcome Negro players on the White Sox and I believe every one of the other fifteen league managers would do likewise. As for the players, they'd all get along, too."[24] That makes him appear to be a racial progressive whose hands were tied, but the words are totally at odds with Hill's 1970 recollection of how Dykes and White Sox players had *acted* toward Robinson and Moreland in 1942. If Dykes actually said those welcoming words, they hardly carried much weight.

Whatever the exact details of the 1942 incident, the White Sox were not about to rock the boat when it came to the integration of baseball. With Robinson entering the army in the spring of 1942, the Sox would not have had a chance to add him to their roster until 1945; even then, the South Side of Chicago would have been a very difficult place for Jackie to break baseball's color line. "It would have been really tumultuous," said novelist and Northwestern University African American studies professor Leon Forrest. "Jackie said the cities that he caught the most hell in were Chicago, St. Louis, and Cincinnati. [His playing for the Sox] would have meant a confrontation of [Black and white] South Siders. As a youngster growing up on the South Side [Forrest was born in Chicago in 1937], I ran into some really rough gangs. And Jackie certainly would have caught hell from white West Siders." Nonetheless, said Forrest, "If he had come to the Sox, it would have been very dynamic. It would have brought [Chicago's race situation] into the open. In the long run, it would have been good."[25]

◆ ◆ ◆

One of the loudest voices shouting "Jim Crow Must Go!" during this period was that of a white man whose political affiliation made many people uncomfortable: Lester Rodney of the Communist *Daily Worker*. Rodney and the *Daily Worker* had been advocating for baseball's integration since the late 1930s. The drumbeat grew louder after the United States entered World War II, with Black soldiers fighting and dying for their country.

In July 1942 Brooklyn Dodgers manager Leo Durocher, a man who was never afraid to shake things up, told Rodney: "I know a lot of managers who would use Negro ball players on their clubs, but the owners wouldn't stand for it."[26] Asked to comment by reporter Joe Cummiskey, Commissioner Landis acted outraged and proclaimed: "I am hereby notifying all parties concerned that there is no rule—formal or otherwise—that says a ball player must be white. . . . It's up to the owners and managers to put their players on the field—the best players they can get—white or Negro. I insist there's no law now or ever against it."[27] At the same time, however, Durocher issued a new statement, no doubt at Landis's insistence. "I have no prejudice against any ball player on account of race or religion," Durocher told Tom Meany of *PM*. "As long as I am manager I will play the best 25 players I can get. Personally, I have seen only one colored player in recent years of major-league caliber. He's a shortstop named [Silvio] García, whom I played against in Cuba. I played against Satchel Paige and other fine Negro stars years ago, but I think these men are too old to play in the major leagues now."[28] This is the same Leo Durocher who three years earlier had told Wendell Smith: "I've seen plenty of colored boys who could make the grade in the majors. Hell—I've seen a million! . . . I would certainly use a Negro ball player if the bosses said it was all right."[29]

Landis's lip service to racial justice was met with derision in the Black press, particularly by the *Chicago Defender*. "The statement of Landis is about as empty as the promise of any major league manager to sign a Negro ball player," wrote Fay Young in a *Defender* editorial titled, "Judge Landis Decision—Bosh!" When the 1942 season ended with no progress toward integrating the white major leagues, the *Defender* issued a warning: "More, too, we continue to pour our money into the [white baseball] box offices without any return. The owners believe we are satisfied. Hurt their pocketbooks by staying away as long as the Negro ball player is kept out of the game and maybe we'll get somewhere."[30]

◆ ◆ ◆

One of the many white major league owners whose pocketbook was being helped by Black baseball was Philip K. Wrigley of the Chicago Cubs. Unlike the White Sox top brass, Wrigley was slow to open his park to Black-white competition. But that changed during World War II; money was a big factor, as MLB teams were hunting for revenue with most of the big stars serving in the military. According to Cubs historian Ed Hartig, about 25 games involving Negro League teams were played at Wrigley from 1942 to 1945.[31]

Two games that took place during the 1942 season may have opened Wrigley's eyes to the revenue that could be earned from games involving Black players. In May veteran promoter Abe Saperstein, founder of the Harlem Globetrotters basketball team, scheduled an exhibition game at Wrigley Field between Satchel Paige's Kansas City Monarchs and the Dizzy Dean All-Stars. Dean was no longer an active player, and the scheduled starting pitcher for Dean's team was the most sensational pitcher in the white major leagues: strikeout king Bob Feller. Feller, who was stationed at the US Navy base in Norfolk, Virginia, promised to donate his appearance fee to the Navy Relief Fund. It shaped up as a dream matchup between the game's two most charismatic pitchers.

Advance sales were brisk for the game, which would be held on Sunday, May 24. The paid crowd of 29,775 was larger than that of all but one American or National League game played that day, and more than 10,000 greater than the 19,198 fans who attended a White Sox–Detroit Tigers doubleheader at Comiskey Park. "Scalpers got several times face value for mere general admission seats," wrote Paul Dickson. "The real story of the game had occurred before it started, as thousands of fans, black and white, had lined up peacefully before the game to get a ticket."[32]

There was one problem: no Bob Feller. At the last minute, the Indians' ace had had his military leave cancelled—a decision that some felt was the work of Commissioner Landis, who as always was no fan of Black-white competition. It was a major disappointment, especially since Feller had planned to donate his fee to a military charity. So Dean, a popular attraction even years after arm problems had cut short his career, started the game himself for the All-Stars, working a scoreless inning; Paige lived up to advance billing by allowing only two hits and one unearned run in six innings. Future Hall of Famer Hilton Smith relieved Paige in the seventh and worked three scoreless innings for a 3–1 Monarchs victory. Writing about the game in the *Chicago Defender*, Fay Young pointed out that "the White Sox were taking a 14 to 0 licking in one game of the double header at Comiskey Park" and added that "brown American fans are baseball hungry but are sick of paying their hard-earned money to see second rate performers."[33]

Two months later, Paige was back at Wrigley Field. On "Satchel Paige Day," Sunday, July 26, he was honored between games of a doubleheader between the Monarchs and the Memphis Red Sox. This time the crowd at Wrigley was estimated at 20,000, once again easily topping the figure of 8,556 fans who were at Comiskey Park for a game between the White Sox and the Philadelphia A's. The Cubs, meanwhile, were playing in front of only 6,954 fans at Philadelphia's Shibe Park for a doubleheader against the Phillies. After the Red Sox had defeated the Monarchs in game one, Paige took the mound for game two, which was scheduled as a seven-inning contest. Satchel shut out the Red Sox for six innings. An error helped the Red Sox score two runs in the seventh, but he was able to close out a 4–2 Monarchs victory.[34]

The Paige-Dean matchup at Wrigley Field was such a success that Saperstein scheduled a repeat performance at Washington's Griffith Stadium a month later. This game drew 22,000 fans; an encore at Griffith in late June attracted a crowd estimated at 30,000. All this was too much for Landis, especially because the white teams were frequently losing to their Black opponents. Forcing cancellation of another Dean-Paige matchup scheduled for July 4 in Indianapolis, Landis banned all future matchups between the Dean All-Stars and Black teams, ordered white major and minor league teams not to use their players for Black-white matchups, and talked the US Army and Navy into refusing to grant leave for such contests to ball players serving in the military.[35]

◆ ◆ ◆

In December 1942 Cubs owner Phil Wrigley (misidentified in the piece as
William K. Wrigley Jr.) talked about the integration of baseball with William L. Patterson, a Black activist representing the Citizens' Committee
for Colored People in the Big Leagues. A Black reporter for the Associated
Negro Press attended the interview. Wrigley began by saying that "Colored
players will be in the big leagues—and soon," adding, "I would like to see
colored players in the big leagues." He continued,

> I know it's got to come. But I don't think the time is now. There hasn't
> been enough publicity yet. What has to be done is laying the groundwork
> for this by educating the public. What must be done is to get people talk-
> ing. If there was sufficient demand at this time, I would put a colored
> player on my team now.[36]

Patterson, a Communist who was speaking for a group that included a
Catholic bishop, two aldermen, and an attorney, responded that "the issue
revolved around bolstering the morale of colored people in wartime."
Wrigley agreed with the sentiment but reiterated that the public wasn't
ready for integration. "If colored are taken into the big leagues without
proper public support, I'm afraid some fights will take place if a colored
player rides high into a white player," he told Patterson. "What I'm afraid
of is a riot."[37]

Patterson wouldn't let Wrigley off the hook. He pointed out that football
and basketball games often included white players opposing Blacks, and
that those games had not been marred by disturbances. Wrigley agreed
but felt that baseball was different: "The temper of people in baseball is
very high." When Patterson mentioned that a committee of the Congress
of Industrial Organizations (CIO) had scheduled a meeting with Wrigley
to press the case of MLB integration, Wrigley said he would be happy to
talk with the group and added that he was an honorary member of the CIO.
He said that he "urged interested parties to push and extend the national
campaign for the inclusion of colored athletes in bigtime baseball." Of
course, the problem wasn't *him*. "They used to say that I wouldn't allow
colored teams on my field but last year Satchel Paige's All-Stars played
there twice," he said. "My ball players on the west coast play with colored.
Almost every year they have mixed games out there."[38]

The unidentified writer who covered the interview was sympathetic
toward Wrigley, writing, "That Wrigley is vastly interested in the question rapidly gaining momentum in baseball circles was indicated when

he invited other committees interested in seeing colored players in the big leagues to visit him." And he gave Wrigley the last word: "'My door is always open,' he said."[39]

A short while later, Wrigley agreed to a second meeting with Patterson, with Clarence "Pants" Rowland, president of the Wrigley-owned Los Angeles Angels of the Pacific Coast League (PCL), sitting in. According to Patterson, Wrigley asked Rowland if he knew of any Black ballplayers who were ready for the major leagues; Rowland responded that there were several but that the player with the most potential was Jackie Robinson, and that there "was talk of Jackie Robinson being acquired by the Los Angeles Angels."[40] This seems doubtful because Robinson was in the army by that time. However, Rowland subsequently told the *Pittsburgh Courier* and several Black players that they "were entitled to and would receive a fair chance" to try out for the Angels.[41] The *Chicago Defender* wrote that Rowland "has been observing Negro players this winter and is understood to have agreed to allow Nate Moreland, local righthand pitcher, to display his ability on the mound."[42]

But when four Black players—Chet Brewer, Howard Easterling, Olin Dial, and Moreland—attempted to try out with the Angels in March 1943, Rowland refused. His reason was that "a number of the farm clubs in the leagues of lower brackets throughout the country had folded with the war and they therefore had an overabundance of pastimers under contract. These players, Rowland said, had to be taken care of before any outsiders could be considered." Rowland tried to shift some of the blame onto the Angels manager, telling reporter (and former Negro League player) Halley Harding that they "would have to persuade Bill Sweeney to see the light, inasmuch as he (Rowland) did not want to cause team friction."[43] Understandably, what the *Pittsburgh Courier* referred to as Rowland's "rather weak-kneed explanation" did not go down well with Black players, writers, and fans. Nate Moreland, who played in both the Negro and Mexican Leagues after leaving Pasadena Junior College, was bitter about being denied a tryout by a Chicago MLB team for the second time. "I can play in Mexico, but I have to fight for America where I can't play," said Moreland.[44]

Throughout the 1943 season there was considerable pressure from writers and fans for the Angels and other teams in the PCL to sign Black players. The *Pittsburgh Courier* and the *Los Angeles Tribune*, two leading Black publications, threatened to take action if the PCL refused to hire Black players; when no tryouts took place, demonstrations and picketing took place outside Wrigley Field in Los Angeles (Herman Hill of the *Courier* was one of the picketers). "Yet the doors of the PCL remained closed," wrote Neil Lanctot, "and Wrigley turned his attention during 1943 to the All-American Girls Softball (later Baseball) League."[45]

♦ ♦ ♦

Although the Cubs' and White Sox' top brass were unwilling to challenge baseball's racial status quo in 1942–43, the game did include one maverick owner who seems to have been willing to do so. Bill Veeck was a Chicago native whose father, Bill Sr., had been a local sportswriter before being named president of the Cubs in 1918 by team owner William Wrigley; the elder Veeck held the role with great success until his death in 1933. After working for the Cubs during the 1930s, Bill Jr. put together a syndicate that purchased the minor league Milwaukee Brewers in 1941. His goal, however, was to own a major league team, and in the winter of 1942–43 he thought he had found his chance.

The team, the Philadelphia Phillies, was near bankruptcy under owner Gerry Nugent after coming off their fifth straight hundred-loss season. According to Veeck, his plan was to purchase the team and then stock it with Negro League stars. But he made a fatal mistake. "Out of my long respect for Judge Landis, I felt he was entitled to proper notification of what I intended to do," he wrote. "The only way the Commissioner could bar me from using Negroes would be to rule, officially and publicly, that they were 'detrimental to baseball.' With Negroes fighting in the war, such a ruling was unthinkable."[46] But when he got to Philadelphia, Veeck was told that the Phillies had been taken over by the National League and that the club had been sold to lumber and sports magnate William Cox for about half of what Veeck was willing to pay. "When I was in [Landis's] office, I had them purchased," Veeck would later say. "I will always believe Landis leaked our plans to [National League president Ford] Frick. Frick wouldn't talk business with us."[47]

The source for the story of Veeck's integration plan was Veeck himself, but the account in his autobiography contained several inaccuracies. In 1998 an article written by three respected writer-researchers of the Society for American Baseball Research found no contemporary confirmation for Veeck's claim and asserted that the story was not true. Yet *The National Pastime*'s debunking of the story was itself challenged by other researchers in subsequent years. The issue was examined at length by Paul Dickson in his 2012 biography, *Bill Veeck: Baseball's Greatest Maverick*. In a 10-page appendix devoted to the subject, Dickson presented all the evidence he could find on the issue, including his own research. Dickson's conclusion: "During the three years that I researched this biography, I came to the conclusion that Bill Veeck was telling the truth—not only on the Phillies story but on other matters of substance."[48]

♦ ♦ ♦

In November 1943, Sam Lacy of the *Chicago Defender* wrote to Landis requesting permission for a group of Black press and political leaders to speak about the integration of the American and National Leagues at the December meeting of MLB owners. Landis agreed to the request, but when the meeting took place in New York on December 3, Lacy was not included, and the spokesperson for the Black contingent was a man who was not a member of the original group: noted Black entertainer and former All-American athlete Paul Robeson. It was a controversial choice: Although Robeson was an eloquent speaker who could share his personal experiences about race relations, he also had strong political views, including pro–Soviet Union and anticolonialist stances. Lacy, who had expected to address the group himself, thought that the choice of Robeson was made by his superiors at the *Defender* and felt that it was a big mistake. "While I have the utmost respect for Robeson," Lacy wrote, "I feel he is definitely out of place in this campaign. The reason: Paul is generally regarded as having Communist leanings."[49] Soon afterward, Lacy left the *Defender* and returned to the *Baltimore Afro-American*.

According to the transcript of the meeting, however, the choice of Robeson was actually made by Landis, who opened the session by telling one of the Black spokesmen, *Defender* general manager John H. Sengstacke, "Mr. Sengstacke, I am interfering with your plans just a little. I have brought Paul Robeson here. . . . I have brought him on my own invitation." Robeson spoke eloquently to the group, which included Wrigley and general manager Jim Gallagher of the Cubs as well as Harry Grabiner of the White Sox. Robeson related his experiences as both an athlete and a stage performer, which often included Black and white performers working together without incident. "I have played in most of the parks, either in football or something else, all over the country," Robeson concluded, "and I sense a different spirit today. I hope that something can be done." After three other members of the contingent had spoken as well, Landis thanked the group, which then left. When he and the owners returned to the subject of integration at the end of the meeting, the only person to speak up was Branch Rickey of the Dodgers, who asked for clarification on what the owners should say about the meeting. After a few minutes of probing, he got Landis to say, "If any of you gentlemen want to hire a Negro player, you are as much at liberty to do that as you are to sign up any other player, be he in human form."[50]

History would show that Rickey took Landis's words at face value. For a brief period, Phil Wrigley showed signs that he felt the same way. Several weeks after Robeson had addressed Landis and the owners, Wrigley agreed to meet with two members of the Chicago Committee for the Integration of Negroes into White Major League Baseball. One of them was William L. Patterson, who had aggressively queried Wrigley about the integration of baseball a year earlier; the other was William P. Harrison, secretary of the committee. At the meeting, Harrison handed Wrigley a list of Black players who he felt could make the grade in the white major leagues; the list included future Hall of Famers Josh Gibson, Buck Leonard, and Willard Brown, among others. Wrigley expressed doubts that the players could immediately step into a National or American League lineup, telling Harrison, "You don't start at the top in any business." But he said that the Cubs would scout Black players. "Some say the woods are full of good Negro players while others say there aren't enough of them," he told Harrison and Patterson. "We don't know. Therefore we are going to find out."[51]

A few weeks later Dan Burley, sports editor of the *New York Amsterdam News*, a Black newspaper, wrote (citing rumors that "a major baseball story was about to break"): "The Chicago Cubs of the National League may be the first major league club to establish a precedent and hire one or more Negro players this summer." Recalling Wrigley's sympathetic comments about baseball integration and his agreement to scout for Black talent, Burley wrote, "[Wrigley's] coast minor league team had been consistently in contact with top Negro teams. Wrigley's expected step is thus viewed as the history-making move baseball is awaiting."[52]

The history-making move would not come until nearly two years later—and when it did, it was made by Branch Rickey's Dodgers, not Phil Wrigley's Cubs. It would, in fact, be more than a decade after his 1942–43 meetings with the Black activists before the Cubs would add their first Black player. Recalling his 1942 interview with Wrigley, Patterson wrote that "[Wrigley] knew the value of the perspective I had outlined—perhaps he saw a pennant or two in the offing. Yet he was afraid to commit himself. Here was a new angle—white racism could be a barrier to greater profits. And yet, business was afraid of the juggernaut it might create."[53]

In the meantime, it was business as usual in the white major leagues. After the meeting with Robeson, MLB issued its usual statement that "each club is entitled to employ Negroes to any and all extents it desires. The matter is one solely for each club to decide without any restrictions whatsoever."[54] What baseball people were saying in private was a different matter. "I heard the ugly talk made by Southern—and some Northern—ball players and managers," wrote Stanley Frank the day after the Robeson meeting. "Their intolerance and ignorance are frightening: the first Negro ball players in the major or minor leagues would be in constant danger of bean balls and spikes and they would be subjected to foul verbal abuse." And why pick on baseball, anyway? "Baseball people privately resent that their business has been made the focal point of agitation for elimination of racial prejudice," Frank continued. "They want to know why the problem is not solved first in more important fields such as medicine and education. The Army and Navy and industry are not meeting the issue squarely: why should baseball?"[55]

♦ ♦ ♦

On November 25, 1944, 11 months after the meeting with Robeson, Kenesaw Mountain Landis died of thrombosis in Chicago. One of the major obstacles to the integration of baseball was finally gone, and the opportunity for change began to grow. That change would come over the course of the following three years, and members of the Chicago press would be part of the fight.

Phil Wrigley's encouraging words notwithstanding, the same could not be said for the front offices of the Cubs and the White Sox.

3

Not in Our Back Yard

After the death of Landis, American and National League team owners appointed a search committee to draw up a list of candidates to become the next commissioner. Phil Wrigley was one of the committee's four members. When the owners met in Cleveland in April 1945, the surprise choice was someone not on the list submitted by the committee: Kentucky senator Albert "Happy" Chandler. In the meantime, the 1945 season was played with war-depleted rosters that were nicely summarized by the title of a book about the period by Kit Crissey: *Teenagers, Graybeards and 4-F's*. The National League champions were Phil Wrigley's Cubs, who lost the World Series in seven games to the Detroit Tigers. No one knew it at the time, but the Cubs would not return to the World Series for 71 years.

On Sunday, June 17, 1945, about seven thousand fans were on hand at Wrigley Field for a Negro League doubleheader between the Memphis Red Sox and the Cincinnati-Indianapolis Clowns. According to Fay Young of the *Defender*, "There were more white people at Sunday's game than at any Negro American League game this season." In the ninth inning of game one, a heated dispute broke out over the call on a play at third base; Memphis players stormed the field, and in the melee Red Sox third baseman Jim Ford slugged the umpire, Roy Young. A near-riot broke out, and nine policeman were needed to escort Ford off the field. According to Fay Young, it was the second time in twenty-one days that umpire Young had been attacked by a player at a Negro League game in Chicago; on May 27 at Comiskey Park, Walter Thomas of the Kansas City Monarchs had belted Young. "Fighting and rowdyism in baseball must go," wrote Fay Young. "Must the owners of major league parks crack down and say Negro teams cannot use the park unless the fist fighting is stopped?"[1]

This was too much for Phil Wrigley, who, as previously noted, had expressed fears about the danger of riots breaking out at integrated baseball games. Without formally banning Negro League games at Wrigley Field, the Cubs found a way to make use of the field undesirable for Negro League clients. According to Cubs historian Ed Hartig, the team had previously charged groups that wanted to rent Wrigley Field a fee of 15 percent of the gate revenue. But after the near-riot on June 17, the Cubs modified the charge to 15 percent of the gate or $5,000, whichever was greater. The $5,000 minimum made it fiscally impractical for Negro League teams to use the park, and the practice ended.

"The *Defender* was quite in favor of what the Cubs had done," said Hartig. "Fay Young had long said that the fans were getting way too rowdy and that the Negro Leagues needed a strong commissioner rather than a league president."[2] Other Black newspapers were also concerned about fights at Negro League games. The *Philadelphia Tribune* mentioned that a number of fights and brawls had taken place at Negro League games at Yankee Stadium, including one in which a patron had been stabbed 17 times.[3] If Wrigley had been thinking about integrating his team once the war ended, the rowdyism at the Negro League games likely put a damper on such thoughts.

◆ ◆ ◆

While Phil Wrigley was no longer talking about the integration of baseball in the summer of 1945, the subject was a hot topic elsewhere. In June Branch Rickey of the Dodgers and Larry MacPhail of the Yankees were named to a committee studying the issue at the request of New York mayor Fiorello LaGuardia. The chairman of the Mayor's Committee on Baseball was Dan Dodson, a Black sociology professor from New York University. Rather than working with the other members of the committee, MacPhail drafted his own four-page statement of opinion titled "The Negro in Baseball"; he sent it to the committee in late September. A few highlights:

- "It is unfortunate that groups of political and social minded drumbeaters are conducting pressure campaigns in an attempt to force major league clubs to sign negro league players now employed by negro league clubs."
- "The principal reasons negro players have not been signed by major league clubs are as follows: (1) Organized Baseball derives substantial revenues from operation of the negro leagues and wants these leagues to continue to prosper. . . . The Yankee organization, alone, nets nearly $100,000 per year from rentals and concessions in connection with negro league games at Yankee

Stadium. . . . (2) The outstanding negro players are under contract or reservation to clubs in the negro leagues."

- "There are few, if any, negro players who qualify to play in the major leagues at this time." For support MacPhail quoted Sam Lacy, "who says: 'I am reluctant to say that we haven't a single man in the ranks of colored baseball who could step into the major league uniform and disport himself after the fashion of a big leaguer.'"
- "If the major leagues of Organized Baseball raid these leagues and take their outstanding players . . . the negro leagues will fold up— the investments of their club owners will be wiped out—and a lot of professional negro players will lose their jobs."
- "I have no hesitancy in saying that the Yankees have no intention of signing negro players under contract or reservation to negro clubs."[4]

MacPhail's statement was distributed publicly, and although there was virtually no reaction to it in the white mainstream press, Black newspapers had plenty to say. Ludlow Werner of the *New York Age*, Dan Burley of the *New York Amsterdam News*, and Wendell Smith of the *Pittsburgh Courier* all wrote columns blasting MacPhail's statement. Most furious of all was Sam Lacy, whose comments had been used by MacPhail as ammunition for the continuation of Jim Crow in baseball. Lacy did not deny writing the words, which had appeared in the 1945 yearbook *Negro Baseball*. However, he added that they were taken completely out of context and were only the first words of a longer and much more nuanced discussion of the possibility of Blacks playing in the American and National Leagues. In the article Lacy had asserted that Black players, "given the same opportunities provided for white candidates, and subjected to the same program of handling and training, would develop into the same quality of player as the average white recruit." He had also noted that, "with organized baseball suffering from the dearth of talent brought on by the war, there can be no question that there are many players on top colored teams who compare favorably with the nondescript lot that makes up several of the American and National leagues' teams today." Lacy compared MacPhail's twisted use of his words to "Nazi propaganda methods of lifting phrases and half statements of American and British leaders" and using them "as ammunition for the guns of fascism."[5]

What MacPhail and most of the Black writers (Smith being a notable exception) did not know was that Rickey had confidentially asked Dodson to form the Mayor's Committee on Baseball and, wrote Jules Tygiel and John Thorn, "provide the illusion of action while Rickey quietly completed his own preparations to sign several black players at once."[6] While Dodson stalled for time, Rickey summoned Jackie Robinson to Brooklyn for their historic first meeting after sending Dodgers scout Clyde Sukeforth to meet with Jackie and evaluate him at a Negro League game at Comiskey Park in Chicago. Sukeforth was impressed and asked Robinson to accompany him to the Stevens Hotel (now the Hilton Chicago) on South Michigan Avenue, where he was staying, in order to get to know Robinson a little. (He had to slip some money to the elevator operator so that Robinson would not be forced to use the freight elevator to get to the room.)[7] Rickey settled on Robinson as his standard bearer.

On October 23 Rickey and the Dodgers announced that Jackie Robinson had signed to play with the club's Montreal Royals farm team in the International League.

And baseball went ballistic.

◆ ◆ ◆

While many people, white and Black, celebrated the Dodgers' signing of Robinson as a great day for baseball—and America—the reaction was quite different in the insular world of white organized baseball. Common critiques were that Rickey was merely bending to the pressure of New York's new antidiscrimination laws and that Robinson wasn't a legitimate white major league prospect. The *Sporting News*, the self-proclaimed "Bible of Baseball," wrote in an editorial that "Robinson, at 26, is reported to possess baseball abilities which, were he white, would make him eligible for a trial with, let us say, the Brooklyn Dodgers' Class B farm team at Newport News, if he were six years younger."[8]

Meanwhile, Larry MacPhail's comments to the Mayor's Committee on Baseball were suddenly being quoted at length in the white press and being treated as the sensible approach to "the Negro in baseball problem" in many circles. This reaction included numerous messages of support from other American and National League executives, especially those who received crucial park rental income from Negro League teams. Among them was White Sox vice president Harry Grabiner. "Believe that you have outlined the picture, perfectly, fairly and adequately," he wrote in a message to MacPhail.[9]

In the white Chicago press, the signing of Robinson was greeted positively for the most part—if noted at all. The *Chicago Sun* applauded the move in an editorial, writing, "Widespread support of Mr. Rickey's important step by the fans and general public will be healthy for democracy both inside and outside the sports world." The *Chicago Daily News* also supported the move in its editorial pages, writing that "Robinson has a unique opportunity to serve his people and advance their cause." In his daily sports column, John Carmichael of the *Daily News* wrote, "From this viewpoint it's just as well that Rickey decided to take the bull by the horns and find out whether (a) a good Negro player is good enough to play major-league ball and (b) what, if anything, will be done about it. There's no time like the present to settle the matter, one way or another." Sports editor Gene Kessler of the *Chicago Times*, who had long been a champion of Black athletes and who had worked as a ghost writer for boxing champion Joe Louis, was supportive of the move but cautious about the competition that Black players would meet from major league stars returning from the war. The archconservative *Chicago Tribune*, however, had no comment on the Robinson signing and ran only brief wire-service stories about the event (including one with the headline, "Rickey Calls Robinson Top Ball Prospect But Doesn't Think He's Big Leaguer").[10]

By the time Robinson made his debut with the Montreal Royals in April 1946, the Dodgers had signed four more Black players for their farm teams (John Wright, Roy Campanella, Don Newcombe, and Roy Partlow). A sixth Black player, Canadian baseball and hockey star Manny McIntyre, signed with the independent Sherbrooke Canadians of the Class C Border League. But in July the American and National Leagues established a committee "to consider and test all matters of major league interest and report its conclusions and recommendations." The committee consisted of the two league presidents and four owners: MacPhail, who was selected as chairman; Tom Yawkey of the Boston Red Sox; Sam Breadon of the St. Louis Cardinals; and Phil Wrigley. The committee looked into a number of issues, most of which concerned player relations. But when it issued its report to the owners at a meeting in Chicago a month later, it also included MacPhail's analysis of baseball's "Race Question."[11]

After praising "the Negro fan and the Negro player," MacPhail got to the heart of the matter. "The employment of a Negro on one AAA League club in 1946 resulted in a tremendous increase in Negro attendance at all games in which the player appeared," sometimes topping 50 percent, he wrote. "A situation might be presented, if Negroes participate in major league games, in which the preponderance of Negro attendance in parks such as the Yankee Stadium, the Polo Grounds and Comiskey Park could conceivably threaten the value of the major league franchises owned by these clubs." In other words, if too many Black fans come out to see a Black player at a white major league game, white fans won't want to go there. MacPhail then covered much of the territory he had covered in the document he had written for the Mayor's Committee in 1945, including the idea that "comparatively few good Negro players are being developed," once again misquoting Sam Lacy, that Negro League games were a $2 million business that also provided substantial park rental revenue, and that the Negro Leagues would be in jeopardy if white organized baseball took their best players.[12] (Regarding the comment that relatively few good Negro players were being developed, the Negro Leagues of 1945–46 included future white major league stars Larry Doby, Roy Campanella, Don Newcombe, Jim Gilliam, Joe Black—and Orestes Miñoso. All of them were in their early 20s or younger in 1946.)

In February 1948 Branch Rickey spoke about MacPhail's document in a speech at Wilberforce State University, a predominantly Black college. "A committee of baseball executives had been named to explore this situation [integration of baseball]," Rickey recalled, "and to draft a statement. Copies were handed out to all of us—and then gathered up again. The theme of that statement, as read by a chairman who I shall not name—and as agreed to unanimously by the clubs of baseball—I did not have the heart at that moment to fight it—was that the signing of a Negro player into organized baseball HAZARDED THE INVESTMENT AND ALL THE PHYSICAL PROPERTIES OF BASEBALL." Si Burick of the *Dayton Daily News*, who was in attendance, wrote that "Rickey hit that line hard."[13]

Rickey's speech, which became the basis for the story that white major league owners had voted 15–1 against integrating their leagues, with Rickey the lone dissenter, created an immediate sensation. It also produced a flood of denials from MLB executives, beginning with Phil Wrigley. Although there is no hard evidence that a formal vote to bar Robinson by the owners actually took place, the committee's statement undoubtedly reflected the sentiment of most of the clubs, including those representing the Cubs and the White Sox. And while MacPhail was obviously the person who was primarily responsible for the report, many were disappointed that the supposedly progressive Phil Wrigley was one of the four owners—all from teams (the Cubs, the Cardinals, the Yankees, and the Red Sox) that would be slow to integrate—who submitted it. "Wrigley went along with the mob mentality, with the pervasive thinking of the day," said author and Ernie Banks biographer Doug Wilson. "I think the most charitable thing you could say was that he was a man of his time, no more, no less. He did what most of the people in the mob mentality did. He went along."[14]

♦ ♦ ♦

When Jackie Robinson made his Brooklyn Dodgers debut in 1947, he became the first Black to play in the white major leagues since Fleet Walker in 1884. A Chicago baseball icon had more than a little to do with keeping baseball segregated over the course of those 63 years.

Author and baseball historian David Fleitz has called Adrian Constantine "Cap" Anson "baseball's first superstar" and "the dominant on-field figure of nineteenth-century baseball."[15] After making his debut with the Rockford Forest Citys of the National Association (the precursor of the National League) at age 19 in 1871, Anson spent four seasons with the Philadelphia Athletics of the NA and then became player-manager with the Chicago White Stockings when the National League began play in 1876. He remained a player-manager of the team for 19 years, leading it to five pennants while becoming the first major league player to accumulate more than three thousand hits.

At the height of their power in August of 1883, Anson's White Stockings, who had won the National League championship each of their three previous seasons, played an exhibition game in Toledo, Ohio, against the city's minor league franchise in the Northwestern League. Toledo's catcher was 26-year-old Moses Fleetwood Walker, one of the few players of color in white organized baseball at that time. Anson threatened not to play unless Walker was kept out of the lineup. The Toledo franchise stood by Walker, and manager Charlie Morton put him in right field. Faced with the loss of gate receipts, Anson backed down but vowed that he would never again take the field against Black players.

In 1884 the Toledo franchise joined the American Association, at the time one of baseball's two major leagues. Fleet Walker and, briefly, his brother Welday both played for the team, but many members of the league were determined to drive them out. They received support from Anson and his White Stockings; when Chicago played another exhibition game at Toledo in July 1884, Walker was forced to sit out the contest. Other protests against Walker's presence in the league continued, and the Toledo team released him in September.

Anson wasn't done. In 1886 and 1887, opposition from Anson helped derail attempts by the New York Giants to sign Black pitcher George Stovey (in both years) and Walker (in 1887). And in 1887 and 1888, Anson refused to let his team play exhibition games against teams featuring Walker. By the early 1890s, no Black players remained in the professional ranks. Cap Anson was hardly alone in working to ban Black players, but as Sol White, a historian of early Black baseball, wrote, "[Anson's] repugnant feeling, shown at every opportunity, toward colored players, was a source of comment through every league in the country, and his opposition, with his great popularity and power in base ball circles, hastened the exclusion to the Black man from the White leagues."[16]

◆ ◆ ◆

Robinson made his Dodgers debut against the Boston Braves on April 15, 1947. By the time he faced the Chicago Cubs for the first time at Ebbets Field two weeks later, he had endured a game against the Philadelphia Phillies that featured a tirade filled with racist taunts from Phillies manager Ben Chapman and his team, an incident which prompted Commissioner Happy Chandler to warn the Phillies that the harassment must cease.

Robinson entered the series against the Cubs in the midst of the first slump of his Dodgers career; he had been hitless in his preceding 13 at-bats while nursing a sore shoulder—an old football injury that he had aggravated while trying to make a throw to second base. The Cubs' starting pitcher on April 29 was Hank Wyse, a 29-year-old righthander who had led the team in wins in 1945 and 1946. Wyse, an Arkansas native, had no fondness for Jackie Robinson. "I remember the first game against him," he recalled to Peter Golenbock. "I don't remember who started [it]"—of course, it was Wyse himself—"but every time he come up, we knocked him down four times. The pitcher would stay in there until it was his turn to come up, and then they'd knock Robinson down four more times. So we changed pitchers during the game. Paul Erickson was the last pitcher, and the last time he came up, Erickson throwed at his head, and he went down. He got back up, and he stuck one in his ribs. All four times he got up, they knocked him down. All four pitches. He didn't say nothing. He just got up and trotted to first."[17]

Wyse was exaggerating, or perhaps boasting, here. Robinson walked only once in the April 29 game, recording three official at-bats while extending his hitless streak to 0-for-16, and Wyse himself did bat once. But Erickson most definitely hit Robinson. Robinson's slump continued the next day, as he went 0-for-4 against Cubs righthander Doyle Lade. He was now hitless in his past 20 official at-bats, and had hit the ball out of the infield only once in that time. There were no reports of beanballs in the April 30 contest, but Cubs players did their best to make Robinson feel uncomfortable. "Of course, we had a lot of southern ballplayers on the club at that time," recalled infielder Len Merullo. "A lot of them, they would make remarks. Hey, we had [Clyde] McCullough, Claude Passeau, Bill Lee, Dewey Williams, we had a bunch of them on that ball club, and they would all make remarks. I was there when he broke in, and you had to be there to appreciate what Jackie Robinson went through."[18]

Robinson finally ended the slump with a first-inning double against Cubs lefty Bob Chipman in the series finale on May 1. Because it rained for several days, the Dodgers did not play again until May 6, when they began a three-game series against the defending World Series champion St. Louis Cardinals at Ebbets Field. The series was played without any major incidents . . . but on May 9, the *New York Herald Tribune* broke a sensational story written by the paper's legendary sports editor, Stanley Woodward.

The gist of the story was that members of the Cardinals had formulated a plan to launch a general strike of National League players in an attempt to have Robinson banished from the league. According to Woodward, the plan had been formed by an unnamed member of the Dodgers. This was almost certainly outfielder Dixie Walker, who had unsuccessfully attempted to gather a petition from Dodgers players in an effort to pressure the team to release Robinson during spring training. The original plan called for the Cardinals to strike on May 6, the first day of their series in Brooklyn. "Subsequently," Woodward wrote, "the St. Louis players conceived the idea of a general strike within the National League on a certain date." Later research by Roger Kahn determined that the general strike would take place when the Dodgers made their first trip to St. Louis on May 20–21. However, Woodward wrote, Cardinals president Sam Breadon got wind of the plan before it could be executed and traveled to New York to inform National League president Ford Frick, who told the players, "in effect":

> If you do this you will be suspended from the league. You will find that the friends you think you have in the press box will not support you, that you will be outcasts. I do not care if half the league strikes . . . and I don't care if it wrecks the National League for five years. This is the United States of America, and one citizen has as much right to play as another.[19]

And with that, according to Woodward, the strike plans fell apart.

Stanley Woodward's story, and the question of how serious the Cardinals and other National League players were about striking to get Robinson thrown out of the league, has been the subject of furious debate for more than 75 years. One basic problem was that Woodward was reporting third-hand news: he'd heard the story from *Herald Tribune* writer Rud Rennie, whose source was Cardinals team physician Robert Hyland. Rennie didn't want to write the story himself because people knew he was a close friend of Hyland, and he wanted to protect his source. So Woodward wrote the story citing no sources and naming no players.

Writer and historian Warren Corbett, who investigated the incident in a 2017 article for the SABR *Baseball Research Journal*, felt that the most likely scenario was that Hyland heard some players talking about striking against Robinson and then told Breadon about it. Breadon informed Frick, who told him that the league would support Robinson and punish any strikers. Breadon subsequently met with Cardinals team leaders Marty

Marion and Terry Moore, who assured Breadon that the strike talk was just a few players venting.[20]

One Cardinals player who felt that the strike talk was serious was Dick Sisler, a first baseman–outfielder in his second season with the club. Sisler was probably more sympathetic to Robinson than many of his teammates; his father, Hall of Fame first baseman George Sisler, had had a long association with Branch Rickey and had personally worked with Robinson in the spring of '47 in learning how to play first base. "Very definitely there was something going on at the time whereby they said they weren't going to play," Dick Sisler told Jules Tygiel. He said that the planning was done by veteran players. "I don't think the younger fellows had anything at all to say."[21]

Stanley Woodward always stood by the essence of his piece, though he admitted that he was mistaken about Frick talking directly to the Cardinals players. Famed sportswriters Red Smith and Roger Kahn, who were colleagues of Woodward at the *Herald Tribune*, stood solidly behind their boss. In 1992 Kahn tracked down the 80-year-old Terry Moore, an Alabama native and the Cardinals' team captain in 1947. Moore, who was suffering from prostate cancer and, in Kahn's eyes, "an old man making peace with his conscience," basically confirmed Woodward's story. "I ain't gonna give you any names," Moore said. "That wouldn't be right. But most of us had got pretty worked up. Stan Musial was against the strike. I can't recall any others that were. Was other teams in the strike deal? Every other team in the whole damn National League except the Brooklyns."[22]

In 1997 the ESPN investigative show *Outside the Lines* looked into the subject as part of a special broadcast commemorating the 50th anniversary of Robinson's Dodgers debut. They were able to contact 93 of the 107 living players who had competed against Robinson in 1947. Six players representing three teams—the Philadelphia Phillies, the Pittsburgh Pirates, and the Cubs—said that their clubs had taken votes on Opening Day about whether to play if Jackie Robinson took the field for the Dodgers. Al Gionfriddo of the Pirates and Andy Seminick of the Phillies said their teams had voted to play. Hank Wyse, Dewey Williams, and an unidentified member of the Cubs said their team voted to strike, whereas Cubs team captain Phil Cavarretta said that the Cubs voted to play. Wyse told ESPN that Cavarretta "had a telegram saying all the other clubs would go on strike if Jackie Robinson played. 'How do you feel about it?' They voted not to play. It was 25 or 24 to one or something." Dewey Williams said that he and his teammates were waiting for a call from Dixie Walker stating that Robinson had taken the field; when the call never came, the Cubs played.[23]

More than 75 years after the incident, there is no clear evidence about exactly what happened. But even if the talk of striking to protest Robinson's presence on the Dodgers never advanced past the level of grumbling and vague plans, talk of such a nature was simply too serious to ignore. "Woodward's allegations, exaggerated or not, marked a significant turning point," wrote Jules Tygiel. "The account of Frick's steadfast renunciation of all efforts to displace the black athlete, following closely after Chandler's warning to Chapman, placed the baseball hierarchy openly in support of Robinson. In addition, the uproar created by the Woodward story dashed any lingering hopes among dissident players that public opinion, at least as reflected in the press, endorsed their opinions."[24]

◆ ◆ ◆

By the time Robinson made his first visit to Chicago as a member of the Dodgers on May 18, his season was looking a whole lot better. Robinson was batting only .227 when the Cubs-Dodgers series at Ebbets Field had ended on May 1, and he'd just snapped out of his 0-for-20 slump. "When Jackie first came up he had a tough time," observed Phil Cavarretta. "They jammed him so easy. He broke more bats. I feel there was so much pressure on this man that he wasn't playing to his true ability."[25] But from May 1 to May 17 Robinson had batted .351 while hitting safely in 14 straight games. There was no longer any question that Jackie Robinson could play in the white major leagues.

When the Dodgers and the Cubs took the field for Robinson's Wrigley Field debut on May 18, the paid crowd of 46,572 was the second largest for a regular-season game in stadium history, topped only by a game in 1930 in the days when overflow crowds were allowed to stand in the outfield. The crowd also numbered more than 5,000 greater than the 41,123 fans who would be on hand for the American-National League All-Star Game, which was held that year at Wrigley Field. There were no disturbances either on or off the field; in fact, a Cubs official called it "the most orderly large crowd in the history of Wrigley Field."[26]

Another 21,875 fans were on hand the following day, the second-largest crowd for a Monday game there in two years. That was typical of Robinson's drawing power in 1947. For the season, the Dodgers' 11 games at Wrigley Field drew an average crowd of 27,634; the Cubs' other 68 home games (the team played two tie games) drew an average of 15,818. Overall, total attendance at National League games in 1947 was 10,388,460, the first time either league had had a total attendance greater than 10 million. Much of that total was driven by Robinson and the Dodgers. For the year, Dodgers games drew more than 3.7 million fans, at home and on the road—more than 35 percent of the league's total attendance.

Given Robinson's success as both a player and a gate attraction, it was not surprising that other major league teams decided to sign Black players. The first was the Cleveland Indians, who were now owned by Chicago native Bill Veeck. On July 5 the Indians purchased 23-year-old infielder Larry Doby from the Newark Eagles of the Negro National League. Unlike the Dodgers, who had given Robinson a season in the minor leagues before adding him to the Brooklyn roster, Doby made his Indians debut the day he signed before a cheering crowd at Chicago's Comiskey Park (he struck out as a pinch hitter). Less than two weeks later, the St. Louis Browns purchased two members of the Negro League Kansas City Monarchs, 32-year-old outfielder Willard Brown and 21-year-old infielder Hank Thompson.

These signings were not successful, at least not in 1947. Doby spent the remainder of the 1947 season as a little-used substitute, batting just .156. While Brown and Thompson were excellent players—Brown was inducted into the Hall of Fame in 2006 based on his Negro League play—both got off to slow starts while providing no boost in ticket sales. Attendance in St. Louis, a city with many southern roots, actually went *down* after the Black players joined the team. Brown and Thompson were abruptly released in late August.

Shortly after the Indians signed Doby, two Chicago papers and the *Sporting News* reported that the White Sox were considering signing right-handed pitcher Gentry Jessup, who as a member of the Chicago American Giants often worked at Comiskey Park. Asked about the report, White Sox vice president–general manager Leslie O'Connor didn't deny it, saying, "I have nothing to say at this time."[27] Any interest the White Sox had in Jessup appears to have been fleeting. He remained a member of the American Giants, while the White Sox, whose roster included several pitchers older than the 33-year-old Jessup, finished in sixth place in the American League.

The Cubs' interest in Black players appeared to be more substantial. In September the *Defender* reported that a group of 150 players whom scouts for the Cubs would be watching in action included two Black players, second baseman Edward Harper and pitcher James Holmes. Both were members of the East Chicago (Indiana) Giants, a Black semipro team of some renown (it featured Satchel Paige on several occasions during the 1940s).[28] Nothing came of it—according to Ed Hartig, the two players couldn't make it to the tryout—but later that month the *Defender* reported that the Cubs had looked over several Black players, including future National League player George Crowe and future White Sox farmhand Gene Collins. The big news, however, according to the *Defender*, was that the Cubs were about to sign John Ritchey, the 24-year-old catcher of the Negro League Chicago American Giants, for their Class A farm team in Des Moines, Iowa.[29]

Ritchey, a San Diego native who had played on mixed-raced baseball and football teams at Memorial Junior High School and San Diego High School, had attended San Diego State College before joining the American Giants in 1947. On September 19 Ritchey worked out for Cubs officials at Wrigley Field. Club official Harold George told the *New York Amsterdam News* that Ritchey "did all right," that "he can move fast, especially for a catcher," that "he has a good arm," and that the Cubs were "interested."[30]

The Cubs weren't quite ready to close the deal, however; they wanted to see more of Ritchey before making up their minds. They figured that Ritchey would either be playing winter ball or, if not, would be willing to work out with their LA Angels farm club in front of a group of scouts. But Ritchey decided not to play winter ball and never did work out with the Angels. When he failed to respond to a request from the Cubs to let him know where they could see him play, Cubs Director of Minor League Clubs Jack Sheehan seemed to lose patience. Sheehan informed American Giants owner J. B. Martin, "Until we have seen Ritchey in action against real competition, I will not be in position to say whether we are interested in him and would advise that if you receive a proposition to your liking that you should accept same."[31]

As it turned out, another team in white organized baseball was quite interested in John Ritchey: the San Diego Padres of the Pacific Coast League, Ritchey's hometown team. This was something of a big deal, because up to that point the PCL had yet to integrate. After first offering Martin $500 for Ritchey's contact, Padres president Bill Starr discovered that the American Giants could not actually produce a signed contract with Ritchey. The team then contacted Ritchey directly and quickly signed him to play with San Diego in 1948. The American Giants—and the Cubs—were out of luck.

Ed Hartig noted that Des Moines, Ritchey's most likely destination if he signed with the Cubs, "was in Class A, while San Diego was a Triple-A team. I think maybe Ritchey saw that as a closer opportunity to make it to the majors. San Diego versus Des Moines, plus he's from San Diego."[32]

Though Ritchey posted good hitting numbers in the PCL and other minor leagues through the 1956 season, he never played in the American or the National League. "Johnny was a very sensitive guy, a real team player and when some of his teammates treated him differently, Johnny felt this intensely," said Ritchey's former San Diego State teammate Jim Gleason.

"I never observed hostility, but I did observe a coolness, a distance that was very apparent to Johnny. The smile on his face disappeared."[33]

By failing to sign John Ritchey in the fall of 1947, the Cubs may have missed out on a chance to have their first Black major leaguer. Given the hostility toward Robinson expressed by members of the Cubs that year, and the apparent willingness of some of them to strike in an effort to drive him out of the league, the sensitive Ritchey would likely have faced a very hostile clubhouse. Off the field, Chicago continued to be a hostile place for people of color in the years immediately following the end of World War II. In 1946, for instance, protests and rioting took place when the Chicago Housing Authority attempted to move the families of two Black World War II veterans into a Southwest Side housing project called the Airport Homes; author and historian Arnold R. Hirsch called the melée that ensued "comparable to Cicero's" in 1951. A year later, violence lasted for days at the South Side Fernwood Park Homes over another attempt to integrate a housing project. "Police unfortunate enough to get in the mob's way were struck by bricks and rocks," wrote Hirsch. "Blacks were hauled off in streetcars and beaten in a fashion reminiscent of 1919."[34]

John Ritchey may have been fortunate that he elected to stay in San Diego.

4

Beginning Their Journey

While Jackie Robinson was making his debut with the Montreal Royals in 1946, Orestes Miñoso was starting his US baseball career with the New York Cubans of the Negro National League. The club was owned by Alex Pompez, a 56-year-old Cuban American who had founded the team as the Cuban Stars, in 1916. Pompez, who was also involved in New York's illegal but popular numbers lottery, traveled frequently to Latin America to scout for baseball talent. He also had a network of scouts on the lookout in Latin countries. The team included Black Latino and African American players.

In the 1940s the Cubans were managed by José María Fernández, a native of Cuba who had been a star catcher and first baseman with the Cuban Stars during the 1920s. In the winter months Fernández managed and then served as a coach with the Marianao team in the Cuban League. Orestes Miñoso, who had made his Cuban League debut with Marianao during the 1945–46 season, made a strong impression on Fernández. He recommended that Pompez add the young third baseman to the New York Cubans' roster. Miñoso, who had never been outside of Cuba before this, took his first-ever flight from Havana to Miami, then took a train to New Orleans, where the Cubans had their spring camp.

Miñoso was the child of Carlos Arrieta and Cecilia Armas, a divorced woman with four children from a previous marriage. Although his birth name was Saturnino Orestes Arrieta Armas, he was known as Orestes from a young age, and he soon had a different last name as well. Developing a close relationship with his mother's first husband, Julian Miñoso—"He loved me as if I was his own," wrote Minnie—and Julian's talented ball-playing sons, young Orestes was often called "little Miñoso" when he played ball with his half-brothers. By the time his formal Cuban baseball career began, he was commonly known as Orestes Miñoso.[1]

Sugar was the main crop in the area around his hometown of El Perico, and most of the residents worked in the fields. Because of divorces and deaths in the family, Orestes often moved around, but his baseball talent became evident at an early age. Making a name for himself was not easy, however. While amateur baseball was very popular in Cuba, the country's amateur clubs were restricted to whites. "If you were Black, the only chance you had was on the semiprofessional level," wrote Miñoso. "Then if you were good enough, there was professional baseball. But your chances were very small, considering there were so few professional teams in the country."[2]

Orestes was talented enough to beat the odds. After playing for a semipro team sponsored by a Cuban cigar factory, Miñoso tried out for and made the Ambrosia Candy Factory team, one of Havana's top semipro teams. After winning the league's batting title, he joined another top team, the Cuban Miners, and had two more outstanding seasons. He was then signed by Marianao. Winning the Cuban League's Rookie of the Year Award in his first season, Miñoso received an offer of $30,000 for two years from Jorge Pasquel, who was attempting to sign American major leaguers, as well as talented Black players, for the Mexican League. It was a tempting offer, but Orestes wanted to play in the United States, and when Pompez and his Cubans came calling, it was on to New York.[3]

Playing in the United States was, at first, a difficult adjustment for young Miñoso; in 1946 he batted only .226 for the Cubans, who finished fourth in the Negro National League. With only a handful of Black players making their white organized baseball debut that year, the caliber of play in the Negro Leagues in 1946 was still quite high. The leagues featured numerous future Hall of Famers, including Larry Doby, Monte Irvin, and Leon Day of the Newark Eagles, Willie Wells of the Baltimore Elite Giants, Josh Gibson, Cool Papa Bell, and Buck Leonard of the Homestead Grays, and Buck O'Neil, Hilton Smith, and Satchel Paige of the Kansas City Monarchs. There were also a number of players who would later make their mark in the American and National Leagues such as Jim Gilliam, Joe Black, Harry Simpson, Al Smith, and Sam Jethroe.

Miñoso would be the only future Hall of Famer on the New York Cubans, but the club had several other notable players. Catcher Ray Noble and pitcher Pat Scantlebury would later join Miñoso in the formerly all-white majors. Left-handed pitcher Luis Tiant Sr. would not only have an outstanding career in Negro and Cuban League baseball but was the father of Luis Tiant Jr., who would have a brilliant career in the white major leagues beginning in 1964. And then there was Miñoso's roommate and mentor, shortstop Silvio García, who had been described by Leo Durocher in 1942 as "the only colored player in recent years of major league caliber."[4]

Playing for the Cubans with a number of his countrymen, including García, as teammates, the language barrier would not be much of a problem for Miñoso, and he soon came into his own. In his second season with the Cubans, he became a genuine star. Playing mostly at third base, Miñoso ranked in the Negro National League's top five in batting average, on-base percentage, slugging, on base plus slugging, and doubles, while earning a starting berth in both Negro League All-Star Games that year. Best of all, the Cubans finished in first place for the first time since joining the Negro National League. They then defeated the Cleveland Buckeyes, four games to one (plus one tie) in the Negro League World Series. (The series was played at several sites, including Comiskey Park for game 5).

With his superb 1947 season and a league championship in hand, Miñoso was beginning to expand his horizons. "With the integration of Major League baseball a reality," he wrote, "my ambition only increased. For the first time, I had a chance to be a big-league ballplayer."[5]

◆ ◆ ◆

If the Cubs, White Sox, and other major league teams needed any more evidence for how well Black athletes could perform at the highest levels of competition, they got a perfect example at Chicago Stadium on February 19, 1948. That night the all-white Minneapolis Lakers, the team that would become the National Basketball Association's first dynasty, took on Abe Saperstein's legendary Harlem Globetrotters, an all-Black squad best known for clowning their way to victory against inferior competition. The Trotters could play it straight when necessary, however, and they needed to do so against the Lakers, who were led by six-foot, ten-inch George Mikan, a Chicago-area native who was revolutionizing basketball as one of the game's first great "big men." The Trotters had no players taller than six-foot-three, and Minneapolis was heavily favored.

On a bitterly cold Thursday night before a crowd of 17,823—"The whole South Side of Chicago came out for that ball game," recalled Trotters star Marques Haynes—the Globetrotters stunned the sports world. After trailing by nine points at halftime, they prevailed, 61–59, on a long, last-second basket from Ermer Robinson. "For a brief moment, there was a hush in the arena, as if people could not really believe the Globetrotters had won," wrote Ben Green about the game-winning shot. "Then, as the [Chicago] *Herald-American* described it, the place went 'mildly insane'."[6]

With their win over the Lakers, the Trotters could legitimately claim to be the best team in basketball, with the skill and athleticism of their players evident to all. In a rematch at Chicago Stadium a year later, the Globetrotters won again, 49–45; one of the keys to victory was the play of six-foot, six-inch Chicago native Nat "Sweetwater" Clifton, who helped neutralize Mikan. When the NBA began integrating during the 1950–51 season, Clifton was one of the league's first Black players.

Along with owning and coaching the Globetrotters, Abe Saperstein also had a long history with Black baseball, primarily as a booking agent and sometimes as an owner. Five of the Trotters who faced the Minneapolis Lakers in the 1948–49 games—Goose Tatum, Ted Strong, Sam Wheeler, Wilbert King, and Clifton—also played Negro League baseball. The most notable of these, from the perspective of Chicago, were Clifton and Strong.

Clifton, who was born in England, Arkansas, in 1922, moved to Chicago as a child and grew up near Washington Park on the South Side, about three miles away from Comiskey Park. As a young teen he was a star softball player, and he continued to excel in athletics at DuSable High. After serving in Europe during World War II, he played semipro basketball before joining the Globetrotters. Although basketball was obviously Clifton's number one sport, he had a brief stint with the Chicago American Giants in 1949. Intrigued by Clifton's athletic skills, Bill Veeck convinced Indians general manager Hank Greenberg to give Sweets a tryout, and the Indians sent him to their Class C farm team in Pittsfield, Massachusetts. In two seasons in the Cleveland farm system, Clifton batted .307 with impressive power. Strikeouts were a problem, but his performance was exceptional for someone who hadn't played baseball since high school. But his baseball career ended when he got the opportunity to join the NBA.

Born in South Bend, Indiana, in 1917, Theodore Reginald Strong Jr. moved to Chicago's South Side with his family as an infant; the Strong family had witnessed the 1919 riots that took place after the death of Eugene Williams. Strong's father, Ted Sr., had played for Rube Foster's Chicago American Giants in the years before the formation of the Negro National League. After starring in baseball and basketball at Wendell Phillips High School on the South Side, Ted Jr. came to Saperstein's attention and began playing basketball for the Globetrotters at the start of the 1936–37 season; his Negro League baseball career began in 1937 with the Indianapolis Athletics, where his father was working as a coach. Strong continued to play both sports through the late 1940s, and his Negro League baseball career was exceptional: a five-time All-Star, he was a key member of three Negro League championship teams with the Monarchs.

In another time, Ted Strong might have had a long career as a star outfielder with the White Sox, and Nat Clifton might have been a power-hitting first baseman. Of course, Clifton's primary game was basketball, and Strong was 30 years old by the time Jackie Robinson made his Brooklyn Dodgers debut. Yet there was plenty of Black baseball talent on the

South Side alone that the White Sox never bothered to scout during the late 1940s. To cite two obvious examples, Ted Strong's younger brother Othello, who had a stellar athletic career at Wendell Phillips High School and then spent a couple of seasons playing for the Harlem Globetrotters baseball team, never got a look from the White Sox. Neither did Othello's lifelong friend and fellow Chicago high school star Alvin Spearman. Both players, who were in their early 20s in 1947–48, wound up pitching for the Chicago American Giants (they would get very minimal trials in the White Sox farm system a few years later). There is no record that the Cubs scouted these players, either.

The final kicker was that Abe Saperstein, who lived in Chicago and who knew the world of Black athletics as well as anyone and could have been a big help to the White Sox or Cubs, instead used his expertise to help the Cleveland Indians, whose president was Chicagoan Bill Veeck. As was the case with the Dodgers in the National League, the Indians' aggressiveness in scouting and signing Black players helped them become a powerful club and remain one well into the 1950s.

Meanwhile, the White Sox and Cubs continued to flounder.

◆ ◆ ◆

A few weeks after the Globetrotters' historic victory over the Lakers, the White Sox and the Cubs headed to spring training in California. Al Vaughn of the *Chicago Star*, a leftist weekly whose board of directors included William L. Patterson, sarcastically reviewed the teams' offseason player transactions. "The Cubs have traded Bob Sturgeon, a .250 batting second baseman, for slugging Dick Culler, a .250 batting shortstop who couldn't even make it with the woefully weak White Sox," wrote Vaughn. "The Negro leagues apparently play eight men on a team, no shortstop, since the Cubs could not find one worthy of a tryout." Turning to the White Sox, Vaughn noted that the team had traded its winningest pitcher, Ed Lopat, to the Yankees for catcher Aaron Robinson (the Sox also got pitchers Bill Wight and Fred Bradley in the deal). "The Sox so desperately in need of a catcher never found time to give [one to] young John Ritchey, former Chicago American Giant star catcher," he continued. "Now that Lopat is gone it would seem that the fair and unbiased Sox management would jump at the chance to give Gentry Jessup, the American Giant star pitcher, an opportunity to plug the hole made by the departure of Lopat. However, at the time of this writing, the Sox have not mentioned Jessup." He concluded by writing that while politicians were saying that "It is the duty of America to keep the world free, . . . right here in Chicago these teams are trying to exclude 10% of our population from Major League baseball because of their color." He called on Chicago baseball fans to "go to work and demand what in our hearts we know is right."[7]

Sadly, the White Sox and the Cubs were part of the clear majority of American and National League teams who had yet to show much interest in integrating their clubs. When the 1947 season ended, there were only three Black players in the AL and the NL: Robinson and Dan Bankhead with the Dodgers, and Larry Doby with the Indians. When the 1948 season began, there were still only three, with the same two teams: Robinson, Doby, and Roy Campanella, whom the Dodgers would send back to the minors after three games in April. Doby, who was converted to the outfield after spending most of his Negro League career at second base, batted .301 with 14 homers and was a key contributor to the Indians' 1948 World Series championship. Robinson, making his own switch in positions from first base to second, had another excellent year, hitting .296 with 85 RBIs and 108 runs scored. After a couple of months in St. Paul, where he became the first Black player in the Class AAA American Association, Campanella returned to Brooklyn in July and soon established himself as the best catcher in baseball.

That same month, Bill Veeck made his boldest move to date: he signed the legendary Satchel Paige to pitch for the Indians. (The deal was negotiated through Abe Saperstein, who was Paige's booking agent and who pocketed a $15,000 commission.)[8] Paige, whose real age had always been a mystery, turned 42 in July 1948 according to most reliable sources. Many thought he was as old as 50, and the move was widely panned. In an editorial in *Sporting News*, publisher J. G. Taylor Spink, after carefully noting that his criticism "obviously is not based on Paige's color," wrote,

> To sign a hurler at Paige's age is to demean the standard of baseball in the big circuits. Further complicating the situation is the suspicion that if Satchel were white, he would not have drawn a second thought from Veeck.
> William Harridge, president of the American League, would have been well within his rights if he had refused to approve the Paige contract.[9]

In response, Veeck pointed out that the Indians were fighting for a pennant in 1948 and "had foolishly believed that nobody could possibly accuse me of signing Paige for a gag." As for Spink's editorial, he wrote that "If Satch were white, of course, he would have been in the majors twenty-five years earlier, and the question would not have been before the House."[10]

Veeck had the last laugh. Used both as a starter and in relief by Lou Boudreau, Paige was a major contributor to Cleveland's successful drive to a championship. His seven starts were major events that drew enormous crowds. Two of them were back-to-back outings against the White Sox in August. The first, a night game on August 13 at Comiskey Park, drew a paid crowd of 51,013, a park record for a night game. An estimated 15,000 more fans had to be turned away. At one of the entrances the pressure of the crowd was so intense that the gate collapsed and hundreds of fans poured into the park, uncounted by the turnstiles. (The author's father, who attended the game, said that his seat was a step in one of the aisles.) Rising to the occasion as he had done so often in the past, Paige shut out the White Sox on five hits, 5–0. One week later he faced the Sox again at Cleveland's mammoth Municipal Stadium before 78,382 fans—and pitched another shutout, this time a 1–0 three-hitter in an hour and 50 minutes. Overall, Paige's seven starts in 1948 (three at home, four on the road) drew a total of 336,767 fans, for an average of more than 48,000 per game.

While Paige was filling seats and helping the Indians win a championship, the White Sox and the Cubs were both finishing last in their respective leagues—the first time in Chicago history that this had ever happened. In a *Sporting News* article on the plight of the White Sox, *Chicago Tribune* writer Ed Burns offered a number of suggestions for improving the team, beginning with selling the franchise to "a syndicate of millionaires." None of Burns's suggestions involved scouting or signing Black players.[11]

Other writers were not afraid to broach the subject. "Negro and white fans who have been loyal to the Chicago American League club want a winning ball club," wrote William Warren in a *Defender* article titled "White Sox Need Negro Players Like Larry Doby!" He continued: "These fans want to know why the Comiskey family plus Leslie O'Connor, the major domo of the organization[,] doesn't get the color line out of the White Sox front office and hire one or two good Negro ball players who might make this team a first class outfit." Another Black newspaper, the *Atlanta Daily World*, commented, "Despite the wealth of Negro baseball talent available which might pump life into a jaded baseball machine, the White Sox have scorned them to vie with the St. Louis Browns, the most lowly, hated and scorned team in the league."[12]

While Chicago's white press generally avoided the subject of integration, one writer who refused to do so was Gene Kessler of the *Sun-Times*, who was no longer worrying that there might be a scarcity of good Black players. After pointing out in an August column how much Larry Doby had helped the Cleveland Indians, Kessler wrote, "Now if the Cubs really are energetic, they can get a double-play combination from the Birmingham Barons in Art Wilson at short and Lorenzo (Piper) Davis at second which will really help them get out of the cellar. These Negro infielders are far superior to anything the Cubs have now."[13]

In response, White Sox and Cubs executives insisted that they *were* scouting Black ballplayers. "The Cubs now have their scouts looking over promising Negro players," wrote Kessler in early September. "Perhaps Jackie Robinson and Roy Campanella opened the Cubs' eyes with their drawing power at the gate." In a longer article for Kessler's paper, John C. Hoffman wrote, "The White Sox are on the hunt for Negro ball players but … 'They're hard to find,' says General Manager Les O'Connor." According to O'Connor, "We have the same trouble with them as we do with many white players. They don't want to take their chances in the minors." He said he wanted to avoid the mistake the St. Louis Browns had made in 1947, when they signed Willard Brown and Hank Thompson "and then had to release them because they weren't ready for the majors."[14]

O'Connor's comments were almost entirely nonsensical, beginning with the notion that few Black players were capable of succeeding in the American or the National League. He should also have known that there were a number of former Negro Leaguers playing in the minor leagues during the 1948 season, including future two-time All-Star Al Smith, 1950 National League Rookie of the Year Sam Jethroe, and future Rookie of the Year, Most Valuable Player, and Cy Young Award winner Don Newcombe, who was completing his third season in the Dodgers farm system. The *Sporting News* reported in October that the Cubs contacted Branch Rickey about purchasing the 22-year-old Newcombe, who had won 17 games for the Dodgers' Montreal farm club. They lost interest when Rickey put a $500,000 price tag on Newcombe.[15]

◆ ◆ ◆

If the White Sox and the Cubs were beginning to show interest in—or at least curiosity about—Black players during this time, they were not alone. But the scouts who were evaluating Negro Leaguers seemed to share the Chicago teams' skepticism about the players' ability to succeed in the white majors. One of them was Frank "Bots" Nekola, a former Yankees and Tigers pitcher who was beginning a long association with the Boston Red Sox; Nekola would sign a number of quality players for Boston in future years, most notably Hall of Famer Carl Yastrzemski. But when he scouted Negro League players in 1948 at the second East-West All-Star Game at Yankee Stadium, his evaluations were largely unenthusiastic. While raving about the talents of Luke Easter, who would go on to become a fearsome power hitter with the Cleveland Indians, Nekola had other concerns. "Easter has all the requisites for greatness," Nekola wrote. But then he added, "I understand his disposition handicaps him considerably,"[16] the sort of dismissive evaluation likely to be given to independent-minded Black players. (In Easter's case, the accusation was totally unwarranted, as he fit in comfortably with his white teammates after joining the Indians; Cleveland star Al Rosen described Easter as a "great big, easy going, devil-may-care jolly, hail fellow well met kind of guy," and pitcher Mike Garcia called him "a real likeable guy.")[17] Nekola reserved his best comments for Luis Márquez and Orestes Miñoso, though he did not predict stardom (he also had trouble spelling their names): "Marguez and Minosa are speed demons—they field well and throw good. I believe they would do a fair job in Big League ball."[18]

The New York Yankees were also compiling scouting reports about Negro League players in 1948, mostly with even less enthusiasm than Nekola. According to an unsigned set of reports made by Yankees minor league scouts, future New York Giants star (and Hall of Famer) Monte Irvin had a "poor arm, runs only fair; not majors." Future National League Rookie of the Year Joe Black had "only fair stuff." Another future Rookie of the year, Jim Gilliam, "looked fair all around." Luke Easter "can be pitched to." Harry Simpson, who would spend nearly a decade in the American League, was a "poor fielder, hits fair." The best reports were for two members of the New York Cubans, Miñoso (spelled "Menosa" in the report) and first baseman Lorenzo Cabrera ("Carrabella"). Both earned the comment, "recommend another look." However, the Yankees were not going to break the bank to land either player. The unsigned cover sheet for the Yankees' report said, "If they insist, offer to take these two for one of our Class D clubs at $150.00 per month. I was told they were getting $750 per month now."[19]

Miñoso, who batted .344 for the Cubans in 1948, had other suitors. Before the start of the 1948 season, he and Cubans teammate José Santiago were given tryouts by the St. Louis Cardinals. "I didn't remain long in camp," Miñoso wrote about the experience. "My style of play at third base was criticized: they said I shouldn't throw so hard to first. . . . It seemed the Cardinals didn't understand that I was already playing in a strong league and I didn't see why they were making me try out, as if I were some sandlotter."[20] Both players returned to the Cubans.

Miñoso and Santiago soon found another major league team interested in their services: Not surprisingly, it was Bill Veeck's Cleveland Indians. Indians scout Bill Killefer, who had previously recommended that Veeck purchase Larry Doby, watched the two players in action and liked what he saw, especially from Miñoso; Gordon Cobbledick wrote that Killefer "turned in a scouting report [about Miñoso] so delirious as to be almost incoherent." In late August the Cubans sold the two players to Cleveland for a reported $25,000, of which Miñoso and Santiago received "perhaps eleven or twelve hundred dollars."[21]

The players were assigned to Class A Dayton, and as previously noted, Orestes made a sensational debut, hitting .525 and then starring in the playoffs. He also had to deal more directly with racism and the language barrier than he had as a member of the Cubans. Unlike the lighter-skinned Santiago, who served as Miñoso's translator and helped him with learning English, Miñoso had to stay with Black families or at a Black-owned hotel when the team went on the road. He reported being accepted by the team's fans—his hitting undoubtedly helped—but also remembered incidents like one in which a bellhop at one of the hotels on the road saw Miñoso sitting on the team bus and commented "how nice it was that the team had a black batboy."[22]

With his batting skills, strong arm, great speed, and joyful style of play, Orestes Miñoso had made quite a first impression (Dayton manager Joe Vosmik reported that Miñoso had scored three times from first base on a single). Despite having played only a handful of games in white organized baseball, many were saying that he could make the Indians' Opening Day roster in 1949.

◆ ◆ ◆

Although the entry of Black players into the white majors greatly contributed to the demise of the Negro Leagues, it also gave hope for new opportunities to young players of color who were beginning to enter the game. One of them was Ernie Banks. As noted earlier, Banks often played catch with his dad, a former semipro ballplayer who loved the game. But Ernie's baseball playing was limited, in part because Booker T. Washington High School—at the time, Dallas's only Black high school—did not have a baseball team. Along with excelling at football and track at Washington High, Ernie played fastpitch softball for teams in the area, and his skill at the game began to attract notice.

One of the people familiar with Banks's athletic skills was a local sports entrepreneur named Bill Blair. After graduating from Washington High, Blair had played sports at Prairie View A&M University and later pitched in the Negro Leagues for the Indianapolis Clowns. Blair, who had encouraged Ernie to try out for the Washington High football team, had also helped Banks improve his softball skills. It took Banks, who was very much on the shy side, a little while to get with the program:

> I was more an introvert. Sit in the back of the class and just listen to people. I just liked listening to people And I didn't play sports. Bill Blair got me on the football team, got me on the softball team, got me to the YMCA to play all sports. I had no interest in many things that most of the young people were doing. I was not a boring person. I just didn't

understand any of that. I read a lot. I stayed in the crowd, but I didn't say very much when I was with the guys, and they had the girlfriends. Everybody would do all the talking. I'd just sit there and listen to them.[23]

One afternoon in 1948 Blair showed up at Griggs Park, where Banks was playing, with two men. One was Hank Thompson, the Negro League infielder who had briefly played for the St. Louis Browns in 1947 (along with Willard Brown) before being released. Banks knew Thompson, who had grown up in Dallas and had played against the Green Monarchs; Ernie had liked the way Hank swung the bat and tried to copy Thompson's stance and swing. The other man, Johnny Carter, was the owner of a semipro Negro League team that was called the Detroit Colts but had its headquarters in Amarillo, a city about 350 miles northwest of Dallas. Both Thompson and Carter were impressed with how Ernie played ball, and Carter asked Banks to join the Colts, which Ernie did after Carter had assured Banks's mother that he would be back in time for the school season.

Still only 17, Ernie Banks spent the summer of 1948 playing for the Colts, who often traveled to other states such as Kansas, Nebraska, Oklahoma, and New Mexico for their games. Often the opposing teams and fans were white. ("They were happy to see us come in and play," he later recalled, "and they were happy to see us get on the bus and leave.") Though Banks was younger and far less experienced than everyone else on the field, he more than held his own. He also had a great time. "I hit a home run in my first game, and they told me to go into the stands and pass my hat around," he recalled. "I made six dollars in nickels, dimes and quarters."[24]

Banks was back in time to return to Washington High in the fall. He would play again for the Colts in the summer of 1949.

5

Pioneers

When the 1948 season ended there were only four Black players on American or National League rosters: Jackie Robinson, Larry Doby, Roy Campanella, and Satchel Paige. In 1949 just four new Black players would join them—Don Newcombe, Monte Irvin, Luke Easter, and Orestes Miñoso—and one of the four, Miñoso, would be sent back to the minors a month into the season. In addition, Hank Thompson would receive a second, and successful, chance to play in the non–Negro League majors, with the New York Giants. The Giants, with Irvin and Thompson, would join the Dodgers and the Indians as the only MLB teams with a Black player on their rosters. (Miñoso's brief debut, at least, made history. When he appeared as a pinch hitter in the Cleveland Indians' season opener on April 19, he became the first Afro-Latino player to perform in the white major leagues.)

At the same time, the number of Black players in the minor leagues increased greatly in 1949, as did the number of major league teams with Black players in their farm systems. According to data compiled by SABR researchers Gary Fink and Robert Schulz, there were six players of color (defined as players whose skin color would have effectively barred them from white organized baseball before 1946) in the minor leagues in 1946. The number doubled to 12 in 1947 and increased to 21 in 1948. In 1949 the total of Black minor league players nearly quadrupled, to 78. And though there were never more than two National or American League teams with Black players in their farm systems in any season from 1946 to 1948, that number also quadrupled in 1949, to eight.

One of the eight teams was the Chicago Cubs.

◆ ◆ ◆

Charles Pope was their first; "Cubs Sign 1st Negro Player" was the head-line of a *Chicago Herald-American* article on March 24, 1949, written by Wendell Smith. "Without fanfare or drum beating, the Chicago Cubs have signed their first Negro player. He is a 20-year-old San Francisco semipro catcher, Charles Pope, and is considered by Wrigley scouts a future star." Jack Sheehan, the Cubs' farm director, said, "We think he's a fine pros-pect," adding that Pope was "not signed because of his racial identity but because he was a good ball player." Pope was assigned to the Cubs' Class C farm team in Visalia, California.[1]

In a feature article about Pope three days later, Smith wrote that Pope had been born in Shafter, California, then moved to Tulare, a small town in the Central Valley about midway between Fresno and Bakersfield, in 1932. At Tulare High, the alma mater of 1948 (and 1952) Olympic decath-lon champion Bob Mathias, Pope was a switch-hitting catcher and out-fielder with speed on the bases; he had also studied to become a draftsman and played tuba in the school band. After serving overseas in World War II, where he was awarded five medals (family members believe he was involved in the Battle of the Bulge), he joined the San Francisco Cubs, a Black barnstorming team, and got the attention of major league scouts. (Future MLB star Bill Bruton would also be discovered while playing for the San Francisco Cubs in the late 1940s.) According to the *Michigan Chronicle*, the Cubs had outbid the Cincinnati Reds and Pittsburgh Pirates for Pope's services.[2]

Pope, who was actually 24 years old (not 20) in 1949, was the sixth of the nine children of John and Elnora Wade Pope. John Pope, who was born in Arkansas in 1887, worked as a laborer and farm worker, often moving from state to state in order to find work. In the years prior to World War I the family moved to Boley, Oklahoma, an all-Black community of several thousand residents in Okfuskee County. Boley, which was founded in 1903, was one of more than 50 African American towns and settlements created in the Indian Territory in the decades following the Civil War (it became the state of Oklahoma in 1889). The largest of these towns, Boley had two banks, three cotton gins, a weekly newspaper, and its own generating plant, water system, and ice plant.

Boley was heavily dependent on farming for revenue, and when the market began to decline in the 1920s, the Pope family moved to California. For a time they lived in Allensworth, another Black community about 50 miles north of Bakersfield. Founded by Allen Allensworth, a former enslaved person and Civil War veteran who was the first Black officer to achieve the rank of lieutenant colonel, Allensworth had its own stores, businesses, and schools and was created to be a self-supporting Black community like Boley. Charles Pope's younger brother Ed, who would be instrumental in the 1970s in having Allensworth designated as a state historic park, recalled the pride that the Allensworth school, with pictures of such Black heroes as Colonel Allensworth and Booker T. Washington on its walls, instilled in him.[3]

By the time Charles Pope made his Visalia Cubs debut in April, he had two Black teammates, both pitchers. One of them, 24-year-old righthander Ken Taylor, had been Pope's batterymate with the San Francisco Cubs in 1948; he had also pitched for the San Diego Tigers, another Black barnstorming team, in 1947. Taylor, a Mississippi native who moved to Los Angeles in the 1940s, was said to have a live fastball and a wide-breaking curve. The other player, righthander Walter McCoy, was much more experienced than either Pope or Taylor; he was 29 years old (his listed "baseball age" was 24) and had pitched for the Chicago American Giants in the Negro American League from 1945 to 1947.

Taylor got off to a promising start with Visalia, throwing five innings of one-hit ball in an exhibition game against the Tulare All-Stars, a semipro team. But then he began to struggle with his control. In early May, Bob Crawford of the *Visalia Times-Delta* wrote that "Taylor has been worse than awful with his scatter arm pitching."[4] On May 8 Taylor walked only two in four and two-thirds innings against the Ventura Yanks but gave up 11 hits and seven runs. The club released him a week later. Taylor was released a second time when he tried to make the Visalia club in the spring of 1950.

Control would also be the undoing of Walt McCoy. In an article about the three Black players for the *Pittsburgh Courier*, Visalia manager Red Treadway praised McCoy's "pitching head" and said, "Give him his control—and I'm not worried about that because he'll have it soon—and he'll be the toughest man in the league to beat."[5] Unfortunately, McCoy's control never came around. In one complete-game start against Modesto, he struck out 12 but gave up seven runs and 11 walks. The club released him on June 3 after he had posted a 2-2 record with a 6.65 ERA with 50 strikeouts (but 38 walks) in 46 innings. McCoy would struggle when he got another chance with the White Sox' Pacific Coast League farm team in Sacramento in 1950. He continued to pitch in the Dominican Republic and Mexico through the mid-1950s.

The Visalia Cubs released both Taylor and McCoy rather quickly after their early-season struggles. One would think that the team would have had more patience with Charles Pope, the first Black player signed by the

Chicago Cubs and a local star. That was not the case, however. Pope was in the starting lineup when Visalia opened its regular season on April 22; he teamed with the club's pitching ace, 21-year-old Harv Brown, on a four-hit shutout and picked a runner off second base. But from that point on he was in and out of the lineup, appearing behind the plate in only 21 of the team's first 52 games. On June 11 Charlie Pope, who was hitting .286 with an excellent .375 on-base percentage, was handed his release. He would never again play in white organized baseball.

"The major reason for [Pope's] release, according to Visalia baseball followers, was his showing behind the plate," said an article in the *Tulare Advance-Register*. "With only 20 scattered games through the season he was having difficulty keeping up a fine edge on catching duties. His tosses to second base were sometimes short and according to a Visalia spokesman, not connected with the Cub ball club, the youthful Negro player was working under the handicap of a sore arm during most of the season."[6]

If Pope was suffering from a sore arm, that might help explain his throwing difficulties and also raise the question of why the Visalia Cubs didn't wait for it to heal. Pope was versatile enough to play other positions; he had played the outfield in addition to catching while in high school, and after joining Tulare-area semipro teams following his release by the Cubs, he often played third base. The bottom line is that seven weeks into the season, the Visalia Cubs had released all three of their Black players—the first ever to perform in the California League, along with Claude Butler of the Santa Barbara Dodgers.

In an interview, Pope's granddaughter, Traci Carr, told the author, "I would expect [Pope's release by Visalia] to be difficult for some to understand . . . but then, being in this skin, I can tell you people come up with a whole lot of things when they don't want to do something. With stuff like this, my grandfather would say, don't believe everything you hear, don't believe everything you read." Carr, who was raised by Charles Pope and his wife Anna, said that one of the few memorabilia that Pope kept from his baseball career was a photo that had run in a number of newspapers showing him easily gripping four baseballs in his large right hand. "That's the only thing that I saw which was related to him playing that sport," she said. "I do recall, something came up one day. And he said he did not like being referred to as a Black man. Because he's a man. And he was smart. And he could do what anyone else could do, and do it better. And that was the end of that conversation."[7]

Pope continued to play semipro ball well into the 1950s; when the Visalia Cubs warmed up for the 1955 season with an exhibition game against the Tulare Aztecs, Pope was one of the players on the Tulare roster. In the meantime, he was building an impressive non-sports career. For a time he worked as a draftsman for a large San Francisco architectural firm, the only Black man working for the company. When Pope applied for a better position with the firm, said Carr, "he was told we hired someone else for the position—a white man—and we would like you to train him. My grandfather quit and bought a truck."[8] Eventually he started a successful company called Charles E. Pope and Sons Trucking. Charles and his wife Anna had 10 grandchildren and helped raise Traci, whose father, James Carr, had died in a drowning accident at age 24 in 1971. Like Charles Pope, James Carr had been a star athlete at Tulare Union High School and played minor league baseball, in his case the San Francisco Giants' farm system.

"People adored my grandparents, adored him," said Carr. "If someone needed something, they would come out to our house. If they needed a job, he would talk with them first, see what they could do, walk them around the trucks. He was smart, super smart. He was kindhearted, but he wouldn't take junk; I'll put it that way. If you brought stuff to him in a bad way, he was going to tell you don't bring that to my house. And you knew not to do it again."[9]

Charles Pope died in Tulare in 2003 at age 77. When the author began research for this book nearly two decades later, the Chicago Cubs were not aware that he had been the first Black player signed by the team.

◆ ◆ ◆

Five other Black players played for Cubs farm teams in 1949.

Right-handed pitcher Robert Luther Burns, more commonly known as "Blood" Burns, was signed by the Cubs' Class B farm team in Springfield, Massachusetts, in late May, becoming the first Black player to perform for Springfield. Two months later he was sent to Chicago's Class C farm team in Sioux Falls, South Dakota, where he finished the season. Burns, who was 23 years old during the 1949 season, was a Springfield, Ohio, native and a military veteran; he joined the Springfield, Massachusetts, club immediately after being discharged from the Marine Corps base at Camp Lejeune in North Carolina. He had spent five years and two months in the Marines, including 23 months in the South Pacific during World War II.

Blood Burns, who lived to be 96, spent much of his life either in baseball or the military. He was a character out of a book, quite literally; he was featured in *First Seal*, Roy Boehm and Charles Sasser's book about the founding of the US Navy Seals in the early 1960s. Burns was not a man lacking in confidence; in a family interview made in 2021, when he was 95 years old, he talked about his baseball career: "I played in Mississippi; I played ball all over the world. I went down to Mexico; I played all winter. I had that talent. I threw that ball 100 miles an hour, easy. Good curveball, good fastball, I'm telling you like it is. I went through a lot of stuff and played ball all through that."[10]

"From all reports [Burns] cannot fail to help the Springfield Cubs in their battle to win high honors in the New England League race this season," wrote Les Stearns of the *Springfield Journal* shortly after Burns joined the team. "Big Jim Murcheson, a North Carolinian who scouts the Southern territory of the Cubs . . . has had Burns under surveillance for some time and is convinced that he cannot miss." Yet Burns appeared in only five games with nine innings pitched in his nearly two months with Springfield.[11]

Transferred to Sioux Falls in July, Burns posted a 7-4 record over the second half of the season. His 4.55 ERA was on the high side, mostly because he walked 81 batters in 91 innings. High walk totals were a common problem for pitchers moving from Black leagues into white organized baseball in the 1940s and early '50s. Many Black pitchers threw big-breaking curveballs, which can be difficult for umpires to judge, but it is also possible that many umpires weren't giving these Black pioneers much benefit of the doubt in calling pitches.

Burns was expected to return to Sioux Falls in 1950, but the Korean War began that year, and Burns went back into the military. He did not return to baseball until 1954. Pitching for Cubs farm teams for the next two years, Burns posted good ERAs, but erratic control once again held him back. With his baseball career not advancing, Burns returned to the service. According to his grandniece Demica Williams, Burns spent a total of 30 years in the armed forces, seeing action in World War II, the Korean War, and the Vietnam War. In the early 1960s he was a sergeant in the army, serving as a no-nonsense Black Hat instructor at Fort Bragg in North Carolina. Burns's colorful encounters with Roy Boehm, who is considered the founder of the Navy Seals, are covered in *First Seal*; according to Boehm, Blood Burns's favorite term for something he disapproved of was "blass-feemy." A few years later he served with the 173rd Airborne Brigade in Vietnam, routinely taking the lead on dangerous missions in order to protect his troops. Infantry sergeant Jim Quisenberry, a veteran of the brigade, said of Burns: "Because of him, many of us are alive today."[12]

Burns returned to North Carolina after his discharge from the service. According to Demica Williams, he was the first person of color to serve as sheriff of Fayetteville. He also spent 17 years as a detective in Fayetteville and later worked as a game warden. Though he never reached the major leagues and often moved from club to club and from country to country,

Blood Burns took it all in stride. "People would say, how much bread do you want?" he recalled about his baseball career. "I'd say, let me talk to the man . . . and sometimes I would say, that's not enough for me. I knew I couldn't sign with another club, but I got on with them. I made money, I spent money and I had a hell of a time. I don't regret a bit."[13]

♦ ♦ ♦

Unlike Pope, Taylor, McCoy, and Burns, Booker McDaniel was a certified Negro League star. Born in 1913 in Blackwell, Arkansas, McDaniel (his name was often listed as McDaniels) joined the legendary Kansas City Monarchs in 1940, and from 1941 to 1945 was one of the top pitchers on a mound staff that included future Hall of Famers Satchel Paige and Hilton Smith. He was also a teammate of Jackie Robinson in 1945. That year, his final full year with the Monarchs, McDaniel led the league in numerous categories, including wins, saves (he often appeared in relief of Paige), innings pitched, complete games, and strikeouts. He also led the circuit in wins above replacement, a statistical tool for estimating a player's overall value.[14]

Following the 1945 season, McDaniel played for Marianao in the Cuban League, where he was a teammate of Orestes Miñoso and the ace of the team's mound staff. After spending the 1946–48 seasons in the Mexican League, McDaniel returned to the Monarchs in 1949. He did not stay long. Tom Baird, who had co-owned the Monarchs with J. L. Wilkinson since the founding of the Negro National League in 1920, had bought out his partner and was keeping the Monarchs in business by selling off their best players.

One of Baird's main clients was Cubs Director of Minor League Clubs Jack Sheehan, and the first player he sold to the Cubs was McDaniel. When he joined the Cubs' Los Angeles Angels farm team in mid-June, McDaniel was both the first Black player to wear an Angels uniform and the first Black pitcher in Pacific Coast League history. According to the *Los Angeles Sentinel*, the city's leading Black newspaper, "All the fans from the eastside greeted the news of the signing of McDaniels [*sic*] with enthusiasm. They have long felt that with Wrigley Field in the heart of the colored district the Angels should recognize their patronage."[15]

McDaniel got off to a hot start with his new team. By mid-July he had a 5-1 record and was the talk of the league, sometimes drawing crowds of over 15,000 to his starts. But then the man known as "Cannonball" went into a tailspin, losing six straight starts. He finished the year with an 8-9 record; however, his 4.22 ERA was the lowest on the Angels staff, and his eight wins were only one fewer than the staff leaders, although McDaniel didn't join the team until the season was nearly half over. He had also missed several starts in August with a knee injury. He would be back in Los Angeles for the 1950 season.

◆ ◆ ◆

Chicago-area product Milton Bohannion, who at 18 was about half Booker McDaniel's age, joined the Cubs organization right out of Argo Community High School in the South Chicago suburbs. Born in Coffeeville, Mississippi, a rural town with a population of less than 1,000, in January 1931, Milton was the firstborn son of Cecil and Johnnie Mae (Brown) Bohannion (the last name was sometimes spelled Bohannon or Bohanion). Years later, a check of Mississippi birth certificates revealed that Cecil's father was actually a man named Neeley who had died when Cecil was an infant. The family, including Milton and his younger sister Sarah, eventually changed their last name to Neeley.

When Milton was three years old, the Bohannion family moved to Argo, a subdivision of a town called Summit. Argo was basically a company town for the massive Argo Corn Products processing plant and an attractive destination for southern Blacks looking for a better life during the Great Migration.

At Argo High Milton Bohannion played basketball and football, but baseball was his best sport. During his senior year Bohannion led his team to the state baseball finals in Peoria. He also was a unanimous choice of Chicago suburban coaches to play against the City Stars in an all-star game at Wrigley Field sponsored by the *Chicago Herald-American*. Although he had great speed and was described as "a terror on the basepaths" who "drove opposing pitchers hysterical," his primary position in high school was catcher. "Bohanion [sic] is as deadly throwing to the bases as a country-boy with a slingshot," wrote Tommy Kouzmanoff.[16]

Signed by the Cubs in mid-July, Bohannion was sent to the club's Class D farm team in Janesville, Wisconsin, a city of about 25,000 located 100 miles northwest of Chicago. When Bohannion made his debut on July 18 as the first Black player in the history of the Wisconsin State League, it was at second base, not catcher. For the remainder of the season he was a jack of all trades; playing second base, third base, shortstop, and the outfield, as well as spending three games behind the plate, Bohannion batted .257 in 53 games. His most impressive asset was his speed, no surprise for a player whose nickname was "Lightning."

Bohannion was not fazed about being the only Black player in a league full of small-to-medium sized Wisconsin cities that were almost 100 percent white. (According to census data, there were only 28,000 Black people in Wisconsin in 1950, 0.8 percent of the population.) "He loved it in

Janesville," said his sister, Sarah Nicholson. "Milton was the type of person who could adjust to anything; he would make it so that it would soon be the same way as it was at home. He could work with almost anybody."[17] Still a teenager, Milton Bohannion would return to Janesville in 1950 for his first full season in white organized baseball.

◆ ◆ ◆

Two other Black players performed for the Chicago Cubs farm teams in 1949. In terms of athletics, at least, they were so similar that they might have been twins. The first, Sammy Gee (pronounced "Ghee"), was a legendary athlete in the city of Detroit even before he began his pro baseball career. Born in Detroit in 1928, Gee was the sixth of the eight children of William and Carrie Gee. At Miller High School, where he played under famed coach Will Robinson, Gee was an all-city shortstop in baseball, and—though only five feet, seven inches tall according to his draft registration card—a member of the Michigan all-state team in football and the Hearst newspapers All-America team in basketball. In 1947 Gee led Miller High to the Detroit City League championship as part of the city's first championship team with an all-Black roster. (Will Robinson, who had begun his coaching career at DuSable High School in Chicago, was the first Black basketball head coach in Detroit high school history and would later become the first Black basketball head coach at an NCAA Division I school, Illinois State University.)

According to a 2003 article by Ted Talbert for the *Detroit Free Press*, Notre Dame football coach Frank Leahy wanted to recruit Gee for his powerful football team, which was ranked number one by the Associated Press in both 1946 and 1947; however, he was talked out of it by alumni who felt that Notre Dame wasn't ready to integrate its all-white team.[18] Gee also could have played college basketball, and Abe Saperstein wrote to Coach Robinson expressing an interest in adding Sammy to the Globetrotters roster.

In the interim there was baseball. After Gee's graduation from Miller High, Will Robinson approached the Detroit Tigers about signing Gee; although Tigers vice president Spike Briggs told Robinson that the team did not have a biased hiring policy, nothing came of the conversation.[19] (The Tigers would be the next-to-last team in the white major leagues to employ a Black player, not integrating their roster until 1958.) Instead, Gee, who had received strong recommendations from both Robinson and Wendell Smith, signed to play with the Brooklyn Dodgers' Class C Canadian-American League farm team in Trois-Rivieres (Three Rivers), Quebec. According to SABR researcher Merl F. Kleinknecht, Gee was only the ninth Black player to perform in the minor leagues since Jackie Robinson had broken the color barrier with the 1946 Montreal Royals.[20] He was also the first Black player in the Can-Am League. Playing his second- or maybe third-best sport in a foreign country was a difficult adjustment for the 19-year-old Gee. Coach Robinson, who had accompanied Gee to Quebec, reported that Three Rivers manager Lou Rochelli had said that Gee was "suffering from a bad case of the jitters."[21] Gee finished his rookie year with a .185 batting average in 37 games.

Things got better for Gee over the next few months. In October he played in a couple of exhibition games in Detroit as a teammate of Jackie Robinson. A month later he signed a contract to play basketball for the Globetrotters. According to Detroit sports historian Bill Hoover, Saperstein put Gee on the team's top unit and even placed Gee's likeness on the cover of the program when the Trotters played a game at Detroit's Olympia Stadium.

When he began his first full season in white organized baseball in 1948, Gee was assigned to Olean, New York, of the Class D Pennsylvania–Ohio–New York League. He had a Black teammate: fellow Detroiter Ron Teasley, a graduate of the city's Northwestern High. Both players got off to good starts: "Sammy Gee and Ronald Teasley 'Murdering' Ball at Olean," said a *Pittsburgh Courier* headline. In early June Gee was hitting .321, and Teasley, though batting .267, had power numbers that ranked among the best in the league. Nonetheless the Olean Oilers abruptly released both players on June 4.

More than 75 years later, the exact reason why the Dodgers released two young Black players, both of whom were showing promise, is still a mystery. According to newspaper accounts, Gee was having some problems in the field; however, erratic defense is not unusual for a young shortstop. Gee's longtime girlfriend, Emily Allen Garland, wrote that Gee had told her that the Dodgers "said I was just too good. They didn't need another Negro player stealing the limelight so soon after Jackie Robinson. Branch Rickey was afraid it may upset the white fans."[22]

When the author spoke with 95-year-old Ron Teasley in the summer of 2022, Teasley was still mystified about the release. "I have no idea," he said. "I was batting around .280 and leading the league in home runs. Sammy was hitting around .335. I was playing every day; Sammy may have missed one or two games. I never could understand why there was not more criticism of that decision, why more people didn't get upset about it. But no one seemed to follow through any further on it."[23]

With the help of Will Robinson, Gee and Teasley signed to play with the New York Cubans of the Negro National League—Orestes Miñoso's team. "You could tell things were not going well for the league," Teasley recalled about the 1948 season, the last year that the Negro Leagues were considered major. "There was not a lot of comradeship there . . . it was just a sad situation." He did help Miñoso on one occasion. "In the first game I was scheduled to play in, Miñoso came to the game, and didn't have his uniform," said Teasley. "He didn't know where it was. I guess he misplaced it or something. And so I guess you know whose uniform they took then. My uniform. First day on the job."[24]

Gee spent the 1948–49 offseason with the Globetrotters and played in their second straight victory over the Minneapolis Lakers on February 28. He also played with another Saperstein barnstorming team, the Kansas City Stars. With help from Saperstein Gee returned to white organized baseball with the Grand Rapids Jets, an independent team in the Class A Central League, in 1949. Given his release about 10 days into the season, Gee signed with the Cubs' Northern League farm team, the Sioux Falls Canaries.

Sammy Gee never did have much luck during his professional baseball career, and whatever chance he had of making an impression on the Canaries—or the Cubs—in 1949 quickly dissipated when he was stricken with appendicitis only two weeks after joining the team. He did not return until late August, when the season was nearly over, finishing the year with a .135 average in 12 games played.

After another offseason with the Globetrotters, Gee was expected to return to Sioux Falls in 1950. Instead, he received his draft notice and was inducted into the army. Following his discharge in 1953, Gee had another brief stint with Sioux Falls, but basketball was clearly his number one sport by then. For the next decade Gee played with various Globetrotter or Saperstein-sponsored basketball squads, along with several semipro hoops teams; he also played for the Globetrotters baseball team—in one game, he was a teammate of Satchel Paige—and had another stint of Negro League baseball with the Detroit Stars in 1955. By then Sammy had discovered a new diamond sport: fastpitch softball. Over the next 15 years he became known as one of the finest softball players in the nation.

On June 28, 1969, 41-year-old Sammy Gee was playing softball at a park in Windsor, Ontario, when he suffered a heart attack; he was pronounced dead at a Windsor hospital later that day. When Gee was honored at a Black Legends of Professional Basketball dinner in 1999, Will Robinson, who had coached or scouted numerous Detroit-area athletes in his six-decade high school, college, and professional career, paid tribute. "Sammy was the best all-around athlete in Detroit history . . . He was *the* best," said Robinson. "I couldn't pick one sport as his best—he was that kind of good at all of them. His quickness and competitive spirit were what made him great. He was spectacular."[25]

◆ ◆ ◆

Sammy Gee's "twin," Billy Hart, joined the Sioux Falls Canaries in the first week of August. There were more than a few similarities between the two players. Both were born in northern states: Gee in Michigan in 1928, Hart in Massachusetts in 1927. Although Gee was five-foot-seven and Hart five-foot-six, both had starred in football and basketball as well as baseball in high school (and for Hart, in college as well). Both were noted for their great speed. Both would have their athletic careers interrupted by military service during the Korean War. And once they returned from the service, both would achieve their greatest fame in sports other than baseball.

William Frank Hart was born in Williamstown, Massachusetts, a city in the northwest corner of the state very close to its borders with Vermont to the north and New York to the west. He was the fifth of six children of Henry and Kate Hart. At Williamstown High Billy played baseball, basketball, and football, serving as team captain of all three sports. In two years at St. Michael's College, a small Catholic school in Colchester, Vermont, he was a .350-hitting center fielder in baseball and the team's leading scorer in both basketball and football.

Hart joined Sioux Falls with about a month to go in the 1949 season. The team had two other Black players, Gee (who was about to return after his appendix surgery) and Blood Burns. That is not to say that he was entering a welcoming environment. On August 11, four days after Billy's first game with the Canaries, the *Sioux-Falls Argus Leader* contained this letter:

JOB PREJUDICE

To the Editor of The Argus-Leader:

Since being here in Sioux Falls (over two months) I find there are no jobs, with the exception of housework, available for Negroes.

People here are always dragging the South down about how Negroes are "treated." I find they aren't "treated" half as badly there as they are here.

There you find the Negro working in every field except government. I know, because I'm from Alabama. I lived there 19½ years with the exception of a few trips East. I attended college at Alabama State and Tuskegee Institute. I've held the position as teacher (5th–6th grades) and also worked as a salesgirl. I've had a business course but no experience in that line of work. I'm only 19½ years old.

Each time I apply for a job the answer I get is "We don't employ Negroes" or "Fill out an application and we'll see about it."

Why don't the people allow the Negro here an equal chance?

GEORGIA WATTS

Sioux Falls[26]

Living (and playing) in Sioux Falls was not a pleasant experience for Hart. "The people up there called him all kinds of names," said Robert Andreatta, a college teammate of Hart's. "That was terrible. Billy was a gentleman. He was class. He didn't deserve that."[27]

Hart began his Canaries career as a pinch hitter in the ninth inning of an 8–1 loss to the Fargo-Moorhead Twins on August 7; the *Argus-Leader* reported that Hart "bunted along the third base line and streaked to first like Jackie Robinson."[28] He came around to score the Canaries' only run. The next day Hart started at second base, went 1-for-4, and made a defensive play that was praised in the game story. But he seldom played after that, starting only seven games and getting only 26 at-bats over the next four weeks (he batted .269). On September 3, with three days left in the regular season, the Canaries handed Hart his unconditional release. They had apparently seen enough to conclude that this brilliant Black athlete couldn't make it in white organized baseball.

The Chicago Cubs offered Hart another chance, at a higher level: He was added to the winter roster of the Decatur Commodores of the Class B Three-I League, which to date had not had a Black player. (The Commodores were known locally as the "Commies," which must have been an interesting team nickname in the early 1950s). The team held spring training in Moultrie, Georgia, in the Deep South. Billy's wife accompanied him on the trip; their daughter, Shelley Arnold, recalled her mother's painful memories of the experience.

> She talked about how they got a flat tire. They pulled up to this gas station, and they waited and waited and waited for somebody to come out. Finally, this man inside the gas station stood up with a shotgun in his hand. And they knew they had to leave right away. So they moved on. And literally like in the movie "42," they could not find places to stay at night. She said she took the train back home alone, and that the porter told her, you shouldn't be on this train by yourself. He put her in a room where she wouldn't be seen and said, don't come out for anything. He would bring her meals to her so that she wouldn't have to come out.
>
> My father had grown up in Williamstown, Massachusetts, and my mother grew up in North Adams, places where everybody knew them. And don't get me wrong, I'm sure some people were racist. I'm sure there were some feelings about Black families. But we grew up there. There wasn't that fear. I said, Mom, I never [knew] you went through all this. But you know, they didn't talk about it.[29]

Hart, who no doubt was affected by the treatment that he and his wife received in Georgia, did not make the Decatur Commies' roster in 1950; he was cut in early April.

His athletic career was far from over. In May 1950 he led a team of college basketball all-stars to a 63–56 win over the Holy Cross Seniors, whose top player was future Basketball Hall of Famer Bob Cousy. After the game Cousy paid tribute to Hart, saying, "We didn't have anybody fast enough to follow him." After spending two years with the US Army in Korea, where he was decorated with the Combat Infantry Badge, Korean Service Medal, Service Star, and UN Service medal, Hart joined the Lenox Merchants, a legendary semipro basketball team that frequently played—and often beat—NBA teams. While with the Merchants, he played a second time against Cousy in March 1952; though Lenox lost to Cousy's Boston Celtics, 88–71, Hart led his team with 17 points.[30]

Hart continued to play semipro basketball, baseball, and football for the next decade. In his spare time, he became an excellent bowler. When he took up tennis, he reached the top three in New England in his age group in both singles and doubles; in 2010, he was inducted into the New England Tennis Hall of Fame. Hart coached Little League and American Legion teams. And he ran the Henry Hart Construction Company after his father's death.

On March 26, 1995, 68-year-old Billy Hart collapsed after a vigorous day that included several hours of tennis. He was taken to the University of Massachusetts Medical Center and died the next day. Hart's lengthy obituary in the *North Adams (MA) Transcript* described a "prominent and respected business and community leader" and listed numerous accomplishments in the sports world and the business world. In 2017 the *Berkshire (MA) Eagle* named Hart number 2 on the list of the 50 greatest 20th-century athletes in the history of Berkshire County.[31]

◆ ◆ ◆

Of the eight Black men who played in the Cubs' farm system during the 1949 season, only Booker McDaniel and Milton Bohannion returned in 1950. None of the eight would ever play for the Cubs or any other white major league team. Given the limited playing time and indifferent treatment that most of them received, it's impossible to say for sure whether any of the eight could have succeeded in the American or the National League. (Playing time lost while in the military was another factor.) The Cubs would add a new crop of Black players to their minor league farm clubs in 1950, several of whom *would* eventually reach the majors—though only one would do so with the Cubs, and then not until the last month of the 1953 season. In the meantime, indifferent treatment of their Black players would remain a constant for the Cubs.

Blood Burns might have called it "blass-feemy."

6

New Men, Old Ideas

Although the Cubs showed only a half-hearted commitment—if that—to the Black players who performed for their farm teams in 1949, at least they *had* some Black players. That was more than could be said of their crosstown rivals, the White Sox. The Sox surely needed help; in 1948 they lost 101 games, the second most in franchise history. But while the South Siders had dramatically overhauled their management team after that disastrous season, they spent much of the next year finding their bearings while often looking for help in the wrong places and holding off on tapping into the bountiful Black talent pool that was easily available to them.

The new men in charge of the White Sox operation were Vice President Chuck (or Charley) Comiskey, general manager Frank Lane, and field manager Jack Onslow. Also holding a position of increasing power was farm director Johnny Rigney, who had been given a spot in the Sox hierarchy after his retirement as a player in 1947. It was a curious and sometimes dysfunctional combination. The 23-year-old Comiskey, who was the grandson (and namesake) of team founder Charles A. Comiskey, had been the heir presumptive to the team's top position since the death of his father Lou in 1939. "There is little doubt that Lou Comiskey intended for Charley to run the White Sox as soon as he was old enough to do so," wrote White Sox historian and author Richard Lindberg. "But he did not state this clearly, or with any great conviction."[1] Lou Comiskey's widow, Grace, never seemed comfortable in giving Chuck total control of the franchise, and she had the power to have her way. Ultimately she would favor—and leave the majority of the club's stock on her death—to Chuck's sister Dorothy, who was married to Johnny Rigney. Things would get complicated over the course of the following decade.

The biggest problems for Chuck Comiskey were a few years down the road, however. He had grown up in a baseball family and spent several years honing his craft working in the White Sox farm system. Comiskey's first major move after assuming the vice presidency was to hire Frank Lane. Lane's previous baseball experience had included various positions (farm club director, business manager, minor league general manager) with the Cincinnati Reds and the New York Yankees when Larry MacPhail was running those franchises; most recently, he had served as president of the minor league American Association. "I knew I was young and there was an awful lot of practical baseball operations I knew I would not be able to handle, so the thing I decided to do was get a good general manager," Comiskey recalled. "The first man I thought of was Frank Lane. I had to go back and convince my mother and the attorneys that I needed someone of that caliber who had been around the farm systems."[2]

Comiskey also hired "Happy Jack" Onslow, who had managed Sox minor league teams while Comiskey was working in the farm system. Onslow, who at 60 years of age was one of the oldest people ever hired as a first-time major league manager, had begun his professional baseball career in 1909 and had been a minor league manager since the mid-1920s. Despite his nickname, Onslow was not the warm and fuzzy type, which was fine with Comiskey. "I go along pretty much with Leo Durocher's angle that good guys don't win pennants," said Chuck. "I mean, you have to be something of a muleskinner to win. Well, Onslow isn't exactly held in affection by all ball players. Some of 'em hate his guts but he does have a way with them. One that I like."[3]

In a glowing article about Comiskey's ascendancy, the *Sporting News* called the new White Sox regime a "revolution in Sox affairs" for the "new look" Sox.[4] In order to begin the revolution, Comiskey, Lane, and Onslow had to start getting rid of the *old* look. Comiskey's first move was to put the entire roster on the waiver list in order to see how many players would be claimed by other major league clubs. Only one claim was made, that for catcher Aaron Robinson. Lane pulled Robinson off the list, and in his first major trade, dealt him to the Detroit Tigers for 21-year-old left-handed pitcher Billy Pierce, who would become the club's ace pitcher for the next decade. In typical Lane fashion, the trades and purchases would continue at a frenetic pace—some helpful, some not, some appearing to be more compulsive than anything else.

About a month into Lane's White Sox stint, the *Atlanta Daily World* reported that the Sox were interested in two Black Brooklyn Dodger farm-hands, Sam Jethroe and Don Newcombe. Like the Cubs, the Sox discovered that Branch Rickey wanted what the *Daily World* called "Rockefeller figures" for Newcombe. The speedy Jethroe, a Negro League veteran who was 31 years old in 1948 while professing to be several years younger, was more affordable; the paper reported that Rickey wanted $40,000 for the "fleetfooted flychaser." That was still too rich for Lane; he would hold off and watch Jethroe's purchase price enter the Rockefeller zone after a sensational season for the Dodgers' Montreal farm club in 1949 in which he stole 89 bases. "Ironically, the Sox could have had Jethroe for nothing two years ago," the *Daily World* reported. "They gave him a trial at Comiskey Park two summers ago but he failed to impress."[5]

"The future will hold that just nine men will be 'first string,' but also that no matter what the racial strain, each of the nine will be afield because he is best at his position," said Chuck Comiskey in an *Ebony* article published before the start of the 1949 season. Frank Lane echoed those sentiments. "We are looking everywhere for players, and we'll sign any player who looks like a real prospect," he told Wendell Smith. "However, we won't sign a player just because of his color. We want good, young players and we're going to stick to that policy." Lane said that he'd received good reports on a number of Negro League players; however, most of them were in the 27–30 age range, and, he said, "We aren't interested in men that old. I think the Cubs have the right idea. They signed Charley Pope, a 23-year-old catcher who has a bright future. We're looking for players that age, too."[6]

Some observers were dubious about Lane and Comiskey's high-minded words. Roger Treat of the *Chicago Herald-American* sarcastically noted that the White Sox had boasted about signing 22 scouts to hunt for talent. "My [*Herald-American*] partner, Mr. Warren Brown," he wrote, "once said it was an unproven belief in the baseball world that few of the 22 scouts of the Comiskey Clowns could find the ballpark, let alone a ballplayer." Treat asserted that Artie Wilson, a 28-year-old former Negro League star who would win the batting championship of the Pacific Coast League in 1949, "is a better fielder and hitter than all the Clown infielders rolled into one; Oreste Minosa [*sic*], signed by Cleveland, will be one of the great third-basemen in history; Monte Irvin, gone to the Giants, would be the best outfielder the Clowns have uniformed in years and years."[7]

After learning that Lane had derided the abilities of Artie Wilson, Doc Young of the *Defender* was equally blunt:

> I'm going to jab you today with the proposal that major league baseball, to a substantial degree, is only a state of mind.
> This idea pops into mind every time I think of the remark which has been credited, or debited, to the Chicago White Sox' energetic general

manager, Frank Lane, to the effect that they weren't interested in Art Wilson, the Birmingham Gentleman, because he wasn't "of major league caliber."

I am not saying he is or was of major league caliber. I'm wondering— just what is major league caliber?

After watching the likes of the St. Louis Browns, the positively pathetic Chicago Cubs, and the New York Yankees and White Sox in a recent night game, I am proposing that too much of major league baseball is nearly bush league, and that if Wilson isn't, or wasn't, of that caliber, maybe it's because he's above it.[8]

In late June the White Sox, who perhaps were feeling the pressure to take some sort of concrete step toward integrating their team, signed former Negro League pitching great John Donaldson as a scout. Three months earlier the Cubs had made a similar move, adding former Negro League pitching star Hal "Yellow Horse" Morris to their scouting staff. Both Morris and Donaldson had pitched for the Kansas City Monarchs; according to Ron Rapoport, Jack Sheehan had added Morris to the Cubs' scouting staff after talking to Monarchs owner Tom Baird, who told him that Morris "was above average intelligence for a Negro." Morris, who worked out of the San Francisco Bay area, may have played a hand in the signing of Black players for Cubs farm teams in 1949, in particular, Charles Pope, Ken Taylor, Walt McCoy, and Booker McDaniel. Donaldson, described by Chuck Comiskey as "an experienced baseball man and a good judge of players," would recommend a number of Black players to the White Sox brass over the next few years, but ultimately would find working for the team to be a frustrating experience, beginning with a teenaged outfielder who was playing for the Birmingham Black Barons. "Donaldson wanted [Willie] Mays [for the White Sox] but couldn't get his front office to commit," wrote John Klima.[9]

The new White Sox regime got off to a good start in 1949; in late May the club was in third place with a 17-15 record. But a slump dropped them to seventh place, and after moving up to sixth in mid-July, they remained there for the rest of the season. The team did improve by 12 wins over the dismal 1948 season, and attendance increased by more than 150,000; however, it was anything but a happy year for the new management team. The apparently misnamed "Happy Jack" Onslow often feuded with his players, sometimes getting into shouting matches in the clubhouse. He also battled with Frank Lane, at one point describing the Sox general manager as "a front office ink-thrower."[10] The two tried to make peace, but Lane, who had never been keen on hiring Onslow in the first place, longed to replace him with Paul Richards. Comiskey eventually came around to the same way of thinking. But Onslow was in the first year of a two-year contract, and Grace Comiskey refused to dismiss him.

While press reports indicated that the White Sox were still interested in Sam Jethroe, the Sox never seemed close to making a deal with Branch Rickey. After Jethroe's big season with Montreal, Rickey's asking price was said to have risen to $200,000 or maybe $300,000. "Jethroe is no spring chicken, and if Rickey asks a publicized $200,000 for his services, he is doing Jethroe a disservice," Lane complained. "He is probably the fastest man in uniform I've ever seen. But who is going to pay an exorbitant price for a man that has not been tested in the majors? Jethroe is not only the property of a baseball team, he is also a human being with a future of his own. Apparently baseball is his business, and he should not be kept in the minors for the best years of his life."[11] (In October the Dodgers traded Jethroe and outfielder Bob Addis to the Boston Braves for three minor league players and cash in the $100,000-$150,000 range, a deal very similar to an offer from the Dodgers that Lane claimed he turned down.)

At the same time that Lane was balking at the high asking price for the likes of Jethroe and Don Newcombe, the White Sox were shelling out huge sums of money to untested young white players, most of them just out of high school. The spending spree began in June, when the club gave a bonus of $52,500 to Jim Baumer, an 18-year-old shortstop from Broken Arrow, Oklahoma. Later that month they signed Gus Keriazakos, a high school pitcher from Montclair, New Jersey, to a contract that included a $60,000 bonus. Two high schoolers from California, pitcher Bill Offield and third baseman Joe Kirrene Jr., received a combined $100,000. Gardner Hamlen, a right-handed pitcher from Marblehead, Massachusetts, received an undisclosed amount. And to prove that the Sox weren't simply giving big bonuses to children, the club spent a reported $30,000 to sign left-handed pitcher Jack Bruner, a 25-year-old World War II veteran who had won All-America honors at the University of Iowa. The 1949 outlay for the six bonus players exceeded a quarter of a million dollars, Chuck Comiskey admitted, but it was money he considered well spent. "We now have landed six of the 12 to 15 youngsters considered ultra-prospects throughout the country this year," Comiskey told the *Chicago Tribune*. He added that the team had spent a "considerable" additional sum to sign other young players.[12]

This is what the White Sox got for the quarter million they spent on the six bonus babies: Jack Bruner, the veteran of the group, appeared in four games for the 1949 White Sox and nine more in 1950 before he was sold to the St. Louis Browns; his career MLB totals, all in 1949–50, were 26 games pitched with a 2-4 record and a 4.91 ERA. Joe Kirrene played in one game in 1950, and after spending three years in the military, nine more in 1954. He did post a .296 batting average for his 10-game major league stint, along with some decent minor league numbers. Gus Keriazakos appeared in one game for the White Sox in 1950 and 27 more for the Senators and the Athletics in 1954–55; his career record was 4-10 with a 5.62 ERA. Jim Baumer played eight games with the 1949 White Sox, and though he went 4-for-10 (a .400 hitter!), spent the entire decade of the 1950s in the minor leagues before he improbably resurfaced with the 1961 Cincinnati Reds; he batted .125 in 10 games before returning to the minors for the remainder his career. Bill Offield and Gar Hamlen never reached the major leagues at all.

The White Sox were hardly alone in giving huge amounts of bonus money to untested amateur players; to some extent every American and National League team took part in the "bonus craze" that took place during years following the end of World War II. Historian Steve Gietschier notes that because of a massive increase in attendance in the postwar period, "baseball moved into an era of unprecedented prosperity." Net income for the 16 MLB teams, which was about $1 million per year in 1944–45— by itself a substantial increase from the Great Depression years—rose to nearly $5 million per year in 1946–47. With money to spend, the result was a bidding war for young talent. "Club owners couldn't help themselves," wrote Gietschier.[13] The bonus craze continued even as overall revenue began to decline and despite several attempts to discourage bonus payments with punitive rules.

The list of bonus players included future greats like Al Kaline, Harmon Killebrew, and Sandy Koufax, but most simply did not pan out. Meanwhile, talented young Black players were still being ignored by MLB teams. To state two obvious examples, Chuck Comiskey's list of the "the 12 to 15 youngsters considered ultra-prospects throughout the country" would not have included Willie Mays and Ernie Banks, both of whom turned 18 in 1949. Other clubs were no wiser. Gietschier notes that in one three-week period in 1952, the Red Sox, who would be the last MLB team to integrate, paid out nearly $500,000 in bonuses to 17 players—all of them white.[14]

Although racism was certainly a major factor in MLB teams' continued failure to tap into the talent pool of Black players, so was out-and-out ignorance. In a May 1949 article for *Ebony*, Cleveland Indians great Bob Feller, who was playing for a team committed to integration and coming off a championship season that featured key contributions by two Black players (Larry Doby and Satchel Paige), wrote,

> There will be no avalanche of Negroes into the big leagues mainly because there are few Negro players who can make the grade.

I have made that statement before. I shall believe it until my judgment is proven wrong. There is one point you have to realize. Baseball is a sport that boasts few Negro stars. Not many Negro youngsters excel in the game of spiked shoes and horsehide gloves. Today clubs are desperately searching for prospective ball players but only a few Negroes are being selected.[15]

Ebony described Feller as a player who "probably has had more firsthand contact with Negro players than any other major leaguer. He has been a friend of Satchel Paige since 1936, has been a teammate of Larry Doby for two seasons and has played in many exhibitions against colored stars."[16]

Who wouldn't believe Bob Feller?

♦ ♦ ♦

Though his career in white organized baseball had consisted of only 21 games (including playoffs) with Class A Dayton at the end of the 1948 season, Orestes Miñoso began 1949 as a teammate of Bob Feller with the Indians. The team's spring training camp was in Tucson, Arizona, and Miñoso and his Black teammates, Larry Doby, Satchel Paige, Jose Santiago, and Artie Wilson, did not find a very welcoming environment. "Although Larry Doby is one of the stars of the world champions, frequently spoken of in the same breath with Joe DiMaggio, and often referred to as the counterpart of the all-time wonder, Tris Speaker," wrote Sam Lacy, "he is required to live apart from the other members of the team—because he is colored of course." While even the rawest Indians rookies stayed at the plush Hotel Santa Rita if they happened to be white, Doby and the others had to stay three miles away at the "humble but clean" home of Chester Willis, a Tucson laundry worker. The hotel management blamed the "Towncats," a powerful Tucson businessman's club, for the segregated housing; the Towncats denied responsibility, but the ban remained.[17]

In early April the team broke camp and headed east, playing exhibition games along the way. In El Paso, Texas, Doby, Paige, and Miñoso (Santiago and Wilson had been farmed out by then) were handed a note saying that they would be staying at a hotel at Prospect and East Market Streets; when they went to that location, there was no hotel in sight. The players had to figure things out on their own. In Texarkana, Texas, where Doby had been given a hard time the previous year, the white members of the team were taken from their hotel to the ballpark in chartered buses; the Black players, who, of course, were forced to stay elsewhere, had to make a lengthy walk to the park, in uniform, because no "colored cabs" were available. The players arrived more than 30 minutes late. "Doby was obviously peeved," wrote Sam Lacy about the Texarkana incident. "Paige, an old trooper, who lets nothing ruffle him, appeared unmoved. Miñoso, carefree in the mold of the average Cuban, laughed about it. The latter was so unperturbed that he slammed a two-run homer to thrill the taxi drivers who passed him up on their way to see the game."[18]

"I think the Indians management is continuing to make a mistake which never should have been made," wrote Jim Schlemmer of the *Akron Beacon Journal* about the treatment that the team's Black players were receiving. "It is the mistake of considering Paige, Doby and Miñoso as bona fide Indians only while they are on the field and treating them as Negroes at other times while in these southland cities."[19]

Of course, it wasn't only in Southland cities that Black players were treated with hostility. As noted above, in 1949 the New York Giants added Monte Irvin and Hank Thompson. A *Sporting News* blurb from Oscar Ruhl conveys how the two players were welcomed to the league. "When the Giants were in Cincinnati," wrote Ruhl, "the Reds' pitchers took turns putting the Giants' two Negro players on the seats of their trousers. Ken Raffensberger let one go in the second inning in the second game of July 31 that smashed Henry Thompson's finger against his bat. Henry was ducking when contact was made and it was ruled a foul. After first aid, he went back and singled for an RBI."[20]

Late in the 1949 season Pittsburgh Pirates manager Billy Meyer, obviously inebriated, was overheard referring to Paige, Doby, and Jackie Robinson with derogatory racial slurs while on a train ride to a Pirates exhibition game. "Those n___s are being moved up too fast and will soon have our jobs as managers and coaches," said Meyer, according to two employees of the railroad. He was also said to have verbally attacked one of the employees, a Black Red Cap. Bill Nunn of the *Pittsburgh Courier* wrote that after the tirade, Ralph Kiner, the Pirates' biggest star, "walked disgustedly away from Meyer when the latter approached him on the train." Meyer subsequently "admitted apologetically that he may have made the remarks," but "being under the influence of liquor at the time, had no way of knowing." He insisted that he had "no prejudices against Negroes playing in [white] organized baseball." However, he then added, "I don't, and I'm sure the Pirate management doesn't go along with the idea of bringing up talent just to exploit them. The Giants tried that with those two boys they brought up and it's not paying off."[21] The two players he was referring to, Thompson and Irvin, would be key contributors to the Giants' pennant-winning teams in 1951 and 1954, and Irvin would be elected to the Baseball Hall of Fame in 1973.

Billy Meyer managed the Pittsburgh Pirates through 1952, a year (or two, depending on whether you count Carlos Bernier) before the team's first Black player took the field. In 1954 Meyer's uniform number 1 was the second number ever retired by the Pirates, after baseball immortal Honus Wagner. After Meyer died in 1957, the ballpark in his hometown of Knoxville, Tennessee, was renamed Bill Meyer Stadium in his honor. In a tribute, *Pittsburgh Post-Gazette* columnist Jack Hernon wrote, "He never carried a dislike for anyone. Never did he speak a harsh word about a friend or associate."[22]

Almost never.

♦ ♦ ♦

After performing sensationally in spring training, Orestes Miñoso made the Cleveland Indians' Opening Day roster in 1949. When he pinch hit for Mike Garcia on Opening Day, April 19, against Ned Garver of the St. Louis Browns, he became the eighth Black player to perform in the American or the National League since Jackie Robinson had made his Brooklyn Dodgers debut in 1947 and the first Afro-Latino. Miñoso drew a walk against Garver, but then did not appear in a game until May 4, when he started in right field against the Philadelphia Athletics; in that game he got his first American League hit, a sixth-inning single off lefthander Alex Kellner. Miñoso started the next five games, all in right field, but after hitting his first homer with the Indians—a 380-foot drive to right center field off Jack Kramer of the Red Sox on May 5—went one for his next 12, which seemed to convince the Indians that he needed more minor league seasoning. When Cleveland had to cut its roster to 25 men on April 19, Miñoso was optioned to San Diego of the Pacific Coast League, where he spent the next two seasons.

Although the Indians were defending World Series champions and perhaps reluctant to insert a rookie into a position (right field) he had seldom played, Miñoso was universally regarded as one of the top prospects in baseball. A typical rave came from Edgar Munzel of the *Chicago Sun-Times*, who wrote that Orestes "could make almost every other team in the majors as a regular."[23] He was almost certainly a better player in 1949 and 1950 than Bob Kennedy, a league-average hitter who played the bulk of the Indians' games in right field. Some of the Indians brass asserted that weak outfield defense was holding him back, but Miñoso's glove work in San Diego was drawing comments like this one from Pacific Coast League writer Ned Cronin: "Miñoso has developed into a fielder who would have a tough time covering more ground if the San Diego management let him play on a motorcycle."[24]

Miñoso took the demotion good-naturedly, even decades later. "Looking at that 1949 Cleveland ballclub, though," he wrote in his 1983 autobiography, "it was becoming obvious that I was 'in the wrong place at the wrong time.' With their lineup, it would be a long time before I made the majors, too long for my satisfaction."[25] He even singled out Bob Kennedy for helping him learn to play the outfield. That sort of generosity was typical of Orestes Miñoso. But Cleveland's handling of this brilliant young talent was mystifying, then and now. It may have cost the Indians a pennant or two.

♦ ♦ ♦

While Miñoso was spending most of the 1949 season with the San Diego Padres, 18-year-old Ernie Banks was playing his second season for the Texas-based Detroit Colts. "He was younger than most of us," recalled Ernie's teammate Frank Adams, "but there wasn't any doubt about him playing with the big boys. When you see a guy who's got it, you know he's got it. Even at an early age all it took was for him to polish up the fundamentals and get a little exposure. Ernie was going places, no doubt about it."[26]

At one point during the season, the Colts played a game against the Kansas City Stars, a club that was basically a farm team for the Kansas City Monarchs. The Stars were managed by former Negro League great Cool Papa Bell, who kept his eye out for players who might be able to help the Monarchs. Banks had a great game against the Stars, getting several hits and sparkling on defense. Afterward, Bell told Banks, "Son, you can play this game!"[27]

Banks, who was in his final year of high school, had an opportunity to go to college—to play football. James A. Stephens, the head football coach at Prairie View A&M University, about 200 miles south of Dallas, was impressed by Banks's pass-catching ability and wanted to recruit him for his team. But Banks was enjoying life with the Detroit Colts, and baseball was definitely now his game. "Things were different in my second summer in Amarillo," Banks wrote.

> Now I felt a genuine acceptance among my older teammates; they treated me as a member of the team, not just another kid player. I didn't have to worry about a hole in the ceiling of my hotel room, or the "let the kid do it" chants of the older players when there was an errand to be run or an odd job to be done.
>
> I was determined to bear down and really improve my game. I was Ernie Banks, shortstop for the Detroit Colts, and I was not about to let anyone question it.[28]

7

At Wid's End

A few weeks after the end of the 1949 season, the Chicago Cubs announced that they were reducing the number of teams in their farm system by five. It was a curious move for a club coming off a second consecutive last-place finish for the first time in franchise history. Yet the team's farm system seemed to have few players considered good enough to become major league stars. The Cubs' short-term solution was to follow the lead of several other MLB clubs: purchase players from Branch Rickey's talent-rich Dodgers. While the team was announcing the reduction of its farm system, it also reported the purchase of two Dodgers for an estimated $100,000. The players, pitcher Paul Minner and infielder-outfielder Preston Ward, would go on to have serviceable major league careers, though neither would ever be considered a star.[1]

Within a couple of weeks, Cubs vice president Jim Gallagher was expressing buyer's remorse, apparently having concluded that Minner and Ward were actually worth $99,999 and change less than their sticker price. "Rickey is the greatest salesman in baseball," Gallagher asserted at a meeting of Chicago's Quarterback Club. "He never sold a player who was worth a quarter. But he has received millions for them." Gallagher's rant also included a critique of Rickey's farm system. He stated that of the key players on the Dodgers' 1949 pennant-winning club, "None . . . was grown on the Rickey farm. [Jackie] Robinson, [Roy] Campanella and [Don] Newcombe came out of the Negro league."[2]

That prompted a response from Gene Kessler of the *Sun-Times*: "If I were Gallagher I wouldn't bring up that last subject. Quite a few [Cubs] fans might ask him this pertinent question: 'Why didn't you sign Robinson, Campanella, Newcombe and other stars when they were playing in

Chicago as members of the Negro league and looking for an opportunity to join any major league club?'"[3] (Kessler could have added Orestes Miñoso, who was starring in the minor leagues for Chicagoan Bill Veeck's Cleveland Indians.)

In December the Cubs' eventful offseason continued when the team announced that it had purchased the historic Newark Bears minor league franchise from the New York Yankees. The Bears, at one time among the mightiest teams in minor league baseball, had been plagued by falling attendance. The Cubs announced that its Class AAA International League franchise would be moved to Springfield, Massachusetts, where they had previously fielded a team in the Class B New England League. The deal included the transfer of several players from Newark to Springfield, among them two Black players, outfielder Bob Thurman and catcher Earl Taborn.

The Cubs weren't done tinkering. In February, as the club was preparing for spring training in California, it announced the appointment of 53-year-old Wid Matthews as its director of player personnel. In the club's official hierarchy Matthews would be taking the place of longtime Cubs manager and executive Charlie Grimm, but in terms of decisionmaking power he was in effect replacing Jim Gallagher, whose new title would be "business manager." Matthews was hired from the Brooklyn Dodgers' organization, where he had been known as an expert at developing young players. Barely two months earlier, Gallagher had been quoted as saying, "Do you know that not a single one of the key men who won the pennant for the Dodgers was developed by Rickey?" Now one of the main people in charge of that development was being hired by the Cubs.[4]

Wid Curry Matthews was born in 1886 in Raleigh, a tiny village in southern Illinois. After serving in the navy during World War I, Matthews began his professional baseball career in 1920, reaching the majors with the Philadelphia A's and the Washington Senators from 1923 to 1925. After retiring as a player, he moved to his wife's hometown of Hattiesburg, Mississippi, which remained his home for the rest of his life.

In 1936 Matthews returned to baseball after offering his services to Rickey, who at the time was running the Cardinals. He soon became one of Rickey's top scouts, moving to the Dodgers with Rickey in 1942. When Brooklyn began scouting Black players, Matthews was one of the scouts asked to evaluate the top prospects, most notably Jackie Robinson. According to Lee Lowenfish, "Matthews had his reservations about Robinson's demeanor on the field. He was too much of a 'hot dog' in his mannerisms, the scout believed." A few years later, Robinson and Roy Campanella recommended a young outfielder they had seen on one of their barnstorming tours, and Matthews was asked to check him out. "Matthews reported back that he couldn't hit a curveball," wrote Ron Rapoport. "So the Dodgers passed on Willie Mays." Author John Klima, noting that Matthews had also filed a negative report on Negro League star Piper Davis—he thought that the fiery Davis had "character flaws"—wrote that "there were signs throughout [Matthews's] career that he didn't care for black players."[5]

◆ ◆ ◆

The Cubs did add more Black players to their farm system in 1950. But as was the case in 1949, their handling of these players showed little commitment to giving them a fair chance to prove their worth or to showing patience with their development. Many were summarily cut in spring training, and only a handful finished the season with their original teams.

One of the few to get a semblance of a fair shot in 1950 was 19-year-old Milton Bohannion, who was in his second season with Class D Janesville and his first full season in the Cubs' farm system. Bohannion batted only .249 with little power, but he tied for fifth most stolen bases (22) in the league, while remaining the Wisconsin State League's only Black player. His versatility, athleticism, and flamboyant style of play made him one of the league's most talked-about players. "Bohannion, though on the 'showboat' side, jumps around like a jitterbug and steals (tries to, that is) every time he gets on," wrote *Green Bay Post-Gazette* reporter Art Daley. "He kicks up his heels on the bases and hurls smart remarks at the opposition," commented another writer. Bohannion played every position on the diamond during his two-year stint with Janesville, even taking the mound and pitching effectively in the last game of the regular season. In another game, while playing the outfield, he drew cheers from the crowd after doing a backward somersault over a fence while in pursuit of a foul fly. Bohannion seemed to excel in big moments; he was one of Janesville's better players in the postseason playoffs and was described as the individual star of the league's All-Star game, in which he played two positions, belted three hits, and "ran the bases like a frightened bunny and fielded spectacularly." Bohannion's performance earned him a promotion to the Cubs' Class C farm team in Topeka for 1951.[6]

In Visalia, California, the three players who had broken the color line in the Cubs' farm system were long gone, but the team had a new Black player: 25-year-old outfielder Napoleon (Nap) Gulley. A native of Huttig, Arkansas, Gulley began his professional baseball career with the Negro League Cleveland Buckeyes in 1943. After serving in the military, he had played briefly with another Negro League team, the Newark Eagles; after that he spent time in the Mexican League and the Provincial League in Canada, and he played with Saperstein's Harlem Globetrotters baseball team. Though only five feet, eight inches tall, Gulley had good power, hitting 14 homers in 106 games with Visalia in 1950; he also drove in 83 runs and batted .292. He had a strong arm in the outfield and an upbeat, outgoing personality; in a fan poll late in the season, he was voted the team's most popular player. Writers who covered the team felt that Gulley deserved the California League's Rookie of the Year award as well as a spot on the league's All-Star team, neither of which happened. But despite his strong performance, Cubs officials did not consider Gulley to be a major league prospect; he would return to Visalia in 1951.

In Los Angeles, Booker McDaniel was back on the mound for the Cubs' Pacific Coast League farm team. McDaniel was used mostly in relief in 1950, and the role did not seem to suit him, as he posted a 6.49 earned run average. McDaniel's career in white organized baseball ended after the 1950 season; in 1951 the Cubs sold him back to the Kansas City Monarchs, where he pitched for two more seasons. It was a quiet ending for a man who had been one of the Negro Leagues' best pitchers.

For a short time in 1950, the Los Angeles Angels had a second Black player on their team, one of the most celebrated all-around athletes in America. While Kenny Washington, who had been Jackie Robinson's baseball and football teammate at UCLA, is remembered primarily for his football career, he was also an outstanding college baseball player. "He was a bigger baseball prospect than Robinson," wrote Joe Posnanski, noting that famed USC baseball coach Rod Dedeaux said that Washington had more power, a better arm, and played better defense than Robinson. Dan Taylor, Washington's biographer, said in an interview that he thought the modern athlete most comparable to Kenny was Bo Jackson. "I don't know how his running speed compared to Bo Jackson," said Taylor, "but I've said to people he was Bo Jackson with John Elway's throwing arm—he had that type of talent."[7]

In December 1945, shortly after the Dodgers had signed Robinson, Wendell Smith wrote to Branch Rickey about signing Washington as well. "I understand that he is a much better ball player than Robinson and that he plays in the outfield and infield," he wrote to Rickey. Whether or not Rickey was interested, the timing was wrong for Washington. "Jackie Robinson once asked me if I'd play pro ball," Washington said in November 1946. "I answered 'No' because I had other plans." The "other plans" were to play football with the Los Angeles Rams, where he and college teammate Woody Strode would reintegrate the NFL by becoming the league's first Black players since 1933.[8]

Washington played for the Rams from 1946 to 1948; he was an electrifying player when healthy, but knee injuries limited his playing time and eventually ended his NFL career. By then, more Black players had entered white organized baseball, and Washington received feelers from both the Pittsburgh Pirates (through Bing Crosby, a part-owner of the team) and the Pacific Coast League San Diego Padres. Once more the timing was wrong; Washington, who had begun a second career as a film actor, had committed to starring in a movie with an all-Black cast called *Thousands Cheer*. But in the spring of 1950, Leo Durocher, who was managing the New York Giants, invited the 31-year-old Washington to try out for his team. He had some impressive moments, including a grand slam homer in an exhibition game, but after being away from competitive baseball for years, he struggled in the field and had trouble hitting breaking pitches. Durocher, however, thought that Washington could play in the Pacific Coast League, and the Angels offered Kenny a contract. It wasn't to be; after going hitless in eight at-bats of mostly part-time duty, Washington was released in late April.

One of the many great Black athletes whose career was marked both by great performances and questions about what might have been, Kenny Washington died in Los Angeles at age 52 in 1971. "Los Angeles in the '30s and '40s was not an easy place for a Black man to live and achieve," said L. L. White, pastor of the Holman United Methodist Church, in his eulogy for Washington. "It was against this kind of background that this man's life [shone] like a star lighting up the sky."[9]

◆ ◆ ◆

In fairness to Wid Matthews and Jack Sheehan, the Cubs ran into bad luck in 1950 with at least one player who would become a major league star with another club: future American League MVP Elston Howard. In March Sheehan wrote to Tom Baird of the Monarchs expressing interest in infielder Gene Baker and catcher-outfielder Howard. Baker was not a problem; Sheehan gave Baird $1,000 for the privilege of giving him a 30-day trial with Springfield and paid Baird an additional $5,500 when he decided to keep him. But Baird told Sheehan that he wanted to "keep Howard this year on account of being short of good hitting outfielders." Sheehan, who assumed that Baird would give him the chance to purchase Howard later, learned in July that Baird had sold Howard to the Yankees (along with pitcher Frank Barnes). Sheehan was furious, writing to Baird, "You know that I have been interested in this player for the last three years, have asked you to set a price on him on two different occasions, and was promised, by you, that you would notify me whenever you were ready to sell him." Sheehan wouldn't give up; on the off chance that the Monarchs still retained an option on Howard, he wrote Baird in November, and after disingenuously claiming that "our only report on him is that he is not a prospect," offered $500 for the right to look over Howard in spring training 1951, and $10,000 if the Cubs wanted to keep him. It was too late; Howard remained in the Yankees' farm system, eventually becoming the team's first Black player in 1955.[10]

The Cubs' handling of another future major league star, Jim Gilliam, was much less clear-cut. In March 1950 the Cubs purchased the 21-year-old Gilliam and another young player, 20-year-old pitcher Howard Leroy (Toots) Ferrell, on a conditional basis from the Baltimore Elite Giants of the Negro American League. Both players were assigned to the team's Class AAA International League team at Springfield, Massachusetts. They joined several other Black players at the Springfield Cubs' training camp in Haines City, Florida.

Despite his youth, Gilliam had played with the Elite Giants since 1946, when he joined the club at age 17. He had played in the East-West All-Star Game in 1948 and 1949 and was considered one of the best players in the Negro Leagues. In spring training he battled for Springfield's second base job with Jack (Red) Hollis, a 22-year-old minor league veteran who had had a big season (.315 BA, 15 HRs, 83 RBIs) in the Class B Southeastern League in 1949. By March 30 the battle was over: The *Springfield Union* reported that Hollis, who had been "hitting the ball hard and fielding brilliantly in addition to teaming well with big Jack Wallaesa around second base," would open the season at second.[11] Although Gilliam made Springfield's Opening Day roster, the Cubs returned him to the Elite Giants a few days later. After another good season with Baltimore in 1950, Gilliam and teammate Joe Black were sold to the Dodgers. Black would win the National League Rookie of the Year award in 1952; Gilliam would win the rookie award a year later, ultimately becoming a franchise icon as a player and coach. After his death in 1978, Gilliam's jersey number 19 was retired by the Dodgers.

The reasons for the Cubs' decision to return Gilliam to Baltimore have always been a bit murky. In his unpublished autobiography, Joe Black wrote, "In 1949 [actually 1950], the Chicago Cubs had signed Jim Gilliam and assigned him to their AAA farm team. Thirty days later, he was back with the Elite Giants. No, it was not because he lacked the playing skills. His drawback was the fact that he had never lived or played in an integrated setting. He would sit at the end of the bench, go to the back of the bus when the team traveled and if it wasn't the manager, he would give a grunt and not be involved in conversation with others." According to Jeff Angus, who wrote Gilliam's SABR biography, "In Black's version, the Cubs returned him with a note saying they were doing the 21-year-old more harm than good by trying to build his baseball skills in that environment."[12]

That makes it seem as though the Cubs thought that they were doing an overwhelmed Gilliam a favor by returning him to Baltimore. But it's also clear that the Cubs did not give Gilliam much of a chance to succeed, much less feel comfortable. A review of spring training box scores from the *Springfield Union*, which covered the team extensively and had reports on all but one or two games, showed Gilliam as the starting second baseman in only 6 of the team's 20-plus spring games; he appeared in seven more games as a pinch hitter or mid-game replacement. Overall he batted .333 (9 for 27), with two doubles, a triple, eight runs scored, a stolen base, and several walks. He did commit three errors in the field, but he also turned three double plays. Those are pretty solid numbers for anyone, especially a 21-year-old player getting his first opportunity in white organized baseball. Yet by the end of March, with more than three weeks to go before the start of the season, the club had publicly handed the second base job to Red Hollis. The Cubs organization didn't even consider giving Gilliam a spot on one of their lower-level farm teams. If Gilliam was sitting sullenly on the bench during his time with Springfield, ready to return to Baltimore, his attitude was understandable.

◆ ◆ ◆

The Springfield Cubs had six other Black players in spring training in 1950; according to the *Springfield Union*, "It looks as though the Springfield club has more Negro players in camp than any other club in baseball with the exception of the Vero Beach setup operated by the Brooklyn Dodgers."[13] But only two of these players made Springfield's Opening Day roster, and only one lasted the entire season with the club.

One of the two was Gene Baker, a 24-year-old infielder who had been purchased from Tom Baird's Kansas City Monarchs. Baker spent the first month of the 1950 season with Springfield, then was optioned to Des Moines of the Class A Western League. He finished the season with the Cubs' marquis minor league franchise, the Los Angeles Angels of the Pacific Coast League. Baker's career is discussed in depth in Chapter 11.

The Black player who received the most attention in the Springfield Cubs' spring camp was outfielder Bob Thurman. An imposing man who was listed as six feet, one and a half inches tall, Thurman weighed well over 200 pounds during his prime years; his muscular physique was often described in such terms as "perfectly proportioned." Ballplayers of his day routinely shaved a couple of years off their actual ages, but Thurman really pushed the envelope: Though his "baseball" birth year was listed as 1923, he was actually born in 1917. Thurman could get away with this ruse more easily because he began his professional baseball career after playing semipro baseball for several years with teams in the vicinity of his hometown of Wichita, Kansas. After serving in the Pacific Theater during World War II, Thurman joined the legendary Homestead Grays of the Negro Leagues at age 29 in 1946. His teammates included future Hall of Famers Josh Gibson, Buck Leonard, and Cool Papa Bell. "When I had a chance to see the guys play, I said that's where I want to play, with the best guys," he recalled.[14] After three seasons with the Grays, Thurman joined the Kansas City Monarchs in 1949. In late July of that year Tom Baird sold the contracts of Thurman and teammate Earl Taborn to the New York Yankees, who, with Larry MacPhail no longer an owner, had begun using Black players in their farm system. The Yankees assigned Thurman to their Class AAA farm team in Newark; as usual with Baird transactions, the purchase price varied with how long the players stuck with the team. According to Fay Young, the White Sox were also interested in both Thurman and Taborn and even sent Baird a check to purchase them; however, Baird preferred dealing with the Yankees because the Monarchs were using the ballpark of the Yankees' Kansas City Blues affiliate in the American Association.[15]

Thurman was an immediate sensation with Newark. In his first game he had two singles and a 415-foot homer over the center field fence that was described as the longest home run in the Bears' home park since the late 1920s. More tape measure shots followed; Rod Marvin of the *Hackensack Record* wrote, "Followers of the Newark Bears are thinking that they may have another Babe Ruth in Bob Thurman, young Negro star." In September the *Sporting News* reported that Thurman's first six home runs had traveled between 390 and 460 feet. The *Pittsburgh Courier* predicted that "Bob Thurman is the lad that will break the New York Yankees holdout against Negro players."[16]

But despite Thurman's outstanding debut (he batted .317 with an .850 OPS in 59 games for the Bears), that never came close to happening. When the Cubs acquired the Newark franchise and moved it to Springfield, they acquired Thurman (and Taborn) as part of the deal, with the Cubs paying Baird $2,500 when Thurman made Springfield's Opening Day roster. By mid-May, when Springfield demoted Gene Baker to Class A Des Moines, Thurman was the team's only remaining Black player. He wound up batting .269, though he had an excellent .376 on-base percentage. While he continued to hit long home runs, he belted only 12 during the season. That, apparently, was not good enough for the Cubs. When the season ended, they sold Thurman to the San Francisco Seals, a Yankees farm team. The

Yankees had little interest in advancing their Black players to the majors, and by the time Thurman finally got a chance to play in the majors with the 1955 Cincinnati Reds, he was 38 years old (but listed as 32). He stayed with the Reds until 1959, never getting as many as 200 at-bats in a season. But he still had that old-time power. In 1957 the 40-year-old Thurman blasted 16 home runs with 40 RBIs in only 190 at-bats. He continued to play in the minor leagues until 1961, then served as a scout for the Minnesota Twins, the Reds, and the Kansas City Royals. He knew talent; "Cincinnati wouldn't have signed Johnny Bench without Bob Thurman," said Herk Robinson, a Reds executive during the time when Thurman worked for the team. Bob Thurman died in Wichita at age 81 in 1998.[17]

Summing up how he was treated during his minor league career, Thurman's wife Dorothy said, "They (management) wanted to use Bob for a workhorse. . . . They weren't concerned about (his) career or whether he advanced beyond that. They felt he should be grateful for playing with white players."[18] Thurman was not a bitter man, however. Writer Robert Objoski, who interviewed Thurman toward the end of his life, remembered him as one of the nicest players he ever talked to.[19] "He never seemed to regret not getting a chance earlier," said Dorothy Thurman.[20]

♦ ♦ ♦

Springfield's other Black players would all be gone by the end of spring training. Obtained by the Cubs along with Thurman, 27-year-old catcher Earl "Mickey" Taborn had played for the Kansas City Monarchs from 1946 to 1949, earning a reputation as an excellent defensive catcher. Monarchs owner Tom Baird first offered Taborn to the Cubs in the spring of 1949, describing him as "a hustling ball player and a favorite with the fans," as well as "the only young catcher in the Negro American League who has major league possibilities in my opinion."[21] Sheehan had some interest, but not on Baird's terms, so Baird sold Taborn to the Yankees. With Springfield, Taborn battled for a roster spot with two experienced catchers, Les Peden and future major league star Forrest (Smoky) Burgess; Taborn was the odd man out. Sold back to the Monarchs at the end of spring training, Taborn played one more year with Kansas City, then joined the Mexican League, where he played for 11 seasons; his hustling, enthusiastic style of play helped him become a franchise favorite with the Veracruz team.

Carlos Bernier, a 23-year-old outfielder who got his shot with Springfield after stealing 89 bases with Bristol in the Class B Colonial League in 1949, is another player who, like Jim Gilliam, displayed speed and talent in spring training only to be cut before the regular season began. Bernier is a bit of a tricky case when discussing baseball's integration. A native of

Puerto Rico, he would almost certainly be considered Black or Afro-Latino today, and in fact is often identified as the first Black player to perform for the Pittsburgh Pirates, which he did in 1953. On the other hand, Bernier was categorized as "Puerto Rican" in 1950 and most likely would have been allowed to play in the pre-1947 National or American League without controversy. However we categorize him, Bernier drew a lot of attention in the Springfield Cubs' training camp. "I haven't seen anything like that in a long time," said manager Stan Hack about Bernier's great speed.[22] His "stellar fielding" in center field also won praise.[23] In late March he was considered neck and neck with Bob Talbot in the battle for the team's starting center field job. Yet despite Wid Matthews's statement that "the greatest asset in baseball is speed," Bernier was returned to Bristol before the 1950 regular season began. His baseball career had a long time to go. Along with his one season in the majors with the 1953 Pirates—he batted .213 but led the team with 15 stolen bases—Bernier played 16 seasons in the minor leagues, finishing at age 38 with Reynosa of the Mexican League in 1965. Over the course of his career Bernier played over two thousand games in the minor leagues, with more than five hundred stolen bases. Plagued by medical, financial, and emotional issues, he hanged himself in his own garage in his hometown of Juana Diaz, Puerto Rico, in 1989. He was 62 years old.

Springfield had two former Negro League pitchers in its spring camp. The, first, 30-year-old Bill Ricks, had pitched for the Philadelphia Stars from 1944 to 1949. Ricks's Negro League credentials were outstanding; he had led the Negro National League in wins and wins above replacement for pitchers in 1944, made the East-West All-Star game in 1945, and led the league in ERA in 1948. In spring training with Springfield, Ricks posted a 3.71 ERA in 17 innings, allowing only 12 hits while recording 16 strikeouts; his main negative was allowing 13 walks. He also gave up three home runs, all solo shots, in his final outing. An April column about Springfield Cubs manager Stan Hack in the *Rochester (NY) Democrat and Chronicle* indicated that Ricks was in consideration for starting the season opener. But just before the start of the season, Springfield returned Ricks to the Philadelphia Stars. After spending the first month of the season with the Stars, Ricks finished the year with the Winona, Minnesota, Chiefs of the semipro Southern Minnesota League, a league considered as strong as some Class A and even Class AA leagues. He had one more shot in white organized baseball with the Granby (Quebec) Red Sox of the Class C Provincial League, going 8-8 with a 4.21 ERA in 1951.

Finally, there was pitcher Toots Ferrell, who had come to Springfield from the Baltimore Elite Giants with Jim Gilliam. Ferrell didn't even make it to the end of March; he was sent back to the Elite Giants after committing two balks in his first appearance and surrendering three home runs in his second. According to Ferrell in a 1985 interview with the *Wilmington Morning News*, he was part of the deal in which the Elite Giants sold Gilliam and Joe Black to the Dodgers in 1951, but this account could not be confirmed. After serving in the army during the Korean War, Ferrell was in the Dodgers' spring camp in 1953 but apparently was released. In the same 1985 interview Ferrell said he had pitched for Montreal and St. Paul in the Dodgers' farm system, but again there is nothing in the record to confirm this assertion. Ferrell did pitch for Black semipro teams in his hometown of Wilmington, Delaware, for several years in the 1950s.[24]

In 1975, long after his baseball career was over, Toots Ferrell was in the news again—under tragic circumstances. On August 17 of that year, Ferrell's 13-year-old daughter Sheila, who was living in Wilmington with Toots's ex-wife, was playing with some friends when they decided to pick peaches from a neighborhood tree. According to *Wilmington News Journal* reporter Wendy Fox, "It wasn't unusual to collect peaches from that tree— until recently the house on 35th St. had been vacant for a year and half, neighbors said, so there was nobody there to mind." While the children were picking the peaches, a car pulled up that was driven by a white man who had been renovating the property on which the tree was situated. The man, who was riding with a female companion, angrily told the children to get out of the tree, then took after them on foot when they started running away. When he drew near Sheila, witnesses heard him shout, "Stop or I'll shoot!" Bystanders heard a gun firing, and Sheila Ferrell collapsed after continuing to run for several hundred feet. She was taken to Delaware Division Hospital, clinging to life. For the next 13 days Toots and Sheila's mother, Carolyn Snow, took turns sitting in her room, hoping for signs of recovery.[25]

The day after the shooting, 24-year-old John Bailey, whose family owned the house and the peach tree, was arrested and charged with attempted murder. When Bailey was released on $25,000 bail less than 12 hours later, many in Wilmington's Black community were outraged. "A dope pusher gets $50,000 bail, and this pig gets only $25,000?," asked one of Sheila's neighbors. For several days there were angry demonstrations in protest of Bailey's release, including confrontations that featured officers on horseback and in riot gear, wielding nightsticks and using tear gas to disperse the crowd. A few of the demonstrators broke windows and threw rocks and bottles at the police. Wilmington, which had erupted into several days of rioting after Martin Luther King's assassination seven years earlier, was on edge. Sheila's parents pleaded for the demonstrators to remain peaceful. Violent protests were "not the way to solve the problem," Toots Ferrell told a crowd at Market St. Mall. "For God's sake, I don't want anyone else hurt. If something does happen we will be defeating our own purpose." The protests finally ended after Bailey was jailed again, with his bail increased to $130,000. No one was killed during the protests, and property damage was fairly minimal. But on August 30, Sheila Ferrell died at Delaware District. John Bailey's charge was increased to first-degree murder.[26]

At Bailey's trial, the defense produced a surprise witness who said he had seen a second shooter, an unidentified Black man, pursuing Bailey; they claimed that it was this second shooter, aiming for Bailey, who had shot Sheila. The jury apparently did not believe this story, but the prosecution was hampered by not having been able to retrieve either the gun or the bullet that had killed Sheila. (Bailey admitted to brandishing his gun, saying that he had thrown it in the Delaware River.) Nor had the prosecution formally identified or interviewed Bailey's female companion. Ultimately the jury convicted Bailey not of murder but of the lesser charge of manslaughter. John Bailey served 17 years of his maximum 25-year sentence before being released in 1993, still maintaining his innocence. Toots Ferrell, a member of the Delaware Sports and Delaware Afro-American Halls of Fame as well as Delaware's last living Negro Leaguer, according to news stories, died in Newark, Delaware, at age 73 in October 2002. None of the post-1975 stories that the author found about Ferrell, including his obituary, mentioned his daughter Sheila or what had happened to her.[27]

◆ ◆ ◆

"The Chicago Cubs, owned by Phil Wrigley, are finally hunting around for a Negro attraction to draw some of that huge South Side patronage to the North side when the little Bears are at home," wrote Dan Burley of the *New York Age* in May 1950; he cited the signing of Thurman, Taborn, Gilliam, Ferrell, Ricks, and Baker. "But the Chicago White Sox are just as far away from signing Negro players as they were back in 1940 [actually 1942] when Jackie Robinson and a UCLA teammate, a pitcher, reported to the White Sox training camp in California and asked Jimmy Dykes, then manager, for tryouts," Burley continued. "Jimmy gave them a lot of hooey, all in keeping with the Comiskey anti-Negro program[,] and it wasn't until Branch Rickey signed Jackie that anything was definitely done in the matter."[28]

A short time later, Chuck Comiskey and his farm director, John Rigney, met with a group that was protesting the Sox' alleged refusal to sign Black players. At the meeting Comiskey announced that he had hired three more scouts. "We're not opposed to hiring colored ball players," Comiskey told the *Chicago Defender*. "We just haven't found the right colored ball player. I'm a business man, and I know that if I could find a good colored ball player for the White Sox, we would fill this park." He told the paper that his club had tried to purchase Thurman and Taborn and told the scouts, "I'm appointing each of you as a scout of the White Sox and if you can find us a good colored ball player, just let us know."[29]

Finally, in early August, the Sox announced the signing of their first two Black players, first baseman Bob Boyd and catcher Sam Hairston. Unlike the Cubs, whose first Black signees were a mixture of young players and Negro League veterans, the White Sox elected to purchase two Negro League vets—both players were 30 years old, though their listed "baseball ages" were several years younger—who seemed to be almost ready for the majors. The Sox signed Hairston and Boyd on the recommendation of scout and longtime Negro Leaguer John Donaldson.

Boyd, the first of the two players to sign, was a native of Potts Camp, Mississippi. He had joined the Memphis Red Sox in 1947 after serving in the Quartermaster Corps during World War II. From the beginning, he was a line-drive, high-average hitter; as early as 1948, a major league team, the Boston Braves, was said to be interested in signing Boyd. It was a struggle for Boyd to get by. "We didn't make any money back in the 1940s," Boyd recalled in 1991. "We'd get two dollars a day and mostly ride the bus. I hardly ever slept in a hotel."[30]

Hairston, a native of Crawford, Mississippi, was the second of 13 children born to Will and Clara Hairston. His family moved to Birmingham, Alabama, when Hairston was two years old, and he got his first baseball experience playing in an industrial league in the Birmingham area. Classified 4-F during World War II owing to a bad toe, he joined Birmingham's Negro League team, the Black Barons, in 1944. He was soon traded to the Cincinnati-Indianapolis Clowns, and with the Clowns he matured into a consistent high-average hitter. In 1950 Hairston won the Triple Crown in the Negro American League, leading the league in batting average, home runs, and RBIs according to statistics released by the Howe News Bureau.[31]

The White Sox assigned Hairston and Boyd to their Class A farm team in Colorado Springs. While Hairston performed creditably for the Sky Sox, hitting .286, Boyd was a sensation with a .373 average. Both men would be in the White Sox spring training camp in Pasadena in 1951.

◆ ◆ ◆

In the spring of 1950 Ernie Banks, who was finishing his senior year at Booker T. Washington High, was at his local YMCA when William (Dizzy) Dismukes came to see him. A former Negro League pitcher in the 1910s and '20s, Dismukes was the traveling secretary and chief scout for the Kansas City Monarchs; he had been instrumental in the signing of Jackie Robinson to play shortstop for the Monarchs in 1945. Now he wanted to sign Ernie Banks. Dismukes asked to meet Ernie's parents, and at the meeting he offered Banks $300 a month to play for the Monarchs as soon as Ernie graduated. That was more money than Ernie's parents were making, and he immediately accepted. The day after his graduation ceremony in May, Banks headed to Kansas City. He made his debut on June 4, going 3-for-7 in a doubleheader against Memphis.

Although the Negro Leagues were in decline, the Monarchs were still a well-run franchise under owner Tom Baird. The team's manager, future Hall of Famer Buck O'Neil, had been a Monarchs player since 1937 and the team's player-manager since 1948; he was, wrote Banks biographer Doug Wilson, "simply one of the most respected black men in America."[32] As a manager, O'Neil was firm but supportive. His upbeat personality was perfect for the 19-year-old Banks. "A teacher and a leader, he was all that and more," said Banks in 2006. "He was the most positive person that I have ever been around. I transferred that into my life."[33]

Banks also benefited from having veteran teammates who for the most part helped him feel comfortable. His first roommate was Elston Howard, who would be the first Black player for the New York Yankees. Another teammate was Curt Roberts, who would be the Pittsburgh Pirates' first African American player in 1954. "It was a wonderful experience, you know, riding on the bus and stopping and eating peanut butter and sardines and, you know, guys just playing their harps and guitars," he recalled. "I'm a type of person that I really enjoy my own comfort area. And I liked being with the guys. I liked their attitude. We cared about each other."[34]

Buck O'Neil also helped Banks deal with discrimination and racism. Although Kansas City had a large Black population, Blacks were largely confined to the east side, with Troost Avenue the dividing line (the "Troost Divide"). The Monarchs players largely kept to their own area, staying at the Streets Hotel, where they were well treated. When the Monarchs visited a town, O'Neil would caution the players about neighborhoods and stores to avoid and inform them whether the city had an active Ku Klux Klan chapter. "Before we got to one city in Kansas, he said, 'Hey, they just had a lynching over here,'" Banks recalled. "That got our attention. I was looking around and wondering what's going on? I mean, this is America."[35]

After the season Banks was asked to be part of a barnstorming team organized by Jackie Robinson; his teammates included Larry Doby and Roy Campanella as well as Robinson, who helped Ernie with batting and fielding tips. Robinson paid him $400 for playing on the tour, a large sum of money to Ernie. But when he returned home, Banks received a notice from his draft board. He was soon inducted into the US Army and would not return to professional baseball until 1953.

8

Window Dressing

On February 18, 1951, the Chicago White Sox entourage left LaSalle Street Station to head to California for spring training. The team would make an eight-day stopover in Palm Springs before setting up in Pasadena. Except for the seasons during World War II when travel restrictions limited major league teams to training camps closer to home, the Sox had trained in Pasadena annually since 1933. Pasadena, the city where Jackie Robinson grew up, had numerous Jim Crow restrictions, with segregated hotels, stores, restaurants, schools, and hospitals. By 1940, a year before Robinson's departure from the city, a *California Eagle* editorial noted that the city had yet to hire "a single [black] policeman, fireman, regular daytime school teacher, meter-reader, or any other type of employee for the utilities; no, not even a janitor or an elevator boy in the city hall."[1] Robinson's brother Mack, a silver medalist as a sprinter in the 1936 Olympics, said that when he applied for work after his return from the Games, the city offered him a job cleaning the Pasadena streets with a broom and pushcart. Mack "irritated a number of white people by sweeping the streets decked out in his leather U.S.A. jacket," wrote Jackie Robinson biographer Arnold Rampersad.[2] Ruby McKnight Williams, a Black schoolteacher who became an activist after moving to Pasadena from Topeka, Kansas, in 1930, wrote, "I didn't see any difference in Pasadena and Mississippi except they were spelled differently."[3]

The White Sox spring camp included three Black players: Bob Boyd, Sam Hairston, and Luis Garcia, a Venezuelan infielder. Boyd, who had impressed the Sox enough to be added to the team's 40-man roster, was battling Eddie Robinson and Gordon Goldsberry for the first base job. "He'll outhit, outfield and outrun both of them," said John Donaldson, the scout who had recommended Boyd's signing.[4] According to the *Chicago*

Defender, Boyd batted .533 in spring training games, but at the end of the month both he and Hairston were optioned to Sacramento of the Class AAA Pacific Coast League.[5] "Boyd and Hairston are two good ball players, and they'll have a chance to play every day at Sacramento," said Sox general manager Frank Lane. "It wouldn't be fair to the kids to take them to Chicago and keep them on the bench all season." Manager Paul Richards was impressed with Boyd. "As soon as he proves he can hit good lefthanded pitching, he's a big leaguer right there," said Richards. "He has everything else."[6]

As Orestes Miñoso was making his historic debut as the first Black player in White Sox history, Hairston was spending the bulk of the 1951 season with Sacramento (batting .253 in 68 games) and Class A Colorado Springs (.389 in 15 games). Meanwhile, Boyd got the sort of welcome to his new league that Black players often received in the early years of baseball integration. On May 11, he was hit in the head by a pitch from San Francisco Seals lefthander Chet Johnson and needed to be rushed to the hospital. "I saw the pitch coming . . . it had a lot of stuff . . . I guess I just froze," Boyd said about the beaning. "I must have nodded my head or the pitch would have struck my jaw and torn my face in two. . . . I was lucky. First time I've been hit this year . . . but golly, those pitchers sure try to keep me loosened up at the plate. High . . . inside . . . I'm looking at those kind of pitches every night."[7] The X-rays were negative, and Boyd was back in the lineup the next day. He proceeded to have an outstanding season with Sacramento, hitting .342 with 41 stolen bases.

As noted, both Hairston and Boyd joined Miñoso on the White Sox roster for brief periods during the season: Hairston in late July, Boyd in September. Boyd would get another shot with the big club in 1952, but Hairston's four-game stint, with two hits in five at-bats for a .400 average, would comprise his entire white major league career. "I went to the major leagues, hit .400, they sent me down to Class A," Hairston said in a 1995 interview. He spent four of the next five seasons (1952–56) with Colorado Springs, where he became a fan favorite as well as a consistent .300 hitter. "I was one of the outstanding players," he told an interviewer. "See, the White Sox didn't keep me because they loved me. They kept me there because I did a job. You're there for one thing."[8]

◆ ◆ ◆

The third Black player in the White Sox spring camp, Luis Garcia, would be considered Black or Afro-Latino today but might have been light-skinned enough to be accepted in the pre-Jackie Robinson days as "Latin" and thus eligible to enter white organized baseball. This kind of differentiation—based primarily on the darkness of a player's skin—had been an issue with Latin-born players almost from the time they first entered white baseball. Garcia was not identified as Black in press reports from the White Sox' 1951 spring camp. On the other hand, the *Pittsburgh Courier* covered Garcia's performance along with those of other Afro-Latino players when he was playing in the minors in 1953, which makes it somewhat questionable that he would have been allowed to play in the American or National League before 1947. It's impossible to know for sure.

In spring training with the 1951 White Sox, Garcia had the benefit of a Venezuelan-born teammate: the lighter-skinned Chico Carrasquel, whose lineage had created no controversy when he joined the White Sox in 1950. Garcia had made his white organized baseball debut at age 19 with the Class D Concord Nationals, a Washington Senators farm club. In 1950 he played for Tijuana of the Class C Sunset League, which included teams from the United States and Mexico. The White Sox signed him in January 1951 for a reported $10,000 bonus, and Frank Lane said he would be assigned to Class A Colorado Springs.

Garcia was late reporting to camp, apparently because of a shortage of funds. He got off to a good start once he arrived; Sox manager Paul Richards tried Garcia, who had previously spent most of his career as a third baseman, at second base and was impressed with his "catlike grace" when teamed with shortstop Carrasquel. But in mid-March Garcia abruptly went home to Venezuela, with reports saying that he had "succumbed to homesickness." An Associated Press story referred to him as "Lonesome Lu." White Sox pitcher Luis Aloma, a native of Cuba who was serving as Garcia's interpreter, said that Garcia "never had gone to school and actually came from a tribe of headhunters in the hinterlands of Venezuela. His parents still live in the deep bush." Aloma said he told Garcia that the White Sox had promised Luis that he could bring his wife to camp, "but it [didn't] help. You know, I understand English better than I understand his Spanish." Garcia said that he would return the $10,000 bonus but denied that he left the team owing to homesickness. "There was nothing in particular that made me leave," he told reporters in Venezuela. "I just didn't feel well and the California climate is too cold for me. . . . I will never go back."[9]

Ten days later Garcia changed his mind, saying that he would return to the team. Still assigned to Colorado Springs, he reported to the club's minor league camp in Hot Springs, Arkansas, on April 6. He was accompanied by his wife, who, it turned out, was pregnant and needed to be rushed to the hospital upon arrival. Garcia began the season with Colorado Springs, but after getting off to a 2-for-22 start while struggling at second base, he went back to Venezuela in early May. Later in the year he was back with Tijuana. In 1952, still only 22 years old, he had an outstanding season with the Aberdeen Pheasants, a St. Louis Browns farm club in the Class C Northern League, hitting .288 with 15 homers, 97 RBIs, 101 runs scored, and 70 walks in only 126 games. Those were numbers that would seem to mark him as a top prospect in most observers' eyes.

Instead, Garcia wandered from one league—and one country—to another over the next few years. In 1953 he was acquired by the independent Toronto Maple Leafs of the Class AAA International League. The Leafs then sent him to the Tampa Smokers of the Class B Florida International League prior to the start of the season. A news report stated that Garcia "was loaned to the Smokers because he spoke no English but could converse with the several Cuban players on the Tampa Bay team." Although the Smokers were managed by Ben Chapman, the manager notorious for the racist taunts that he and his players had hurled at Jackie Robinson in 1947, Garcia again played outstanding ball; in 81 games through early July, he batted .304 with 10 homers, 62 RBIs, and a .394 on-base percentage while batting cleanup and excelling in the field. "He is a fancy Dan in the field and has amazing wrist power at the plate," said the *Tampa Tribune*.[10]

But despite the promising start to his career, Garcia never got a chance to play in the white major leagues. Promoted to Class AAA in midyear 1953—he finished the season with Charleston of the American Association, a White Sox farm team (though he apparently was still the property of Toronto)—his numbers declined, and in 1956 the 26-year-old Garcia accepted an offer to play in the Mexican League. He continued to play in Mexico, Cuba, Venezuela, and the United States for the next decade, usually at a high level. He also excelled in winter league play, particularly in the annual postseason Caribbean Series. After his retirement in 1966, Garcia was elected to the Caribbean Baseball Hall of Fame (2000), the Venezuelan Baseball Hall of Fame (2003), the Navegantes del Magallanes (Magellan Navigators) Hall of Fame (2012), and the Latino Baseball Hall of Fame (2014); he was also a finalist for the Mexican Baseball Hall of Fame, an organization that has never inducted a Venezuelan player, on four occasions.

Given the great success of Latin players in US baseball since the 1960s, it is reasonable to think that Luis Garcia might have become a major league star under different circumstances. Perhaps the arc of his American baseball career would have been different with a little more patience and care on the part of the White Sox in the spring of 1951. There seemed to be no consideration that a dark-skinned, non-English-speaking man from a remote part of Venezuela with a pregnant wife might be feeling a little overwhelmed. (The White Sox, of course, were hardly unusual in this regard.) It's not hard to see Garcia as a teammate of the Venezuelan Chico Carrasquel and the Cuban Orestes Miñoso, a key member of the Go-Go Sox of the 1950s. As with so many players during this transitional period of baseball history, the times weren't quite right.

◆ ◆ ◆

Along with Boyd, Hairston, and Garcia, the White Sox had nine other Black players in their farm system in 1951. These players ranged from Negro League veterans to prospects signed right out of college. None of them ever reached the American or the National League, and their handling by the White Sox makes it difficult to think that the Sox considered any of them to be serious prospects to play for the big club.

The Class A Colorado Springs club had seven Black players on its roster over the course of the season: Jesse Douglas, Melvin Duncan, Ben Lott, Bill Powell, and Curley Williams, plus Hairston and (very briefly) Garcia. Along with Garcia, Powell was the player who had the most distinguished playing career. A Georgia native who had grown up in Birmingham, Alabama, Powell played semipro ball in the Birmingham area and served in World War II before joining the Birmingham Black Barons of the Negro American League at age 27 in 1946. Over the course of the next five seasons he was one of the best pitchers in the Negro Leagues; his accomplishments included starting two games against the Kansas City Monarchs in the 1948 Negro League World Series. With the 1951 Sky Sox he posted a 14-8 record with a 4.69 ERA that was one of the best on a team playing in Colorado's high altitude; his 157 strikeouts led the staff. Powell pitched for the White Sox' Class AAA Toledo and Charleston farm teams in 1952–53 and remained in the minor leagues until 1961, when he was 42 years old. He also excelled in winter league play. Including Negro League play (regular season and nonleague games), minor league games, and winter ball, Powell is estimated to have won nearly 250 games during his professional career.[11] He played against Satchel Paige and Josh Gibson and pitched to the young Hank Aaron (in the minors). His Negro League teammates included Willie Mays; his minor league teammates included Brooks Robinson and Curt Flood. But he never got a chance to pitch in the white majors. "It was tough then, man; segregation was *bad*," Powell said. "Good ballplayers in the minor leagues and they don't bring them up. It's rough. You have to be almost perfect."[12]

If white major league teams could use Bill Powell's age as a reason not to give him a trial, the same could not be said of infielder Ben "Honey" Lott, who was 26 when he split the latter stages of the 1951 season between

Colorado Springs and the Sox' Class B farm team in Waterloo, Iowa. Lott, an infielder who had played three seasons (1948–50) with the Negro League New York Black Yankees and part of the 1951 season with the Indianapolis Clowns, stood only five foot eight and weighed 145 pounds, according to his draft records, but he could hit with surprising power. He could also steal bases. A 1950 article about a Black Yankees exhibition game described Lott as "another Jackie Robinson." Negro League player Raydell Maddix recalled that "every time we played in New Orleans, [Lott] hit two home runs."[13] Lott was a .300 hitter (or close to it) with power and speed pretty much everywhere he played—Negro Leagues, US minor leagues, the ManDak League in Canada and the Dakotas, winter ball—yet he found himself looking for a new job almost every year. His batting totals for 163 games in the affiliated minor leagues (a full season nowadays) show a .287 average, .367 on-base percentage, 135 runs scored, 23 homers, 101 RBIs and 28 stolen bases. Those are impressive numbers. Yet Lott's performance seemed to interest no one, including the White Sox. After hitting over .300 in his brief stints with Sox farm teams in 1951, Lott went to the ManDak League in 1952. His last year in professional baseball was 1957.

Another Negro League veteran, middle infielder Jesse Douglas, was 35 when he joined the Sky Sox in July of the 1951 season. A native of Longview, Texas, the five-foot, six-inch Douglas was a true baseball vagabond. He played in the Negro Leagues with the New York Black Yankees, the Kansas City Monarchs, and the Chicago American Giants from 1938 to 1945, spent two seasons (1946–47) in the Mexican League, returned to the Negro Leagues with the Chicago American Giants (1949–1950), and then spent 1950 and part of 1951 in the Panamanian League. Douglas barnstormed with Satchel Paige in 1939 and played in the East-West All-Star game in 1950. With the Sky Sox he got into 72 games, batting .262. In 1952 he headed north to the ManDak League, a popular haven for Black players with the deterioration of the Negro Leagues; in three seasons in the league he played for the Winnipeg Giants, the Winnipeg Royals, the Brandon Greys and the Carmen Cardinals. Returning to the United States in 1956, Douglas finished his career two years later, playing nine games with Yakima, Washington, of the Northwest League.

Although pitcher-outfielder Melvin Duncan had spent nearly three full seasons with the Kansas City Monarchs (1949–51), he was only 22 years old when he joined the Sky Sox in late July 1951. Duncan, who was born in Ann Arbor, Michigan, grew up in Centralia, a city in southwestern Illinois about 60 miles east of St. Louis; he recalled playing ball as a youngster with the brothers of Hall of Famer Red Schoendienst, who lived about 20 miles away in Germantown. Duncan joined the Monarchs in 1949 for

$300 a month, with three dollars a day for food. He pitched only briefly for Colorado Springs in 1951; a search of box scores listed his record as 1-2. After that he played in Mexico, Venezuela, and Canada, with a brief return to the Negro Leagues in 1955. Very few stats are available for Duncan because most of the leagues he played in compiled sketchy records. But he fondly recalled his years in the Negro Leagues, especially his time with the Monarchs under Buck O'Neil. "I never knew a better bunch of guys than I played with—not just the team I played on, the teams I played against, too," he told author Brent Kelley. "We had fun and we respected everybody."[14]

Shortstop Willie "Curley" Williams was 25 years old when he became the third Black player (after Boyd and Hairston) signed by the White Sox in December 1950. Previously Williams had played in the Negro Leagues for the Newark (and later Houston) Eagles from 1945–50; like Boyd and Hairston, Williams had been scouted by John Donaldson. Preseason stories indicated that Williams would be the Sky Sox' regular shortstop in 1951, and he homered in the team's home opener on April 21. In 20 games he batted .297 with a .547 slugging average and four home runs. But he also committed 12 errors in 14 games at shortstop, and that apparently was too much for the Sky (and White) Sox. By midseason Williams was back with the Eagles, who were now calling New Orleans home; he was the starting shortstop for the West in the 1951 East-West All-Star Game.

Williams wasn't done with white organized baseball, however. In September 1951 the Eagles sold Williams's contract to the St. Louis Browns, now owned by Bill Veeck. When playing for Class AAA Toledo and Class AA Scranton in 1952, Williams's hitting fell off, and his defense continued to be an issue. When he felt he wasn't getting a fair shot in spring training in 1953, Williams walked out and signed with a team in the Dominican Republic. He continued to play in Canada (including part of the 1953 season in the ManDak League) and the Dominican Republic into the 1960s. Asked by Brent Kelley if he had any regrets, Williams said,

> No. The only thing I regret was that things would have been a little better in the first year in organized baseball. It would've made it a *lot* better. You're afraid to say anything; you get out there, you play your heart out, and after the game you're just alone. Nobody to talk to—your teammates go their way, you go your way. That's sad. . . .
>
> I'll tell you another thing that really [made me angry]. They'd have players—sort of light-colored players—from the Dominican Republic and Puerto Rico and all and they could stay *any*place. They always put us someplace—in a black neighborhood. That kind of got to me too. That's just the way it was then. It shouldn't have been that way, but I'll

tell you one thing—they missed out on some of the greatest players who ever lived.[15]

◆ ◆ ◆

White Sox farm teams had four more Black players in 1951: Gideon Applegate and Gene Collins with Waterloo, Iowa, of the Class B Three-I League, along with Crawford Neal and Frank Ensley with Superior, Wisconsin, of the Class C Northern League. All were young enough in 1951 (Collins at 26 was the oldest) to have some expectation that the White Sox might consider them to be prospective major league players. If they did, their expectations would soon be dashed.

Neal and Ensley were teammates at Grambling College (now Grambling State University), a Black college in Louisiana which would launch the careers of numerous African American athletes, particularly in football under legendary coach and athletic director Eddie Robinson. Neal, a power-hitting third baseman–outfielder, was a native of Bernice, Louisiana, a small town about 25 miles north of Grambling. In 1950 he had batted .483 with 15 home runs for the Grambling baseball team and had drawn the attention of several major league teams including the New York Yankees and the Pittsburgh Pirates. He was called "one of the best looking prospects in college ball."[16] Ensley was born and raised in Rustin, Louisiana, a city of about ten thousand people a few miles east of Grambling. A multisport star, he was the captain of the Grambling baseball team and co-captain of the football team. A shortstop and outfielder, he was known for his great speed.

In the spring of 1951 White Sox scout Doug Minor, who had seen Neal and Ensley play, brought them to the attention of John Donaldson. The former Negro League star came to Grambling, and after several days of negotiation, signed both players to contracts. Terms weren't announced, but Neal said that the White Sox had outbid the Pirates for his services. The Baton Rouge *Weekly Reader* reported that "Minor and Donaldson left convinced that the boys, even without needed experience in the 'bushes' would be much more than bench ornament in the majors."[17]

In mid-May Neal and Ensley were sent to the Sox' Class C farm team in Superior, Wisconsin, of the Northern League. Both players struggled in what was likely their first time outside the South, as well as their first experience with racially integrated competition. Ensley batted .208 in 34 games for Superior; Neal hit .209 in 18 contests. That was enough for the White Sox; in mid-July Superior released both players. The pair quickly signed with the Negro League Kansas City Monarchs. Neal did not last;

in late August he was inducted into the army, and he did not return to professional baseball after his discharge in October 1953. After earning a master's degree in education at the University of San Francisco, Neal worked for 16 years as a physical education teacher at Havenscourt Junior High School in Oakland. He also opened a real estate agency. "Crawford meant so much to the junior high kids," said a Havenscourt Junior High colleague. "He could have taught at the high school level but he was committed to the younger ones."[18]

Unlike Neal, Frank Ensley stayed in professional baseball after being let go by Superior. After playing for the Monarchs in 1951–52, he was traded to the Indianapolis Clowns for infielder Sherwood Brewer, who became the double play partner of and mentor to Monarchs shortstop Ernie Banks in 1953. Ensley remained with the Clowns through 1955, earning a reputation as an excellent center fielder and one of the league's fastest players. During his time in the Negro Leagues, Ensley played against Banks and Henry Aaron; he was also a teammate of female players Toni Stone, Mamie Johnson, and Connie Morgan with the Clowns. In 1956 Ensley returned to white organized baseball at the age of 29 with a two-year stint in the Milwaukee Braves farm system; his batting averages were around the .250 level, but he was praised for his speed, versatility, and defensive prowess. After a brief second stint with the Monarchs, Ensley went back to Louisiana, where he coached and taught in Franklin Parish; he also served as a dorm counselor and assistant baseball coach at Grambling.

◆ ◆ ◆

The final two Black players who performed in the White Sox farm system in 1951, Gene Collins and Gideon Applegate, joined Waterloo in July. Collins, who was born in Kansas City, Kansas, but had grown up in Detroit, was a Negro League veteran who had spent four and a half years with the Kansas City Monarchs. With the Monarchs he both pitched and played the outfield, but it was his pitching that brought him to the attention of American and National League scouts. In 1949 Collins was given a tryout by the New York Yankees, who were under pressure to start signing Black players; however, the Yankees sent him back to Kansas City. When the 26-year-old Collins got off to a sensational start in 1951—an article in the *Sporting News* credited him with 54 strikeouts in his first 32 innings[19]—the White Sox bought him on a conditional basis and sent him to Waterloo, where he went 7-2 with a 3.27 ERA over the remainder of the season.

Collins remained in the Sox farm system through 1953. He posted some impressive numbers both as a pitcher and as an outfielder and was invited to spring training with the big club in 1952. But his years as a Sox farmhand were not a happy experience for Collins. The White Sox kept shifting him from club to club: He played for three different Sox farm teams in 1952 (Colorado Springs, Superior, and Wisconsin Rapids) and two in 1953 (Superior and Colorado Springs). Collins didn't feel that the Sox were helping him develop or taking him or other African American players seriously as major league prospects; he described their roles as "window dressing." Matters finally came to a head in 1953. "Considering the treatment I was getting from Superior," he recalled, "I got an offer from Santo Domingo, Dominican Republic. The money was up front, they wired it to me right away, and the next thing I knew I was in Miami waiting for a plane." Apart from a brief return to the Monarchs in 1954, Collins spent the remainder of his career playing for Latin American teams, primarily in Mexico, where he ended his career in 1961. "We encountered no prejudices in Mexico or other Latin American countries," Collins said. "It was quite relaxing to be able to play."[20]

Finally, there was Gideon Applegate. Though he was only 23 years old in 1951, Applegate was already a professional baseball veteran. A native of Newport, Rhode Island, he attended East Providence High School, where he was a multisport star (baseball, football, basketball, hockey, and track). As a senior, he was one of only two Black students at the school. "You were always aware of prejudice," he told a friend several decades later. "You were born into it. You knew it from grammar school."[21]

In 1945, while still in high school, the 17-year-old Applegate played part of the season as a third baseman for the New York Black Yankees of the Negro National League under the fictitious name of John Spearman. He served in the navy for two years after finishing high school, then attended Brown University in Providence for two years. In 1949 Applegate was signed by the Boston Braves, one of the first National League teams to recruit Black players. When he took the field at the Braves' minor league camp in Myrtle Beach, South Carolina, he became the first Black player to appear in a Braves' training camp (two other Black players, Welford Williams and future National League player George Crowe, would join him a few days later).

Applegate began the 1949 season with the Braves' Pawtucket, Rhode Island, farm team, then spent the rest of the season with an independent minor league team, Kingston (Ontario) of the Class C Border League. He was the first Black player to perform for Kingston. Despite some impressive stats as a hitter (his on-base-plus-slugging percentage with Kingston was an excellent .891) he was converted to the mound late in 1949; according to Applegate, he recorded 17 strikeouts in his first mound appearance. By 1951 the move was an unqualified success; between Kingston and

Waterloo, which he joined in July after the Border League disbanded in midseason, Applegate posted a 15-5 record for the year.[22]

After the season, Applegate, who was six weeks shy of his 24th birthday, was asked to speak before about one hundred members of the Cosmopolitan Club of Haven Methodist Church in East Providence. The subject was the color line in sports. Applegate told the group, "We're accepted on the field—as long as we produce—but off the field, there's always the line." He said when on the road, Black players "have no chance to get a decent place to eat, sleep or relax." He said that only one hotel in Iowa would register Black players, "and then they had to make sure not to fraternize with other hotel guests." Whenever heckled by fans, Applegate said, the only thing for a Black player to do was keep quiet. "You can't fight back," he said, "because you want those coming behind you to have a chance."[23]

Gideon Applegate would be back in the White Sox farm system in 1952 for what would prove to be a very memorable season.

9

The Problems We Must Solve

When Orestes Miñoso took the field at Comiskey Park on May 1, 1951, the White Sox became only the sixth of the 16 American and National League teams to integrate in the five seasons since 1947—and one of those teams, the St. Louis Browns, had quickly abandoned integration after their short experiment with Willard Brown and Hank Thompson in 1947. Progress remained very slow.

Yet there were a few positive signs. According to Gary Fink, a SABR researcher who maintains a list of African Americans in white organized baseball during the early years of integration, the number of Black players in the American and National Leagues (including Afro-Latino players) more than doubled in 1951 from nine (the total in both 1949 and 1950) to 19 in 1951. The number of Black players in the minor leagues continued to increase steadily, from 21 in 1948 to 78 in 1949, 140 in 1950, and 248 in 1951.[1] While a lamentable number of these players were undoubtedly what Gene Collins referred to as "window dressing," the needle was moving in the right direction. The 1951–55 period would feature the MLB debuts of such enduring stars as Willie Mays, Hank Aaron, Ernie Banks, Roberto Clemente, Jim Gilliam, and Elston Howard, along with excellent players such as Vic Power, Al Smith, Bill Bruton, Sam Jones, and Brooks Lawrence.

Of the Black players in the Chicago White Sox farm system in 1951, only Bob Boyd would get a real opportunity to play regularly in the white major leagues, and that would not happen for several years. But at least the Sox had Black players in the majors; the Cubs had no Blacks in the majors and only seven in the minors. All seven were either summarily dismissed after short trials or kept in the minors, with little or no advancement no matter how well they performed.

The Cubs' most notorious case, 26-year-old shortstop Gene Baker, was beginning the second of his four seasons with the club's flagship farm team, the Los Angeles Angels of the Pacific Coast League. The other extreme was represented by 28-year-old Jesse Sheron Williams, an outfielder–first baseman who had previously played in the Negro Leagues with the Cleveland Buckeyes (where he had a teammate who was also named Jesse Williams). Williams was given a one-week trial by the Cubs' Class A farm team in Grand Rapids, Michigan, and then released. Another recruit, 21-year-old infielder Bill McCrary, got only 21 games at the end of 1951 to show the Class D Janesville, Wisconsin, Cubs, what he could do. (Two years earlier McCrary, at that time a pitcher, had been the first Black player in the Class C Northern League.) Though McCrary had grown up in nearby Beloit, where he had starred in high school and American Legion ball, he was released after batting .197. He never played in white organized baseball again.

Like Baker, outfielder Nap Gulley was a player whom the Cubs kept in the same place despite his continued excellent performance. For Baker, it was Class AAA Los Angeles, for Gulley Class C Visalia. Gulley, who was 26 years old in 1951 (his listed "baseball age" was 24) had basically the same season for the Visalia Cubs in 1951 (.288 with 13 homers) that he'd had in 1950 (.292 with 14 homers). His reward was to be given yet another season with Visalia in 1952. Although Gulley's performance merited promotion, he was very popular with the fans—"basically, I could put a few thousand people in the seats every night," he commented—and the Cubs were content with the status quo. And even with shaving a couple of years off his age, he was getting to be a little old to be considered a prospect, especially one who was still at the Class C level. Gulley himself said that longtime manager and executive Fred Haney, who was managing the Hollywood Stars of the Pacific Coast League, wanted Nap on his team in 1950. Moving up to the PCL might have helped Gulley draw attention from a major league club, but he was told that Stars owner Bob Cobb wasn't ready for a Black player.[2]

After his third season with Visalia in 1952, Gulley played for Victoria in the Class A Western International League in 1953, returned to Visalia in 1954, played for Spokane in the Class B Northwest League in 1955, and finished back in the California League with Salinas in 1956. A broken wrist suffered that year effectively ended Gulley's career. His batting average for seven minor league seasons was a splendid .317. "I was accepted in all the cities by the fans, except Bakersfield," he recalled about his time in the California League. "They let black cats out on the field and that kind of stuff. You can't let that annoy you; you just go ahead and play."[3]

Nap Gulley became a fixture in Visalia, not necessarily by choice; Arnie Green, another infielder in the Cubs farm system, decided on his own to plant his roots in Cedar Rapids, Iowa. Born in Abbeville, Louisiana, in 1923, Green played semipro ball in Louisiana after serving in World War II. In 1951 he began the season with the Cubs' Class D farm team in Janesville. "There was [a] considerable stir here early Wednesday when Arnold Green reported," wrote the *Janesville Daily Gazette*. "No one in camp, it seems, knew he was a Negro." Green made a good impression and quickly was promoted to the Cubs' Topeka farm team in the Class C Western Association. After a few weeks with Topeka he was sent to the Sioux Falls Canaries of the Class C Northern League, then sent back to Janesville in mid-June. This time his arrival was welcomed. "Followers of the Janesville Cubs who enjoyed for two seasons the work of Milt Bohannion, especially his baserunning, have another thrill in store," the *Daily Gazette* proclaimed. "Arnold Green, 22-year-old Negro rookie infielder [he was actually 27], has joined the club." Green lived up to the billing; in 78 games with Janesville, he batted .331 and stole 18 bases.[4]

In 1952 Green spent the entire season with Topeka, where he was the only Black player on the team and one of only three Black players in the Western Association. He again batted over .300, but a year later, when he spent most of the 1953 season with the Cubs' Cedar Rapids farm club the Class B Three-I League, batting .256, he was no longer being treated as a prospect. His age was one issue. "Didn't you used to catch Satch Paige when he was just starting out?" a teammate kiddingly asked him.[5] After the season, Green retired from professional baseball and took a job at the Wilson & Company meatpacking plant, a leading employer in Cedar Rapids and one of the largest meatpacking plants in the world. Wilson had a team in the M & J (Manufacturers and Jobbers) semipro league, and Green became the team's first Black player. He played for Wilson for a number of years and remained in the Cedar Rapids area for the rest of his life.

The other two Black players in the Cubs farm system in 1951 were Milton Bohannion and Solly Drake, both 20 years old and teammates with the Topeka Owls. They became close friends. Drake, a native of Little Rock, Arkansas, had been a multisport star at Philander Smith College in Little Rock before joining the ManDak League in 1949. The Cubs signed him prior to the 1951 season. Playing in 85 games for Topeka, Drake batted .324 and earned a reputation as one of the top prospects in the system. He received his draft notice in August, however, and spent most of 1952 stationed at Fort Leonard Wood in Missouri. He was one of the stars of the annual National Baseball Congress tournament in Wichita, where Fort

Leonard Wood reached the finals. With the war in Korea still ongoing in 1953, Drake was sent overseas. He would return to the Cubs farm system in 1954.

In his third season as a Cubs farmhand, Milton Bohannion had his best year yet, batting .274 with a .370 on-base percentage and 13 stolen bases while splitting his time between the infield and his original position of catcher. In spite of his youth, the Cubs' plans for him were best reflected in the fact that he only got into 67 games in 1951; he was decidedly the team's second-string catcher behind light-hitting (.238) Donald Hoskin, a non-prospect in his sixth season in the minor leagues. After the season Bohannion joined the Air Force and did not return to the minor leagues until 1956. At Wichita, Milton's sister Sarah recalled, "Milton didn't get to play as much as he wanted to. Back then that's the way things were. It was hard. I think that was one of the reasons that he went into the Air Force."[6]

While stationed in England, Bohannion was able to play a little bit of ball, and when he got out of the Air Force, he spent three seasons (1956–58) with Duluth-Superior of the Northern League, a Chicago White Sox farm team. He was only 27 when his professional baseball career ended after the 1958 season. "Milton felt that he was skipped over a lot of times because he was Black," said his sister. "He thought, 'If I hadn't been a Black man, they would have used me.' But it didn't stop him because he felt he was good enough to play."[7]

After his time in baseball Bohannion got a job at the Argo Starch Company near his home, married, and coached a little baseball. Until his death in Argo Summit at age 62 in 1993, Milton (Bohannion) Neeley, who had adopted his father's surname, remained close to his former Topeka teammate Solly Drake. "Milton and Solly kept in touch, and he thought that when Solly finally made it to the majors [in 1956], he would be next," recalled Sarah Nicholson. "Everybody thought that Milton would make the majors. It just didn't work that way."[8]

◆ ◆ ◆

While the Black players in the Cubs' farm system were experiencing a frustrating season in 1951, year two of the Wid Matthews regime was creating its own level of frustration—not to mention confusion—back in Chicago. In June, with the club in seventh place, Matthews traded one of the Cubs' biggest stars, outfielder Andy Pafko, to Wid's former employers, the Dodgers, as part of an eight-player deal that ultimately netted the Cubs nothing of consequence. (The most notable player acquired by Matthews in the trade, infielder Eddie Miksis, would best be remembered for a slogan hung on him by Branch Rickey that ultimately became a chant of derision: "Mik-sis will fix us.") In mid-July Matthews announced that manager Frankie Frisch, a man described as "a snarling, ranting Captain Bligh in the dugout and clubhouse" by sportswriter Edgar Munzel, "definitely is the manager and no change is contemplated." But after several anonymous Cubs play-ers ripped Frisch in an interview with a *Chicago Daily News* reporter, Captain Bligh was cast adrift by the Cubs. He was replaced by veteran first baseman Phil Cavarretta, with owner Phil Wrigley announcing that "Phil definitely will be replaced next year. He fully understands that and has taken the job on that condition." Under player-manager Cavarretta, the Cubs dropped into last place, finishing the year with a 62–92 record. He was then rehired to manage the team in 1952.[9]

As the Cubs continued to flounder on the field, they were also lament-ing the lack of players in the minor leagues who were true major league prospects. "It's always been a problem with the Cubs that the personnel director, whatever his title, has not been astute in judging talent," said future major league star Jim Brosnan, who was playing in the Cubs' minor league system during the early 1950s. "And of course, they compounded it by not having teachers of fundamentals to improve whatever talent they get."[10] Brosnan might have been speaking for the Black players who were treading water in the Cubs' farm system.

Early in 1951 the talent-hungry Cubs wrote to J. B. Martin, president of the Negro American League, asking for the addresses of franchise own-ers, as well as the rosters of the teams. While the Negro Leagues were a shadow of what they had been just a few years earlier, the Negro AL still contained a number of talented players who would play successfully in either the majors or the minors over the next few years. Among others, Negro AL rosters included Connie Johnson, Sandy Amoros, Joe Black . . . and the man the Cubs had sent back to the Negro Leagues in 1950, Jim Gilliam. The Cubs would strike gold with Negro Leaguer Ernie Banks a couple of years later, but in 1951, they apparently thought they had enough Black players in their farm system.

◆ ◆ ◆

Elsewhere in baseball, and in American sports in general, opportunities for Black athletes were increasing overall, albeit with the same sort of slow progress that was the case in baseball. In the late summer of 1950 Althea Gibson, a 22-year-old Black tennis player, won the Eastern Indoor Champi-onships, a prestigious tournament. The victory made it obvious that Gibson was talented enough to play in National Grass Court Championships at Forest Hills, the predecessor of the current US Open. Forest Hills officials insisted, however, that Gibson first needed to make a good showing at an outdoor qualifying tournament, and none would permit a Black player to take the court. With the support of many people in the sport, particularly longtime women's champion Alice Marble, Gibson received a somewhat grudging invitation to play in a qualifying tournament. After performing well, she became the first Black player to receive an invitation to play at Forest Hills. Although eliminated in the second round, Gibson went on to win five Grand Slam titles in her career and was elected to the International Tennis Hall of Fame in 1971.

In pro basketball, Chuck Cooper of Duquesne became the first Black player to be drafted by a National Basketball Association team when he was selected by the Boston Celtics in the 1950 draft. During the 1950–51 season Cooper, Earl Lloyd (Washington Capitols), and former Chicago high school star Nat Clifton (New York Knicks) became the first Black players to perform in the NBA (a fourth player, Hank DeZonie, appeared in five games for the Tri-Cities Blackhawks during the season). As with Black pioneers in other sports, the process was anything but smooth. Along with dealing with such difficulties as substandard accommodations, problems getting served in restaurants, and other forms of demeaning treatment, these players felt that they were expected to play a subservient role on the court: rebound and defend, leaving the scoring to their white teammates. "[My father] always said the NBA was ready to integrate in 1950 but they weren't ready for a black star," said Cooper's son Chuck Cooper III.[11] Clifton, Cooper, and Lloyd have all been inducted into the Naismith Memorial Basketball Hall of Fame.

In pro football, the opposing teams in the 1951 National Football League championship game, the Los Angeles Rams and the Cleveland Browns, featured Black players in important roles; however, most NFL teams (including both Chicago teams, the Bears and the Cardinals) remained all-white during the 1951 season. In the NFL draft after the season, the Cardinals selected Black halfback Ollie Matson of the University of San Francisco with the third overall pick. Matson would star for the Cardinals for six seasons and play 14 NFL seasons overall; he was inducted into the Pro Football Hall of Fame in 1972. With the 20th overall pick in the second round, the Bears selected Eddie Macon, a Black halfback from the College of the Pacific. Macon spent two seasons with the Bears, then played several years in the Canadian Football League before returning to the States to play for the Oakland Raiders in their inaugural season of 1960. Macon said he felt accepted by most fans, teammates, and opponents but that the Detroit Lions, NFL champions in 1952 and '53, "beat me in the face, twisted my legs." Macon also recalled that during his seasons with the Bears, he lived at a local YMCA, where he was not permitted to use the swimming pool.[12]

College football featured many integrated teams in 1951, yet one of the season's most powerful teams, the University of San Francisco Dons, was denied a bowl bid despite winning all nine of its games after refusing to leave its two Black players, Matson and Burl Tolar, at home. (A book about the team was titled *Undefeated, Untied, and Uninvited.*). Matson's white teammates Gino Marchetti and Bob St. Clair would later join him in the Pro Football Hall of Fame. Tolar, who had to retire as a player owing to a serious knee injury, became the NFL's first Black referee.

The most-discussed sports incident of 1951 involving race took place at a college football game on October 20. On that day the Drake University Bulldogs, who had won their first five games of the season, were in Stillwater, Oklahoma, to face the Oklahoma A&M Aggies (1-3). Two years earlier Johnny Bright, Drake's biggest star, had been the first African American to play on A&M's home field. (Oklahoma A&M's first Black student, Nancy Randolph Davis, had enrolled at the school in the summer of 1949.) The 1949 game, an easy A&M victory, had been played without incident, and Bright was even allowed to stay at the same hotel as his white teammates.

The atmosphere was very different when Drake arrived for the 1951 game. The Aggies were now coached by Arkansas-born J. B. Whitworth, a tough-minded southerner, and when Bright, who a week earlier had broken the collegiate record for total scrimmage yards gained in a career, tried to check into the hotel where he had stayed with his teammates in 1949, he was denied accommodations. He had to stay with a local Black minister. Pregame reports indicated that Bright would be targeted for rough treatment. Three students who had watched A&M practice sessions reported that a coach repeatedly yelled, "Get that n___" when the team ran plays with a member of the B team portraying Drake.[13]

On Drake's first play from scrimmage versus A&M, Bright took a direct snap and handed the ball to his fullback. Although Bright was clearly out of the play, Aggies lineman Wilbanks Smith ran up and brutally smashed him in the face with his right forearm. Bright was not wearing a facemask, and Smith's blow broke his jaw. Bright slumped to the ground and lay on the field for several minutes receiving medical attention. He was able to continue and threw a 61-yard touchdown pass on the next play, but after enduring several more hard hits, he needed to leave the game for good midway in the first quarter. Oklahoma A&M won, 27–14, but the outcome of the game was forgotten in the furor over Smith's hit. The incident had been photographed in detail by two *Des Moines Register* photographers using high-speed cameras, and their publication created a national sensation.

(The photographers would win a Pulitzer Prize for their work.) Many insisted that race had nothing to do with the rough hits on Bright. Oklahoma A&M vice president Oliver Willham, wrote Rob Darcy, "claimed he saw all the plays. He saw nothing unusual or out of the way. He knew all the players. They were all fine men."[14] The *Chicago Defender* was having none of that.

> We know and every other American who is familiar with racism knows why Johnny Bright was attacked. The boys who have been brought up on white supremacy propaganda simply cannot stand to see their illusions threatened. The Negro quarterback struck fear into them, fear that this presumably "inferior" should make monkeys out of them. Too many whites are afraid that in a true test of individual merit, their racist convictions will be shattered.[15]

Within a few days Drake University requested a hearing with Missouri Valley Conference officials over what it called "malicious and intentional attacks" on Bright. When the officials chose to take no action against Smith or Oklahoma A&M, Drake elected to withdraw from the conference and cancelled all remaining games with A&M. Bradley University also withdrew from the MVC, citing the Bright case as the reason. (Both schools rejoined the conference several years later.)

Although Bright was able to play in only one more game after his jaw was broken, he finished fifth in the 1951 Heisman Trophy voting and was the number one draft choice of the Philadelphia Eagles. He turned down Philadelphia's offer, instead signing with the Calgary Stampeders of the Canadian Football League. "I would have been their first Negro player," said Bright said about the Eagles, "but there was a tremendous influx of Southern players into the NFL . . . and I didn't know what kind of treatment I would receive."[16] Bright starred for 13 seasons in Canada, where he helped lead the Edmonton Eskimos to three Grey Cup league championships (1954–56) and won the league's Most Outstanding Player Award in 1959. He became a Canadian citizen in 1962 and was elected to both the (American) College Football and Canadian Football Halls of Fame.

In 2005, 54 years after the incident and 22 years after Bright's death, the president of Oklahoma State University (formerly Oklahoma A&M), Dave Schmidly, wrote to Drake president David Maxwell to apologize. "The incident was an ugly mark on Oklahoma State University and college football and we regret the harm it caused Johnny Bright, your university, and many others," Schmidly wrote.[17] But when reporter Kyle Fredrickson contacted Wilbanks Smith in 2012, the man who had broken Bright's jaw insisted that the hit had not been racially motivated. ("There's no way it *couldn't* have been racially motivated," Bright had said in 1980.)[18] Smith said he been told that the forearm shiver was a completely legal hit—it was not, even in 1951—and that he was only doing what his coaches had taught him. When Fredrickson asked him about Schmidly's apology, Smith said, "I could just never understand why they would do that. I didn't know what they were apologizing for."[19]

◆ ◆ ◆

"With nine Negroes on big league teams and more coming up, Negroes are there to stay," proclaimed an article in *Our World* in the fall of 1950. "They have proved they can hit, field and run; and that's the measure of a big league player. . . . Negro ball players are in major league ball to stay and the future will see more."[20] As noted at the top of the chapter, the number of Black players in MLB had more than doubled to 19 by the end of 1951. Optimism was in the air, and what Jules Tygiel would call "Baseball's Great Experiment" seemed to be working fine.

In 1951 the man who had begun the experiment, Jackie Robinson, had another outstanding season, batting .338, the second-highest average of his Dodgers career. But the season included an ugly reminder of the treatment that Robinson continued to endure. When the Dodgers traveled to Cincinnati for a Sunday doubleheader on May 20, Robinson was met by two FBI agents who told him of threatening letters that had been addressed to him. The letters, signed by the "Three Travelers," told Robinson that he would be assassinated on the field that day. He chose to play in both games and recorded three hits, including a home run, and scored five runs as the fired-up Dodgers swept both games, 10–3 and 14–4. Before the games Dodger captain Pee Wee Reese had attempted to lighten the tension by suggesting, "I think we will all wear 42 [Robinson's uniform number] today, and then we will have a shooting gallery."[21] Decades later, Major League Baseball would honor Robinson by having all players wear number 42 on the anniversary of Robinson's debut, April 15.

Elsewhere in baseball, the man who had signed Robinson, Branch Rickey, moved from Brooklyn to the Pittsburgh Pirates after Walter O'Malley gained control of the Dodgers late in 1950. Rickey's hiring as Pirates general manager aroused hopes not only that the team, which had finished last in 1950, would soon become pennant contenders, but that they would also be adding Black players. According to Rickey biographer Lee Lowenfish, Rickey made a major commitment to scouting Black players, hiring 22 new scouts from Black colleges and high schools. He even hired Grambling athletic director and football coach Eddie Robinson, whose school had (briefly) sent two Black players to the White Sox in 1951. Yet

Pittsburgh would not have an African American player until 1954, when former Negro Leaguer Curt Roberts joined the club. Economics, Lowenfish wrote, was a factor in Rickey's losing out on several talented Black players in the early 1950s, among them future Cubs Ernie Banks and Gene Baker. At the same time that they were failing to sign Black players, however, the Pirates were paying huge bonuses to a number of white high school and college players who mostly failed to pan out—the same mistake made by the White Sox in 1949.[22]

In June Bill Veeck, the man who had joined Rickey in breaking baseball's color line in 1947, returned to baseball as head of an ownership group that acquired the lowly St. Louis Browns. As was the case with Rickey in Pittsburgh, Veeck was expected to aggressively pursue Black talent for his new team. Almost as quickly as Veeck had taken control of the Browns, the *Defender* was predicting that Satchel Paige and Sweetwater Clifton would soon join him in St. Louis. They were right about Paige, who was a Brownie by mid-July. Once again, the signing was ridiculed as another Veeck stunt, but after pitching poorly in 1951, Paige was brilliant as a Browns reliever at age 46 the following year, making the American League All-Star team (where his teammates included Larry Doby and Minnie Miñoso). Clifton, however, was content with playing basketball. Like Rickey, Veeck was unable to acquire more Black players for the Brownies after signing Paige, most likely because of a lack of funds. In his autobiography, Veeck wrote that he tried to buy Ernie Banks from the Kansas City Monarchs in 1953 but couldn't come up with Tom Baird's asking price.

While Rickey and Veeck largely failed in their efforts to add Black players to their new teams in the early years of their regimes (Rickey would eventually hit the jackpot with Roberto Clemente), there was good news in other cities. In May one of baseball's immortals, Willie Mays, made his debut with the New York Giants and helped lead them to their first National League pennant since 1937. After trailing the Dodgers by as many as 13½ games in August, the Giants staged an epic finish to beat Brooklyn in a best-of-three playoff, with both teams receiving crucial help from Black players. In the World Series, which the Giants lost to the New York Yankees in six games, the Giants featured the first all-Black outfield in major league history: Monte Irvin, Hank Thompson, and Mays.

In the minor leagues, history was made in 1951 when 36-year-old Emmett Ashford took a leave of absence from his job as a letter carrier with the US Post Office to try out as an umpire in the Southwestern International League. When he took the field for his first game, Ashford's fellow umpires walked off the field rather than work with him, and substitutes had to be found. But Ashford made the grade as the first Black umpire in white baseball. He would endure a long minor league apprenticeship including 12 years in the Pacific Coast League before reaching the majors in 1966.[23]

◆ ◆ ◆

Ernie Banks spent 1951 as a member of the US Army. After receiving his draft notice late in 1950, Banks was sent to Fort Bliss in El Paso. At the start of basic training, Banks suffered an injury to his left knee that required several weeks of hospitalization. He was able to avoid surgery; instead, he was confined to bed with heavy weights immobilizing the leg. After his discharge from the hospital, he joined the 45th AAA Gun Battalion, an all-Black unit that had served in combat during World War II. At the time, the Korean War was raging, but fortunately for Ernie, the 45th's headquarters were in Germany, where a large contingent of American troops were stationed. Ernie was sent to Germany early in 1952, and while there he had an opportunity to play baseball for the 242nd Antiaircraft unit. His sports talents drew attention almost immediately, and eventually he became the base athletic director. For Banks, his service stint was his first experience working and playing with whites.

◆ ◆ ◆

In December 1951 the poet, playwright, and author Langston Hughes, who regularly contributed columns to the *Chicago Defender*, wrote a year-end column titled "The Progress Made in 1951 Spotlights the Problems That Face Us in 1952." The incidents he wrote about included the blow to Johnny Bright's jaw, Harvey Clark's battle to move his family into an apartment in the Chicago suburb of Cicero, and the refusal of New York's famed Stork Club to provide service to the Black singer-dancer Josephine Baker. He concluded,

> Did someone say that a night club or a football game is not important? Doesn't the Constitution guarantee, "The right to life, liberty and THE PURSUIT OF HAPPINESS?" Happiness includes enjoyable meals in public places without insult, and the right to play football without the deliberate breaking of one's jaw. Let's try to make 1952 a Happy New Year for the Clarks, for Johnny Bright, and for Josephine Baker should she visit our shores again. They are symbols of the problems we must solve for a really Happy New Year in America—since only in decent human relations does happiness lie. Happy New Year![24]

The first Afro-Latino player to play in the white major leagues, Minnie Miñoso became the White Sox' first Black player when he was acquired in a trade in 1951. (Courtesy National Baseball Hall of Fame and Museum, Cooperstown, NY)

Known as "Trader Lane" for his compulsive dealing, Frank Lane signed the White Sox' first Black players in 1950 and traded for Minnie Miñoso a year later. (Courtesy National Baseball Hall of Fame and Museum, Cooperstown, NY)

The White Sox manager from 1951 to 1954, Paul Richards managed the team's first Black players and was instrumental in the trade for Minnie Miñoso. (Courtesy National Baseball Hall of Fame and Museum, Cooperstown, NY)

Selected as baseball's first commissioner in the wake of the 1919 Black Sox scandal, Judge Kenesaw Mountain Landis was considered a major impediment to the integration of baseball during his 24-year term (1920–44). (Courtesy Library of Congress Prints and Photographs Division)

While the White Sox and the Cubs were slowly beginning their integration process, bus driver Harvey Clark and his wife Johnetta were waging a long legal battle after being prevented from moving into an apartment in suburban Cicero. (Courtesy Chicago Daily News/Chicago Sun-Times collection, Chicago History Museum, ADN-0000064)

Pioneering Black baseball writer Sam Lacy helped lead the battle for the sport's integration while working for the *Chicago Defender* and the *Baltimore Afro-American* in the 1930s and '40s. (Credit: National Baseball Hall of Fame and Museum, Cooperstown, NY)

The first Black member of the Baseball Writers Association of America, Wendell Smith was instrumental in helping make the integration of baseball a success. (Courtesy National Baseball Hall of Fame and Museum, Cooperstown, NY)

The Cubs' owner from 1932 until his death in 1977, Phil Wrigley expressed verbal support for integration of the game but was slow to add Black players to his own team. (Courtesy National Baseball Hall of Fame and Museum, Cooperstown, NY)

A brilliant three-sport athlete from Massachusetts, Billy Hart was one of the first Black players to sign with the Cubs, but he was released after an 11-game trial. (Courtesy St. Michael's College, Colchester, VT)

As White Sox manager in 1942, Jimmy Dykes refused to give a tryout to Jackie Robinson and another Black player. In the 1950s Dykes was accused of making racial taunts at Minnie Miñoso and of ordering his pitchers to throw at Miñoso. (Courtesy National Baseball Hall of Fame and Museum, Cooperstown, NY)

The first African American player to perform for the White Sox, Negro League star Sam Hairston spent more than 40 years in the White Sox system as a player, coach, and scout. (Courtesy National Baseball Hall of Fame and Museum, Cooperstown, NY)

Considered one of the greatest third basemen in Cuban history, Héctor Rodríguez joined Miñoso and the White Sox in 1952 but lasted only one season with the team. (Courtesy SABR-Rucker Archive)

(Left to right): Director of Player Personnel Wid Matthews, Owner-President Phil Wrigley, and Manager Phil Cavarretta led the Cubs' slow march to integration in the early 1950s. (Courtesy *Chicago Sun-Times* collection, Chicago History Museum, ST-17667741)

Expected by many to be the Cubs' first Black player, Gene Baker spent four seasons with the team's Los Angeles Angels farm team before finally making his white major league debut in September 1953, a few days after Ernie Banks. (Courtesy National Baseball Hall of Fame and Museum, Cooperstown, NY)

A Negro League pitching star for the Kansas City Monarchs in the 1940s, Connie Johnson was the first Black pitcher to play for the White Sox. (Courtesy National Baseball Hall of Fame and Museum, Cooperstown, NY)

Negro League star Bob Boyd was one of the first Black players signed by the White Sox, making his Sox debut in 1951. (Courtesy National Baseball Hall of Fame and Museum, Cooperstown, NY)

The 1953 Danville Dans, a White Sox farm team, employed nine Black players over the course of the season, including three in the team's Opening Day lineup (T. J. Brown, Jim Zapp, and Lonnie Davis). (Courtesy Danville Dans)

The Cubs' first Black player, Ernie Banks went directly from the Negro Leagues to the white major leagues in September 1953, going on to become a franchise icon and Hall of Fame player. (Courtesy National Baseball Hall of Fame and Museum, Cooperstown, NY)

SAM JONES

The first Black pitcher to play for the Cubs, Sam Jones was the first pitcher of his race to throw a no-hitter in the white major leagues. (Courtesy National Baseball Hall of Fame and Museum, Cooperstown, NY)

The first Black member of the White Sox who had not played in the Negro Leagues, Earl Battey made his Sox debut at age 20 in 1955 but had his greatest success as a member of the Minnesota Twins in the 1960s. (Courtesy National Baseball Hall of Fame and Museum, Cooperstown, NY)

The daughter of Harvey and Johnetta Clark, Michele Clark became the first Black female national news correspondent for CBS News and was considered a rising star at the network before her death in a plane crash in December 1972. (Courtesy Emmett Wilson)

10

A Trying Year

After his outstanding rookie season with the White Sox in 1951, Orestes Miñoso returned to his native Cuba and another season of winter baseball with the Marianao Tigers of the Cuban League. Frank Lane and Paul Richards felt that playing year-round baseball was too much of a strain on players' bodies, and they convinced Miñoso to restrict his play during the 1951–52 Cuban League campaign to a half-season. Minnie didn't exactly rest up during the break; he returned to the sugar cane fields where he had toiled as a young man, working alongside his father. "I even told my father to take a vacation for a week while I was there and I'd do the work for him," Miñoso wrote.[1]

When Miñoso reported to the Sox spring training camp in Pasadena, he had two new Cuban teammates. One of them, slick-fielding shortstop Willy Miranda, had little chance of playing regularly with Carrasquel entrenched at the spot. The Sox traded him to the St. Louis Browns in June. (Richards, who loved Miranda's glove, traded for Willy and made him his team's regular shortstop after becoming manager–general manager of the Baltimore Orioles in 1955.)

The other player, 31-year-old third baseman Héctor Rodríguez, was expected to win the White Sox third base job, freeing Miñoso to play full-time in the outfield in 1952. Rodríguez was a baseball legend in Cuba. An Afro-Latino like Miñoso, he had made his Cuban League debut with the Almendares Blues in 1942–43; he would play in the league for 18 seasons with Almendares and Habana, becoming the all-time league leader in numerous categories. Apart from one season with the New York Cubans of the Negro National League in 1944, Rodríguez spent his non–winter league baseball seasons in the Mexican League. Only five feet, eight inches tall, he was not a power hitter. His forte was defense. "Héctor Rodríguez is considered to have been the greatest defensive third baseman Cuba ever produced," wrote Cuban-born writer and historian Roberto González Echevarría. "Rodríguez was a magician at third, with quick reflexes and a strong arm. He was as swift and graceful as a ballet dancer coming in on a bunt or a slow roller."[2]

In 1951 Rodríguez entered white organized baseball with the Class AAA Montreal Royals, a Brooklyn Dodgers farm club. (His manager was future Hall of Famer Walter Alston.) Héctor batted .302 with 95 RBIs for Montreal and won the league's Rookie of the Year Award, beating out teammate Jim Gilliam for the honor. The Dodgers already had an excellent third baseman in Billy Cox, and in December 1951 they traded Rodríguez to the White Sox for first baseman Rocky Nelson. "If Rodríguez can hit .275, and I think he can, the White Sox will have their best infield in many years," Lane predicted.[3] Rodríguez spoke almost no English, and Miñoso took him under his wing, helping his teammate with language issues. He even arranged for Rodríguez to live with the Lewis family on the South Side while Minnie moved to the Wedgewood Hotel at 64th and Woodlawn.

A third Black player in the Sox spring training camp, Bob Boyd, likely had no chance of making the club in 1952, though he was coming off an outstanding season with Sacramento of the Pacific Coast League. Boyd was a first baseman, and the Sox had an All-Star at the position in Eddie Robinson. So the Sox sent Boyd, whom Paul Richards described as "a good hitter with power and fast, but desperately in need of fielding experience," to Seattle of the PCL. Boyd, who said, "I know I need to work on my defensive play," did not complain; he went to Seattle and had another great year, winning the league batting title while stealing 33 bases. He would be back for another trial in 1953.[4]

◆ ◆ ◆

As the White Sox were beginning spring training in March, Cicero police chief Erwin Konovsky was standing trial in Cook County Criminal Court for malfeasance in office and palpable omission of duty. Konovsky had been cited with failing to protect Black bus driver Harvey Clark and his family when the Clarks tried to move into an apartment in Cicero in July 1951. Clark testified that when he tried to move in, Konovsky told the truck driver carrying his family's belongings, "Get out of here fast and don't come in." Clark said that when he persisted in attempting to move in, one Cicero police officer waved a revolver at him, and another officer shoved and threatened him. But when testimony ended after five days, Judge Frank Leonard issued a directed verdict of acquittal before the jury could deliberate. "It is the duty of the state to prove the defendant guilty beyond a reasonable doubt," Leonard said. "This has not been done."[5]

In an editorial, the *Chicago Sun-Times* sharply criticized the "mediocrity" of State's Attorney John S. Boyle and his assistant James A. Brown in conducting the prosecution of the trial. The editorial continued,

> In the final analysis, the fact that justice has not been served in the Cicero case is more important than who is to blame for the failure. It is frightening to realize that mobs can prevent anyone—not only Negroes—from moving into certain neighborhoods in Cook County without fear of punishment under our statutes.

"What do you expect?" Harvey Clark commented about the directed verdict. "I'm not a bit surprised. I hope for better luck in the federal case against Konovsky."[6]

The federal trial involving Konovsky and six other defendants would begin in May.

◆ ◆ ◆

On the night of April 7 the White Sox played an exhibition game against the Pittsburgh Pirates at Pelican Park in New Orleans. When Miñoso and Rodríguez took the field for the White Sox, it marked the first time in New Orleans history that Black and white players had performed together in a racially integrated baseball game. This was a major event: The paid crowd of 9,502 fans, many of them Black, was so large that some fans had to stand on the outfield grass. Both Miñoso and Rodríguez played well in the game, and news reports said that their performance drew cheers from the white patrons in attendance.

The game drew national attention. "It was more than merely another spring exhibition game," wrote *New Orleans Item* sports columnist Hap Glaudi in a column that was reprinted in numerous publications. "It was a sports event which contributed more for the betterment of race relations in this area than do organizations dedicated to the same purpose. And it will assist tremendously in erasing the impression that some organizations give our people that there is something wrong with the way God distributes his color."[7]

Howard Roberts of the *Chicago Daily News* wrote that Miñoso and Rodríguez "played brilliantly" and that when Minnie was removed from the game after hitting a double in the sixth inning, "the whites seated behind the Sox bench back of first base arose and gave him a tremendous ovation." Roberts called the events of April 7 "easily the spring's greatest thrill."[8] Writing in the *Pittsburgh Courier*, Wendell Smith republished an entire column about the game written by his *Chicago Herald-American* colleague Warren Brown. "This was the night in which baseball broke down one more barrier of racial intolerance," Brown had written. "The main items were that they played in the ball game; that the largest crowd ever to witness an exhibition game in New Orleans attended; that the realization must have come to everyone present: 'What's wrong with this? Why hasn't it been done before?'"[9]

Less noted was the fact that the game did nothing to affect the barriers of Jim Crow for the Black citizens of New Orleans. At the end of a piece that quoted liberally from Hap Glaudi's column, the *Sporting News* reported that "a total of 2,882 Negroes saw the game from their section of the stands in Pelican Park." In his column about the game, Charles Doyle of the *Pittsburgh Sun-Telegraph* wrote, "The sportsmanship shown by the Negro section definitely made a good impression on the white folks attending the game." And Warren Brown almost casually mentioned that the welcome given to Miñoso and Rodríguez extended only to the playing field. "The one restriction that was placed on Miñoso and Rodríguez for the night was that they could not dress in the clubhouse with the rest of the White Sox," Brown wrote.[10]

In 1950 Sam Lacy wrote about his experiences in Florida as a Black writer covering the Dodgers. "Regardless of any impression you may have gotten to the contrary," Lacy wrote, "the South has not accepted interracialism in baseball. It is merely tolerating it. . . . Once we leave Dodgertown, the city within the city of Vero Beach, we are on our own. White members of the organization go in one direction; we cross the railroad tracks and go the other way. Whenever and wherever possible, Dixie whites waste no time reminding us of what has been the status quo for more than 84 years."[11]

♦ ♦ ♦

The White Sox opened the regular season on April 15 against the Cleveland Indians, with Rodríguez in the starting lineup at third base and Miñoso in left field. In an as-told-to article for Sam Lacy before the start of the season, Paul Richards praised Minnie's "utter lack of fear. . . . The (opposing pitchers) hit him 16 times last season, in the head and about the arms and legs. He was struck more often than any other player in either league. Yet up to the very last game of the season, he was in there, crowding the plate and taking every inch the rules allow. No matter how often they knocked him down, they weren't able to stop him taking his cut." In a feature article about Miñoso for *Look*, author Tim Cohane called Miñoso "the most exciting ballplayer in the American League today."[12]

Miñoso got off to a slow start in 1952, and so did the team. The Sox lost their first four games of the season and were still below .500 in early June (23-24). Nearly a month into the season, Miñoso was hitting only .213 with no home runs and only one stolen base. Rodríguez, on the other hand, got off to a great start; he batted .354 in April and kept his average over the .300 mark until late May. "Let me tell you something," raved Paul Richards. "When he walks to that plate, those pitchers better take up another notch in their belts . . . because he's goin' after them."[13]

The White Sox recovered from their slow start to finish the season with an 81-73 record and in third place, one spot higher than in 1951. Miñoso recovered as well; while his season-end .281 average was a 45-point drop from 1951, he made the All-Star team and led the league in stolen bases (as well as times being hit by pitches). Rodríguez, however, slumped after his hot start; he finished the year with a .265 average and only one home run. According to Miñoso, Rodríguez suffered a leg injury during the 1952 season but insisted on staying in the lineup, which made the injury worse and hampered his mobility at third base. That, and his lack of home run power, cost him his job with the White Sox.

After the season the White Sox sent Rodríguez back to the minor leagues. He continued to play at the Class AAA level until 1961, when he was 41 years old, but he never played major league baseball again. He ended his career in the Mexican League in 1966. "The problem with Héctor was that he was not a power hitter," said Roberto González Echevarría in an interview. "In the major leagues at both first and third you need to be a power hitter. Rodríguez spent one year with the White Sox and did well enough. He was a superb defensive third baseman, but he was also Black, and major league teams had their quotas. He continued to play in Triple-A, but he should have been in the major leagues throughout that time."[14]

◆ ◆ ◆

On May 19 the trial of seven Cicero officials charged with violating Harvey Clark's civil rights began in Federal Court in Chicago before an all-white jury. The defendants included the town president, police chief, fire marshal, town attorney, and three police officers. Clark essentially repeated the testimony that he had given in the Criminal Court trial of Konovsky in March. He said that Konovsky had told him, "Get out of here fast and don't ever come back"; that one of the officers had brandished a pistol and told Clark he could not move in because he was Black; and that police had stood by while a mob cursed at, jeered at, and spat on him as well as setting fire to his car. Clark's wife Johnetta testified that when she and her children approached the building, a man asked, "Where will your kids go to school? I want to know so I can have my kids beat them up." Another witness testified that when he asked a policeman why nothing was being done to prevent mob violence, the officer told him, "Colored people are trying to move in. Our chief warned these people to stay out of here."[15]

When the trial concluded in early June, the jury deliberated for five hours before convicting Konovsky, town attorney Nicholas Berkos, and two police officers. Charges against the other defendants had been dismissed earlier by Judge Walter J. LaBuy. The *Chicago Defender* applauded the verdict, writing, "It gives promise and hope to those who suffer racial violence that their citizenship will not forever be abused."[16] In July Judge LaBuy set aside the conviction of Berkos, citing insufficient evidence. The other three defendants filed appeals.

◆ ◆ ◆

The White Sox had a total of 11 Black players in their minor league farm system in 1952, one fewer than in 1951. As was the case in previous years, they apparently considered few of these players to be legitimate prospects to play in the major leagues. Whatever their chances of advancing to the majors, the way the White Sox handled these players was often hard to understand.

Some of the most frustrated players were former Negro Leaguers who were aware that time was running out on their chances to reach the white major leagues. Connie Johnson, a 29-year-old former Kansas City Monarchs pitching star, won 18 games for Class A Colorado Springs in 1952, leading the league in strikeouts. Johnson would prove to be an effective major league pitcher for the next few years, but there's no reason to think he could not have helped the White Sox in 1952. At least Johnson eventually got his chance to pitch for Chicago. His Colorado Springs batterymate Sam Hairston, who was 32 years old and playing his third season with the Sky Sox in 1952, wasn't as fortunate. While Hairston probably could not have beaten out Sherman Lollar for the regular White Sox catching job, he might have been very useful as a reserve catcher and pinch hitter. He never got the chance.

Willie Pope, who had pitched for the Homestead Grays in 1947–48, was 33 years old in 1952 and in his first year in the White Sox farm system after spending three seasons in the independent Provincial League in Canada. Pope spent four seasons in the system (1952–55); like Hairston, he kept toiling away at Colorado Springs, putting up good numbers and hoping for a chance to move up. Pope, whose younger brother Dave played several seasons as an outfielder with the Cleveland Indians and Baltimore Orioles, was invited to spring training with the White Sox in 1954. In one spring outing he struck out six Cincinnati Reds hitters in three innings, but before the season started, he was optioned to Class AAA Charleston. "What does a fellow [have to] do to impress a manager?" he asked a reporter. After Pope and Hairston had formed the first Black battery in American Association history in 1954, both players were back with Colorado Springs in 1955. After the 1955 season, Pope decided to retire. "[The White Sox] kept telling me they were going to bring me up, kept promising me," he said four decades later.[17]

Two of the former Negro Leaguers found themselves being shuttled from one White Sox farm team to another. Gene Collins, whose career was discussed earlier, played for three different Sox farm clubs in 1952 (Colorado Springs, Superior, and Wisconsin Rapids) and two more in 1953 (Colorado Springs and Superior). Thirty-three-year-old catcher Bill "Ready" Cash, who had spent eight seasons with the Philadelphia Stars of the Negro National League, played for Colorado Springs, Waterloo, and Superior in 1952, his only year in the White Sox farm system. "It was really demoralizing to play for the White Sox," said Cash, who said that the club's farm director Glen Miller had lied to him about where he would be playing. "You know, you don't have to lie to the ballplayers," he said.[18] In 1953 Cash signed a contract with a team in the Dominican Summer League, and then spent the rest of his professional career playing in Latin America.

The younger Black players performing in the White Sox farm system didn't fare much better. To be fair, Dick "Campy" Lewis, who had starred in baseball, basketball, and football at Detroit's Northern High, had miserable luck. A stocky catcher who was only five feet, eight inches tall, Lewis joined the Class D Wisconsin Rapids White Sox at age 18 during the latter stages of the 1952 season. Playing for the same team in 1953, Lewis was struck in the face while warming up a pitcher in the bullpen, resulting in a broken nose and an injured eye that took a long time to heal. Shortly after returning, he received his draft notice. Lewis missed nearly two years while in the service, and soon after returning to the Sox' farm system with Waterloo in 1955, had to leave the team owing to his mother's illness. That was Lewis's last season in white organized baseball.

Outfielder Mitchell June, a Birmingham, Alabama, native with a sprinter's speed, was signed by Sox scout John Donaldson in the summer of 1952. He played briefly for the Sox' Wisconsin Rapids farm team in 1952–53, but in June 1953, press reports stated that June had "decided to give up baseball."[19] That was decidedly untrue; what June was giving up was playing in the White Sox farm system. The following year June signed with a Cleveland Indians farm team. He spent eight seasons in the Cleveland system, reaching the Class AAA level and recording four seasons with 20 or more stolen bases, including a 1960 season with 26 homers, 27 steals, and 100 RBIs. While he never made it to the major leagues, June clearly had skills that the White Sox seemed unable to recognize.

Probably the most promising young players in the White Sox farm system in 1952 were two Cubans: Alfredo Ibáñez, a 22-year-old pitcher, and José Bustamante, a 20-year-old third baseman. Both were recommended to the Sox by Roberto Maduro, owner of Gran Stadium in Habana as well as the Cienfuegos Cuban League franchise. Both players spent the 1952 season with Class C Superior, Wisconsin, of the Northern League and performed extremely well: Ibáñez went 18-4 with a 2.26 ERA, and Bustamante batted .313 with a .430 on-base percentage and 32 stolen bases. Both made the league All-Star team, and Ibáñez finished second in the league's Rookie of the Year voting behind an 18-year-old shortstop for the Eau Claire Bears named Henry Aaron. Those would be outstanding performances regardless of circumstance, but they were even more impressive given that both players were playing outside of Cuba for the first time, while struggling to decipher a new language.

Both Ibáñez and Bustamante held their own when moved up to Class B Waterloo in 1953. But in 1954 the White Sox made a curious deal that resulted in the two players' spending the year with the Modesto Reds, a Yankees farm team, while still technically belonging to the Sox. Out of sight seemed out of mind; by 1955 Ibáñez and Bustamante were performing in the Mexican League. How these two young players went from top prospects to Mexican Leaguers in such a short time is something of a mystery. But, as was the case with Luis Garcia in 1951, if the Sox were doing much to nurture their skills or showing sensitivity toward young men who were Black, Latin, and trying to find their way in a totally different world, it was hard to see. "It happens to all of us," the Cuban star and Hall of Famer Tony Oliva once said about the experience of Latin players in the United States. "We all get released. . . . To the Americans, we are like some stray dog, like a rudderless ship at sea."[20]

Finally, there was Gideon Applegate, the New Englander who had pitched brilliantly in 1951 and then spoken eloquently about the color line in sports after the season. Applegate began the 1952 season with the Waterloo White Hawks of the Class B Three-I League. He struggled with his control and was demoted to Class C Superior in mid-May. In his first start for Superior on May 18, Applegate threw a no-hitter against the Sioux Fall Canaries, facing only 29 men. Four weeks later he threw a second no-hitter, this one against the St. Cloud Rox (because it was the first game of a doubleheader, the game was only seven innings long). Applegate struck out 11 St. Cloud hitters and hit two doubles as a batter. Facing St. Cloud again on July 7, Applegate nearly pitched a *third* no-hitter; the only St. Cloud hit of the game was a single in the eighth inning. For the season, Applegate posted a 14-6 record and a 3.36 ERA while leading the Northern League with 188 strikeouts. His pitching helped Superior win the league championship. It was truly a season to remember.

Or perhaps not; less than a year later, Applegate was no longer pitching in white organized baseball. Control had been an issue with Applegate even in his brilliant 1952 season, when he led the Northern League in walks allowed. Slated to pitch for Waterloo in 1953, he was sent back to Superior after failing to throw a strike on 27 consecutive pitches in a spring training game. He struck out 12 batters in his first start for Superior, but in late June he was demoted to Class D Danville, despite a winning record (5-3). Applegate did not report to Danville; instead, he went to South Dakota to pitch for the Pierre Cowboys in the Basin League, an independent semipro league. At age 25, his career in white organized baseball was over. "They said I threw my arm out," Applegate told a friend decades later. "But I could see the handwriting on the wall. And you can't be bitter. I hoped some of the things I've done in my life made it easier for someone else."[21]

After his stint in the Basin League, Applegate returned to Rhode Island. He got married, had two sons whom he coached in Little League, and officiated Division II and III college football games. He died at age 89 in December 2016. "He wasn't bitter," said his son Josh, a former member of the US Alpine Ski team and later its strength and conditioning coach. "He was always telling my brother and I that he had played against this guy, knew that guy. He had stories about riding on rickety old buses. Stories about having fun."[22]

◆ ◆ ◆

During the 1952 season Black players on the Colorado Springs Sky Sox endured an incident that would not be remembered as fun. In a game against the Omaha Cardinals on July 18, the Sky Sox accused Omaha player-manager George Kissell and his players of hurling racial taunts at Sam Hairston and Connie Johnson. Sky Sox president Chase Stone and general manager Bill MacPhail—a future television sports executive and the younger son of Larry MacPhail, who had done much to resist baseball integration in the 1940s—protested the abuse in a telegram to Western League officials:

> This club does not feel there is a place in the Western league or in baseball for discriminatory remarks directed against our players nor for profanity directed at our fans, nor for general poor sportsmanship.

We have no legal rights to bar the Omaha manager, George Kissell, from this field, but unless we are immediately assured by the Western league that there will be no repetition of these tactics the Colorado Springs club will request a hearing before the National Association of professional baseball leagues.[23]

Kissell denied both making derogatory remarks to the players and directing any profanity at the fans. But Omaha Cardinals team president Robert H. Hall did not back away from the charge; on the contrary, he seemed to lean into it. "Games are won on the field and not by appealing to the president of the league," Hall wrote in a formal statement. He continued,

> Baseball is a game for men, and over the years the fans know that those participating must play the game to the hilt. Players worthy of a uniform must be able to take it as well as dish it out. This is notice to Colorado Springs and all everywhere that in keeping with that philosophy and in the fine tradition of our Cardinal team, that whenever and wherever the Omaha Cardinals play, that we ask no quarter and give no quarter—and in the parlance of the baseball world, "We come to play ball."[24]

Chase Stone fired back, calling Hall's statement "pure Nebraska corn" and suggesting that perhaps Hall was unaware that "Kissell and his team lead the league in fines levied by the Western league for actions detrimental to the proper conduct of the game."[25]

The president of the Western League, Edwin Johnson, was a career politician who held the post from 1947 to 1955 while also serving as a US senator from Colorado (1937–55); Johnson also served three terms as Colorado's governor (1933–37, 1955–57). As a senator, Johnson had won notoriety in 1950 for repeatedly assailing actress Ingrid Bergman, who had borne a child out of wedlock with director Roberto Rossellini. Johnson had also introduced a bill creating a licensing bureau for films that he said would curb "immorality and lewdness" in the movies.[26] He was not someone likely to tolerate abusive language from ballplayers and managers.

After taking statements from one of the umpires and a Western League official who had attended the July 18 game, Johnson issued a formal apology to Colorado Springs baseball fans. He wrote that "vile and abusive language has no place in Western league parks and will not be tolerated." He did not take action against either the Omaha franchise or manager George Kissell, but he wrote that "Manager Kissell of the Omaha club tolerated this conduct and heard this language and did not stop it, but to observers apparently encouraged it." He added, "There will be action, and plenty of it, if such is repeated in the future."[27]

By all accounts the manager at the center of this controversy, George Kissell, never repeated the ugly actions of 1952. Kissell worked for the St. Louis Cardinals organization as a player, coach, manager, and executive from 1940, when Branch Rickey signed him for $125 a month, until his death from injuries suffered in a car accident in 1988. During the 1960s the Cardinals earned a reputation as one of Major League Baseball's best teams in nurturing and developing Black players. Kissell himself managed numerous future Black MLB players, including Bobby Tolan, Willie Montañez, Coco Laboy, Walt Williams, and Johnny Lewis. Author Rob Rains wrote that "when it came to developing 'the Cardinal way,' nobody was more influential than Kissell—who wrote the team's organization manual about how to practice fundamentals, about the importance of acting as a professional, and the necessity of concentrating on doing all of the little things right in order to be successful."[28]

◆ ◆ ◆

In November 1952 Harvey Clark was interviewed by *Chicago Daily News* writer Frank Hayes. The Clark family was living in the Michigan Garden Apartments at 47th St. and Michigan Avenue, only two miles from Comiskey Park. The former CTA bus driver was now working as a salesman.

"If anything, my faith in America is stronger than ever," Clark said. "After the press had told my story to the world I learned, through hundreds of letters and messages, how many friendly people there are in my country, and in other countries." Clark said that he had received threatening letters, but that they were vastly outnumbered by letters of sympathy and encouragement. He talked about how, after the riots in Cicero had prevented his family from living there, the city of Norwalk, Connecticut, had invited the Clarks to live there; when the Clarks graciously declined the offer, Norwalk gave his nine-year-old daughter Michele a music scholarship. "You can't be poisoned against America when things like that happen," Clark said.[29]

11

The Forgotten One

As 1952 began, Wid Matthews was a man on the spot. The Cubs' director of player personnel was beginning his third season with the team, and it was hard to see any progress. In 1949, the year before Matthews arrived in Chicago, the Cubs finished last with a 61-93 record. In 1951, year two of the Matthews regime, the Cubs finished last with a 62-92 mark. But while Cubs owner Phil Wrigley showed signs of restlessness at times, he largely stood by his man. "When you set out an asparagus bed you wait a couple of years or so to see what comes up," Wrigley told a reporter.[1]

When the season got under way in April, the asparagus appeared to be sprouting at last. Over the first third of the season, the Cubs were one of the biggest stories in baseball. On the morning of June 15, the North Siders boasted a 34-19 record and were in third place, only four games behind the league-leading Dodgers. A slump followed, but with a strong finish the Cubs ended the year in fifth place with a 77-77 record. It was the first time the team had finished the year with a .500 or better record since 1946.

Suddenly Wid Matthews was taking bows. In June the *Sporting News* devoted publisher J. G. Taylor Spink's "Looping the Loops" column to a full-page interview with Matthews. When the Cubs were floundering, he told Spink, "I would wrestle with myself, wondering whether I was going too far with the youngsters and should bring in some veterans. . . . I would tell myself, 'You've got to stay hitched, you've got to stick with the kids.'"[2]

While the improved record gave Matthews some cover, most of top players on the 1952 roster weren't kids at all. The team's best position players were 35-year-old Hank Sauer, who won the league's Most Valuable Player Award, and 33-year-old Frankie Baumholtz. The relief ace was 43-year-old knuckleballer Dutch Leonard. Most of the "kids," such as pitchers Bob Rush, Randy Jackson, Warren Hacker, and Paul Minner, were 26 or older, and only Rush would continue to perform at a high level. The Cubs were particularly weak in the middle infield. Second baseman Eddie Miksis, whom Matthews had described to Spink as "the best infielder in baseball," batted .232. That was 10 points higher than his nominal double-play partner, Roy Smalley.

Cubs fans also couldn't help noticing that their crosstown rivals, the White Sox, had surged into pennant contention after adding their first Black player, Minnie Miñoso, in 1951. Or that four of the six National League pennants since 1947 had been won by teams (the Dodgers and the Giants) who had received major contributions from Black players. Meanwhile the Cubs, who had had seven Black players in their minor league farm system in 1951, were down to three in 1952. Two of them, Nap Gulley and Arnie Green, were players whom the Cubs clearly did not consider prospects to reach the majors. But the third player, Gene Baker, was finishing his third season as a member of the Cubs' Los Angeles Angels farm team in 1952. Baker was a highly regarded middle infielder, an area where the Cubs definitely needed help.

Many were asking: Why was Gene Baker still in the minor leagues?

◆ ◆ ◆

Eugene Walter Baker was born in Davenport, Iowa, on June 15, 1925, the eldest son of Eugene O. and Mildred (Freeman) Baker. Davenport is one of the "Quad Cities" on the Mississippi River along with Bettendorf, Iowa, and Rock Island and Moline, Illinois. In 1950 the total population of the area was about two hundred thousand, more than 95 percent of it white. Most of Baker's early fame as an athlete came on the basketball court. In 1942 and 1943, he helped lead Davenport High to the semifinals in the state basketball tournament. He was also selected first-team All-State by the Iowa Daily Press Association in 1943. The IDPA press release noted that Baker was six feet tall and, at 142 pounds, the lightest player on the team. "Most improved player on this year's Davenport cage team," said the release. "Clean type of player, fouling infrequently. So alert that he caused opposing guards to foul. Best passer in Mississippi Valley loop."[3]

With World War II raging, Baker was inducted into the US Navy in October 1943. He was stationed primarily at Ottumwa Naval Air Station in Iowa, where he starred on the station's basketball and baseball teams. "I never really got interested in baseball until I enlisted in the Navy," said Baker, who previously had concentrated on basketball and track.[4] After his discharge in May 1946, Baker played American Legion and semipro baseball in the Davenport area. When the Kansas City Monarchs came to Davenport in 1947 for an exhibition game, he asked for a tryout; the Monarchs were impressed, and the following year Baker joined Black baseball's premier team. He quickly became the team's regular shortstop. Managed by Buck O'Neil, the Monarchs were a powerhouse team featuring a number of players who had played or would play in the American and National Leagues—Willard Brown, Elston Howard, Hank Thompson, Connie Johnson, and Baker's double-play partner, second baseman Curt Roberts—along with several players who reached the high minors. The 1948 Monarchs won the Negro American League pennant before losing one of the final Negro League World Series to the Birmingham Black Barons, four games to three.

Baker began a second season with the Monarchs in 1949, and his play drew the attention of several major league teams, including the Cubs. In July of that year, Cubs director of minor league clubs Jack Sheehan wrote to Monarchs owner Tom Baird about Baker, stating that Cubs scout Jimmy Payton had recommended Baker for the Cubs' Los Angeles Angels farm team. Nothing happened in 1949, but in May 1950 Sheehan wrote Baird once again, expressing interest in both Baker and Monarchs catcher-outfielder Elston Howard. As previously noted, Baird said he wanted to keep Howard for the time being, then infuriated Sheehan by selling him to the Yankees. The Cubs were, however, able to get a $1,000 option for Baker to have a spring training trial with their Class AAA Springfield farm team. They agreed to pay Baird an additional $5,500 if they elected to keep him after 30 days of Springfield's regular season. "You will have two of the best infielders in our league if you take Baker," Baird wrote. "Gilliam, [the] boy you got from Baltimore, is a hell of a good ball player."[5] The Cubs missed their chance with Jim Gilliam, but they sent the $5,500 to Baird to complete the purchase of Baker.

After spending the first month of the 1950 season with Springfield—getting into only three games—Baker was demoted to Class A Des Moines. Although he was the first Black player ever to play for Des Moines, Baker was a well-known athlete in Iowa, and his hustling style of play helped make him popular right from the start. In his first game against Sioux City on May 16, he singled, doubled, drew a walk, and stole a base. On one play he raced from first to third on a short throw, finishing with a slide that his manager, former Cubs pitching star Charlie Root, called "the most beautiful I've ever seen in my life."[6] When he made his home debut on June 1, Maury White of the *Des Moines Tribune* wrote, "Des Moines fans, some 1,861 of them, took their first look at shortstop Gene Baker Thursday night—and liked what they saw."[7]

Baker also quickly won over his teammates. In mid-June *Des Moines Tribune* columnist Gordon Gammack wrote:

> The Jackie Robinson story is being repeated in the case of Gene Baker, the Des Moines Bruins' shortstop. All the players now have made it absolutely clear that Baker is not only a teammate but a friend.
>
> The spirt was exemplified recently when one of the Bruins, a South Carolinian, went to Business Manager John Holland and said, "I'd appreciate it, sir, if you'd arrange for Baker and me to room together.[8]

It soon became apparent that Baker was too good for Class A ball. After hitting .321 and playing well defensively in 49 games for the Bruins—the *Des Moines Register* wrote that his fielding "verged on the miraculous at times"—he was promoted to the Cubs' Class AAA team in Los Angeles.

He would stay there for four seasons.

◆ ◆ ◆

As we have seen, southern California was not especially welcoming to people of color. When a Black man named O'Day Short purchased property in the city of Fontana in the fall of 1945, he was threatened by vigilantes and warned by deputy sheriffs not to move in. The Short family moved in anyway, and in December an explosion at the house resulted in the death of several members of the family. Although evidence strongly indicated that arson was the cause, a grand jury investigating the explosion adjourned without issuing a report. In the subsequent months Black homeowners who had moved into white neighborhoods were subjected to threats, violence, and cross burnings. Local civil rights organizations attributed much of the violence to the Ku Klux Klan, which had marched in downtown Los Angeles in 1939 and surged in popularity after the war ended.[9]

Even famous Black entertainers had to battle prejudice. In 1948 the popular singer Nat King Cole, a man who had grown up on the South Side of Chicago, began shopping for a house in the posh Los Angeles neighborhood of Hancock Park. After local residents heard the news, an anonymous caller told their real estate agent that she would be forced out of the business; another caller told her she would "meet with a serious automobile accident within a few days." When the Coles persisted and purchased a home on Muirfield Road, a sign was placed in their yard that read "N__ Heaven." A year later, a shot was fired into their window. The Coles refused to be intimidated, and Nat Cole lived in the Hancock Park home until his death at age 45 in 1965.[10]

While Black athletes playing for southern California sports teams were permitted to play with whites, they often struggled to win acceptance.

Despite Jackie Robinson's multisport heroics during his career at UCLA, a football teammate once injured Robinson's knee with a tackle that observers felt was a deliberate attempt to injure him. "There were some players on that team who weren't fans of Jackie Robinson," said a writer who was covering the team.[11] When Robinson's college teammates Kenny Washington and Woody Strode joined the Los Angeles Rams in 1946 as the first Black players in the NFL in more than a decade, they did so under political pressure to field an integrated team in the publicly funded Los Angeles Memorial Coliseum. Strode, who was added to the team at Washington's insistence, said that he was looked down on by Rams officials because of his interracial marriage and seldom given a chance to play. "Integrating the NFL was the low point of my life," said Strode, who would go on to a distinguished career in Hollywood as an actor. "There was nothing nice about it."[12]

When Gene Baker joined the Los Angeles Angels during the 1950 season, they had one other Black player, Booker McDaniel; Kenny Washington had been released after playing for the team earlier in the season. At the time there were only a handful of Black players in the Pacific Coast League. Nonetheless, Baker, who had a low-key personality and was used to playing on integrated teams, soon became one of the team's, and the league's, most popular players. One factor in his favor was that the Angels' home ballpark, Wrigley Field in Los Angeles, was located in an area close to much of the city's Black population. "It has long been held that Los Angeles might benefit more from the employment of a truly formidable Negro baseball star than any other club in this league," wrote John R. Williams of the *Chicago Defender*.[13]

Baker seemed to be that player. During most of the 1940s, the Angels' regular shortstop was Bill Schuster, a popular and colorful player known as Broadway Bill. Although well known for his antics on the field, such as sliding back into home plate when he knew he would be a sure out at first or cutting across the diamond instead of running to second on a sure double play, Schuster was an excellent player who had twice been voted Most Valuable Player in the Pacific Coast League. Although the Angels had traded the 36-year-old Schuster to Seattle in 1949, he was still considered the benchmark for Angels shortstops. "The thought of somebody taking Schuster's place was somewhat unfathomable for the average Angel fan," recalled future major league scout Artie Harris, who attended many Angels games during Baker's time there. Baker soon won Harris over. "People would say no, he can't be better than Schuster; Schuster's the most popular player in this city. But when Baker came along, he was 1,000 percent better than Schuster," said Harris.[14]

After joining the Angels in July 1950 Baker got into 100 games, batted .280, and won numerous plaudits for his speed and defensive ability. Angels beat writer Frank Finch wrote that "unless a lot of competent judges of diamond talent are completely out of their minds, Baker won't miss the boat to the Big Time." Gene Kessler of the *Chicago Sun-Times* wrote that Baker "is given an excellent chance to run Roy Smalley out of the [Cubs] shortstop job."[15]

In 1950 Smalley had played in all 154 Cubs games, and while he batted only .232, his power numbers (21 homers, 85 RBIs) were excellent, especially for a middle infielder. So it was no shock that Baker was sent back to Los Angeles in the spring of 1951. But when Smalley broke his leg in April and went on the injured list for two months, Baker was not recalled to take his place. In June Doc Young of the *Los Angeles Sentinel* wrote that Branch Rickey's Pittsburgh Pirates were interested in Baker, while questioning the Cubs' interest in Black players. Young noted that Stan Hack, Baker's manager with the Angels, had been skipper of the Cubs' Springfield farm team in 1950, when the club had had seven Black players in spring training but had kept only one. When the Cubs fired manager Frankie Frisch in July and speculation was rampant that Hack would become the team's manager in 1952, Young wrote, "Although Hack has done a good job with the Angels this season, the 'peculiarity' of his style insofar as Negro players are concerned forces one to wonder if his promotion won't kill whatever chances Gene Baker might have with the Cubs."[16] Young was probably being unfair to Hack, who would give extensive playing time to several Blacks, including Baker and Ernie Banks, after becoming Cubs manager in 1954. But given the Cubs' track record with Black players to that point, his suspicion was understandable.

In 1952 Hack was still managing the Angels, and despite the Cubs' middle-infield problems, Gene Baker was still his shortstop. Wid Matthews assured people he was committed to having Baker join the Cubs. When Paul Fagan, owner of the PCL's San Francisco Seals, made a $30,000 offer for Baker during the 1952 season, Matthews was quoted as saying, "Not even $100,000 would get Baker's contract . . . we're bringing him up in '53 as the first Negro ever to wear a Cub uniform."[17] In the meantime, Baker remained an Angel. In August he set a record that probably underscored his frustration: He played in his 394th consecutive game for the Angels, the most in franchise history. The streak eventually reached 420 games before Baker finally sat out a game.

As the 1952 season was coming to an end, Bob Hunter of the *Sporting News* wrote, "It looks like Gene is destined not only to become the Cub shortstop, but the team's first Negro performer." A few weeks later,

Sporting News writer Ed Burns wrote, "Shortstop has been the Cubs' main aches and pains station for years" and contrasted "the fragile Cub shortstop crop" with Baker's ironman feats. In November the publication stated, "The Cubs may become the seventh major league team to present a Negro in their lineup next season. Gene Baker, 26-year-old shortstop belonging to Los Angeles (Pacific Coast), will be given a trial by the Bruins during spring training and transferred to the Cubs if he shows up well." Baker's promotion to the Cubs in 1953 seemed inevitable.[18]

Or maybe not. *"Baker may be a year away,"* said Matthews in February 1953, "but our shortstop spot is wide open. Eddie Miksis, Roy Smalley and Baker will fight for it."[19]

Did the Cubs really think that Miksis and Smalley were better players than Baker? There are some reasons to think so. Matthews's affection for Miksis, the .236 career hitter whom Wid had called "the best infielder in baseball," was well-known . . . and highly ridiculed. When the Cubs traded longtime star Andy Pafko to the Dodgers in 1951 for a package of fringe players with Miksis as the Cubs' key acquisition, a Willard Mullin cartoon in the *Sporting News* showed Mullin's famous Brooklyn bum character hypnotizing Matthews and telling him, "Yez are Sandy Claurs . . . and this is Criss-mus." Matthews seemed to have a similarly high regard for Smalley, at one point calling Roy the equal of Phillies shortstop Granny Hamner, a three-time All-Star. Yet when Smalley broke his leg in 1951, the Cubs instead gave playing time to obscure players like Jack Cusick and Bob Ramazzotti. Along with posting unimpressive career statistics, Miksis, Smalley, Cusick, and Ramazzotti shared one obvious trait: All of them were white.

Would the Cubs really send Baker back to Los Angeles for a fourth season? If they did, a lot of people would be asking questions.

◆ ◆ ◆

While Baker was spending 1952 in Los Angeles, his future double-play partner Ernie Banks was playing baseball for his army team in Germany. It was a plum assignment; members of the 242nd AAA Group Barons traveled frequently to games against other bases, had their own floor in the barracks, and got first crack at the chow line. Banks's performance at shortstop and at bat drew raves. He was featured in an article in the military newspaper *Stars and Stripes,* and his performance began to draw the attention of major league teams. "Everybody knew right away that he was sensational," recalled Jim Knutson, an army teammate.[20] According to Banks, he received letters from the Brooklyn Dodgers and the Cleveland Indians inviting him to try out for their teams when his service stint was complete. Banks, however, would not begin to appear on the Cubs' radar for another year.

◆ ◆ ◆

During this time, the Cubs weren't the only major league team feeling some heat over their failure to add a Black player. The Cubbies could at least point out that there were Black players in their farm system. The Detroit Tigers, playing in a city that, like Chicago, had both a large Black population and a proud Black baseball history, had not even gone that far. "In Detroit in the 1920s players found winter jobs in the local automobile plants," wrote Jules Tygiel. "Turkey Stearnes and other Detroit Stars found work in factories owned by Detroit Tigers co-owner Walter O. Briggs, glad to hire them in his legendarily grimy and unsafe paint shops, but not on his baseball team." By the early 1950s, nothing had changed. "The question of hiring a Negro has never bothered us," Tigers general manager Billy Evans told a Black reporter in 1951. "The Tigers got along many years without Negro players." It wasn't only Black *players* that the Tigers weren't interested in hiring. "There isn't even a Negro selling peanuts in Briggs stadium," a fan complained to the *Detroit Tribune*.[21]

Early in 1952 the National Negro Labor Council wrote to Walter O. (Spike) Briggs Jr., son of Walter O. and the man now running the franchise. It asked the team to comment on what it called the club's "lilywhite" policy. "There is no discrimination against Negro players here," said Charlie Gehringer, who had succeeded Evans as the team's general manager. A Tiger great who had been elected to the Hall of Fame in 1949, Gehringer recalled conversations with Briggs Sr. in which Walter O. had said, "We'd have Negro players if we could get good ones."[22] In an interview with the *Detroit Tribune* in April, Gehringer said, "We would buy or trade for [Larry] Doby if we could"—but of course Doby was not available. Gehringer backed the thoughts of team manager Red Rolfe, who had said, "There hardly are any good ball players left: not only colored, but white as well."[23] (The Tigers would eventually make a trade for Doby—in 1959.)

"General Manager Charlie Gehringer, who stated earlier this year that the Tigers would hire capable Negro players if located, will have to be armed with radar indicator and search warrant if he does," commented the *Detroit Tribune*. "That's the way it looks. Red Rolfe's statement that all of the top Negro players have been discovered is [a] lot of hogwash."[24] Meanwhile, the team was floundering. Rolfe was fired midway through the 1952 season, a year in which the Tigers lost a franchise record 104 games and finished in last place for the first time in team history. Gehringer left after the Tigers finished sixth with 94 losses in 1953.

According to Wendell Smith, the Tigers were one of only three major league teams with no Black players in either the majors or in their minor league farm systems in 1952. The others were the St. Louis Cardinals and the Boston Red Sox. The Cardinals would begin acquiring Black players after August Busch Jr. and Anheuser-Busch purchased the franchise in 1953. But like the Tigers, the Red Sox would long resist pressure to integrate their team. In April 1945, after Boston city councilman Isadore Muchnick had threatened to withdraw permission for the Red Sox and the Boston Braves to play home games on Sundays unless the teams held tryouts for Black players, the Red Sox had conducted a public tryout for Jackie Robinson and two other Negro League players, Sam Jethroe and Marvin Williams. As was typical for major league teams who held "tryouts" for Black players during that time, Red Sox officials thanked the players and then did nothing. (While Robinson would remain bitter toward the Red Sox for the rest of his life, a claim by Boston sportswriter Clif Keane that a Red Sox official had shouted, "Get those n___rs off the field!" did not surface until 1979. The claim was never corroborated by the others who attended the tryout, including Robinson.)[25]

In 1950 the Red Sox purchased Negro League star Lorenzo "Piper" Davis, a player whom Chicago sportswriter Gene Kessler had long urged the Cubs or the White Sox to sign, from the Birmingham Black Barons. The purchase price was $7,500, with a promise to double the figure if Davis remained in the Red Sox organization past May 15. Because Boston's Class AAA and AA farm teams, Louisville and Birmingham, played in Jim Crow states, Davis was assigned to Class A Scranton of the Eastern League; in truth, he was probably qualified to play for the Red Sox without a minor league stint. But on May 13 Scranton released Davis for "economic reasons" despite the fact that he was batting .333 and leading his team in home runs and RBIs. The team did not even offer Davis return train fare back to Birmingham. "I knew that was a joke," Davis said about the excuse that he had been released for monetary reasons, "because [Red Sox owner] Tom Yawkey's one of the richest men in the East."[26] In an article for the *Scranton Tribune* written after his release, Davis told Chic Feldman,

> I am leaving Scranton this morning, for my home in Birmingham, and I can truthfully state that nothing in this life has made me sadder. Because in the short time I have been here the people of Scranton have been most wonderful. Democratic, fair and above all true sportfolk who appreciated what I tried to do.
>
> . . .
>
> Now I am an unemployed baseball player with a family to keep. My boy is nine, my daughter seven. I heard professional baseball was a tough

game. I never thought it was as tough as my experience with Scranton and the Boston club makes it appear.[27]

Davis would be the last Black player to perform for a Red Sox farm team until 1953, when the team signed pitcher Earl Wilson to a minor league contract. In his report on Wilson, Red Sox scout Tom Downey described him as "a well-mannered colored boy, not too black, pleasant to talk to, very good experience, conducts himself as a gentleman."[28] Wilson would eventually pitch for the Red Sox, but not until 1959.

♦ ♦ ♦

As was the case with the Cubs vis-à-vis Baker, some of the teams that had Black players in their minor league systems, but not in the majors, were in no hurry to change the status quo. The New York Yankees, who, like the Cubs, had had Black players in their farm systems beginning in 1949, were the most notorious example.

In 1952 one of the most promising players in the Yankees' farm system was Vic Power. A 24-year-old Afro-Latino from Puerto Rico, Power batted .331 with 16 homers and 109 RBIs for the Yankees' flagship farm team, the Kansas City Blues of the Class AAA American Association. Asked if he planned to invite Power to the Yankees' spring training camp in 1953, general manager George Weiss was noncommittal. "Power may be asked to report to the Yankees, and then again, he may not," Weiss said. "There are divergent opinions on his abilities. We are eager to find a Negro player of Yankee class. But we are not going to have a Negro player merely as a concession to pressure groups. Our mail on that subject show a 3 to 1 edge in support of that policy. The first Negro player will land the job on merit."[29] Privately, Weiss was telling a different story. Roger Kahn wrote that Weiss told him in 1954 that the reason the Yankees did not have any Black players "is that our box seat customers from Westchester County don't want to sit with a lot of colored fans from Harlem."[30]

On November 30, Jackie Robinson was a guest on a New York television show called *Youth Wants to Know*. The format involved Robinson answering questions from young audience members. "Mr. Robinson," a young man asked, "do you think the Yankees are prejudiced against Negro players? I ask this because I am a Yankee fan and I'd like to know."

After letting out an audible gasp, Robinson answered, "Yes. I think they are. I don't mean the players are—they are a fine bunch of fellows and sportsmen and I really had a good time talking to those fellows when they get on base and at other times. But I think the Yankee management is prejudiced. They haven't a single Negro on the team and very few in the

Yankee organization. You asked the question and I answered it honestly. That's my opinion."[31]

Robinson's statement created considerable controversy. The Yankees, of course, denied the charge, with George Weiss repeating the usual mantra that the team would be happy to have a Black player when they found one "good enough to win a place on the Yankees."[32] Yankees manager Casey Stengel echoed Weiss. New York–based sportswriter Dan Daniel, a frequent Yankees apologist, wrote, "Club owners in both leagues believe it is not the business of a ball player to blast rival clubs over TV, especially as the basis for the blast is in heated controversy, and the fundamental issue is doubtful."[33]

A frequent criticism of Robinson was that he was aligning himself with the "agitators" and "rabblerousers" who were pressuring teams such as the Yankees to integrate. "What's he getting ready to do . . . run for Congress?" an anonymous major league executive said about Robinson. "He's getting to be a better agitator than a second baseman."[34] Even Wendell Smith was skeptical of Robinson's criticism; he wrote that the Yankees, the "most successful club in the history of the big leagues," had always been slow to promote young players. "Robinson may be absolutely right about the Yankees, but we are inclined to believe otherwise," he continued. "They are such sound, practical baseball people—and the records prove it—we don't believe they will overlook or ignore any player, regardless of his color."[35]

While Robinson stood by what he had said during the television show, the baseball world by and large closed ranks behind the Yankees and the nine other clubs that had yet to have a Black player on their major league roster. The last team to add a Black player to its roster had been the White Sox in May 1951. No other teams seemed to be in any hurry to join the club, including the Chicago Cubs.

12

The Arc of History

"Negro Players were barred from big league baseball for something like 68 years," wrote Wendell Smith in the *Pittsburgh Courier* in January 1953. (Note: a more accurate total would be 62). "Such great stars as Oscar Charleston, Smoky Joe Williams, John Henry Lloyd, Joe Redding, Mule Suttles, Willie Wells, Josh Gibson and hundreds of others were victimized by the vicious policy, or 'understanding,' which forbade the employment of Negroes." But since Jackie Robinson broke baseball's color line in 1946, Smith continued, "Negro players have profited handsomely." According to Smith's calculations, the top 11 Black players in the major leagues were scheduled to earn an estimated $233,000 in 1953, with the salaries of reserve and part-time players increasing the total to over a quarter of a million dollars. "Obviously, the Negro player has been making giant strides on the field and in the direction of the bank since he arrived in 1947," Smith concluded. "In this instance, baseball is fast atoning for its past sins."[1]

But as players reported to spring training to prepare for the new season, it was apparent that full equality was a still a long way away. In Vero Beach, Florida, there were signs that even on Jackie Robinson's team, Black players were still fighting to win acceptance. The Brooklyn Dodgers' most promising rookie in 1953 was second baseman Jim Gilliam, the player whom the Cubs had sold back to the Negro Leagues in the spring of 1950. In order to get Gilliam into the lineup, Dodgers manager Charlie Dressen planned to move Jackie Robinson to third base. That put a popular white veteran, Billy Cox, on the bench. Cox, understandably, was not happy, but neither were some other Dodgers players, and race was clearly an issue. When the team put four Black players (Robinson, Gilliam, Roy Campanella, and Joe Black) on the field at the same time during a spring training game, an anonymous Dodger was quoted as saying, "I don't mind them in the game, but they're really taking over." Another said, "Good thing we sent that Pendleton [Jim Pendleton, a Black player] to Boston or we'd have one in the outfield, too." When the Dodgers team bus passed a Black minor league pitcher the next day, a player said, "How come he ain't on our roster?"[2]

The Dodgers insisted that their team had no racial problems, but in his classic book *Boys of Summer*, Roger Kahn said that when he spoke to Cox about the situation, Billy asked him, "How would you like a n___ to take your job?"[3] Ultimately Dodgers general manager Buzzy Bavasi met with the teams' veterans, who worked to restore team unity. The Dodgers went on to win another National League pennant in 1953, the team's 105 wins set a franchise record that was not broken until 2019, and Jim Gilliam won the National League Rookie of the Year Award.

While the Dodgers were dealing with the issue of people thinking they had *too many* Black players, the ten teams that had yet to integrate seemed some distance from adding even one to their roster. To be fair, Branch Rickey's Pittsburgh Pirates opened the season with Puerto Rican outfielder Carlos Bernier as part of their team . . . but as noted previously, Bernier was not recognized as Black at that time, and would not be regarded as Pittsburgh's first Black player until many years later. (Contemporary sources would consider Curt Roberts, in 1954, as the Pirates' first Black player.) The most widely publicized of the holdouts, the New York Yankees, sent Vic Power back to Kansas City for his third season at the Class AAA level. As usual, there was a big difference between the Yankees' public and private pronouncements. Publicly, the team brass continued to say, "Power isn't ready." Privately, Yankees general manager George Weiss was telling Roger Kahn, "Maybe he can play, but not for us. He's impudent and he goes for white women."[4] Power had another great season for Kansas City in 1953, winning the American Association batting championship with a .349 average. Rather than go through more controversy, the Yankees traded Power to the Philadelphia Athletics in December.

◆ ◆ ◆

In Mesa, Arizona, the Chicago Cubs were dealing with their own controversy over a Black player who supposedly "still wasn't ready" to play in the majors. Although the Cubs had invited Gene Baker to the team's spring camp for the first time, Baker's supporters were finding reasons to be concerned. The Cubs gave Baker only five scattered starts during the spring training season, while quietly passing on negative comments about his performance. One day a reporter was told that Baker "is a slick fielder but he can't hit." A different writer heard that Baker "hits in spells but falls down frequently on defense." The doubletalk exasperated Sam Lacy. "What looms as the prize stinkeroo of the 1953 spring training season is the hypocrisy being practiced by the Chicago Cubs in connection with their lone tan player, Gene Baker," wrote Lacy. Supporters of Baker, he continued, "point out 'the guy playing over him [Roy Smalley] isn't any ball of fire up there at the plate. Gene couldn't do much worse than Smalley's .222 [batting average] of last year, if he tries batting with a pencil.'"[5]

A few days later the Cubs sent Baker, who had batted .143 (3 for 21) in his sporadic spring training opportunities, back to Los Angeles; Smalley, who had batted .369, won the team's shortstop job. The top brass didn't change their mind even after Smalley was hospitalized with an infected ankle that forced him to miss the first three weeks of the season. Rather than recalling Baker, the team moved Wid Matthews favorite Eddie Miksis from second base to shortstop until Smalley could return. Meanwhile the Cubs, who had raised hopes with a .500 record in 1952, fell back to seventh place with a 65-89 record, despite a June trade with Rickey's Pirates for a package of players that included seven-time National League home run champion Ralph Kiner.

With Baker still playing for Los Angeles in August—he had his best season to date with 20 homers, 99 RBIs and a .284 batting average—Wendell Smith wrote a column in the *Pittsburgh Courier* titled "Critics Roast Cubs About Gene Baker." Along with calling Baker "the most talked-about baseball player in this sprawling, windswept city," Smith published the comments of opposing Pacific Coast League managers solicited by Smith's fellow *Chicago American* staff member, Jim Enright. The question Enright asked was, "If you were a major league manager, would you consider Gene Baker ready for an immediate opportunity to play in the majors?" Six of the seven managers answered that they thought Baker was ready. San Francisco Seals manager Tommy Heath was impressed with Baker's defense but doubtful about Gene's hitting; however, he added that he had not seen Baker play since the first of May. Noting that the Cubs were floundering in seventh place, Enright asked, "Are they more interested in finishing third at Los Angeles than they are winding up seventh in Chicago?"[6]

In response to this, an "obviously irritated" Wid Matthews told Smith, "We did not feel Baker was ready in 1951, nor last season. That is the only reason he has not been called up by the Cubs. He has been playing very good ball this season with the Angels and it appears now that he may be able to make the grade. We'll find out for sure at spring training." Matthews called Baker "a great prospect" and added: "Anyone who says we have held him back purposely because he is a Negro, is not telling the truth."[7]

The pressure to promote Baker may have had an effect. On September 1 the Cubs announced that they were recalling Baker from Los Angeles; Gene was scheduled to make his debut on September 14, the day after the Pacific Coast League season ended. One week later, they said that Baker would be breaking in along with another Black player, one whom the Cubs had purchased from the Kansas City Monarchs.

The other player was Ernie Banks.

◆ ◆ ◆

The Cubs most certainly didn't acquire Banks simply because Gene Baker needed a roommate, which was one theory about why they were keeping Baker in the minors. They purchased Banks because they thought he could succeed in the major leagues. So did several other MLB teams.

After receiving his discharge from the army in March 1953, Banks rejoined Buck O'Neil's Kansas City Monarchs. Although the Negro Leagues were a shadow of what they once were, he quickly became the league's hottest prospect. To be sure, some major league observers weren't impressed with Banks. Pittsburgh Pirates scout Don Caniglia highly recommended that Branch Rickey sign Banks, but when Rickey sent his sent his son Branch Jr. to watch Banks play, the younger Rickey wrote, "Tremendous glove, fast, but won't hit major league pitching."[8] A scout from the St. Louis Cardinals wrote, "He can't hit, he can't run, he has a pretty good arm, but it's a scatter arm. I don't like him."[9] John Donaldson, the former Negro League star who had been working as a scout for the White Sox since 1949, recommended that the Sox sign Banks, and so did Sox pitcher Connie Johnson, who had been a teammate of Banks with the Monarchs in 1950. But Frank Lane, who had heard the same negative report on Banks as the one filed by the Cardinals, elected to pass. Donaldson was so enraged about the White Sox once again ignoring his advice that he quit working for the team.[10]

The Cubs seemed to have few reservations about Banks. In July, Cubs scout Hugh Wise watched Ernie play 13 games for the Monarchs; responding to the question, "Years before major league?" he wrote, "Can play now."[11] Two other scouts, Ray Hayworth and Ray Blades, were similarly impressed. Blades suggested that Wid Matthews himself watch Banks play. After seeing Banks in action in a couple of games, Matthews asked Monarchs owner Tom Baird to name his price for Banks and an 18-year-old Monarchs pitcher named Bill Dickey. Baird said he wanted $20,000—$15,000 for Banks and $5,000 for Dickey. Matthews, who was prepared to go higher in order to land Banks, said yes to the deal. It was said to be the biggest sale in the history of the Negro Leagues.[12]

◆ ◆ ◆

When Baker and Banks joined the Cubs in mid-September, the adjustment understandably was easier for Baker, who had been with the team in spring training and who also had played in the minor leagues with several members of the club. Baker had no issues with switching from shortstop to second base to accommodate his new teammate. By most accounts—including Ernie's in his 1971 autobiography—Banks was given a good reception by his new teammates, particularly veteran stars Ralph Kiner and Hank Sauer. But he was entering a new and different environment, one very much out of his comfort zone. In a 2000 interview, Banks said,

> I didn't want to come to the Cubs. . . . I'm a type of person that I really enjoy my own comfort area. And I liked being with the guys. I liked their attitude. We cared about each other. And I was being taken out of that and going to a new dimension, and it was a big adjustment, although I came with another black player named Gene Baker. He and I came up together. I didn't know him. He didn't know me. But we connected when we joined the Cubs, and we became real good friends.[13]

In the same interview Banks said, "When I came to the major leagues, you know, I kind of felt nobody liked me. . . . I mean they might say it but they don't even know who I am, so they kind of left me to kind of feel my way on, around the park and so forth."[14]

On the day Banks arrived at Wrigley Field, the Cubs were playing the Brooklyn Dodgers. Banks spoke to Jackie Robinson, who gave him some encouraging words. When Ernie stepped into the batting cage before the game, he hit the first pitch on to the ramp in the left field bleachers. That turned a few heads.

Banks did not play against the Dodgers that day, nor in the first two games of a series against the Philadelphia Phillies. He finally made his debut on Thursday, September 17, batting seventh in the Cubs lineup against lefthander Curt Simmons, a talented pitcher who would win 193 games in the majors (including seven as a teammate of Banks in 1966–67). Baker was recovering from an injury to his side, so Banks had the honor of becoming the first Black player in Cubs history. The Cubs lost what *Chicago Tribune* writer Ed Prell called "an hilarious 16–4 [Phillies] victory," and Ernie's performance did not receive good reviews. Prell wrote, "Banks, first Negro to play for the Cubs in a league game, was unimpressive in the field, making an error in the field and failing to hit in three at-bats." Neil Gazel of the *Daily News* wrote, "Obviously nervous, Banks, the first Negro to play for the Cubs, made a mechanical error and was shy of taking charge of two balls that a veteran might have picked off." Jack Griffin of the *Sun-Times* wrote, "Banks, the Negro shortstop, seemed nervous in the field, making one error in seven chances. Touted as a heavy hitter, he flied out three times and walked once." Cubs manager Phil Cavarretta was kinder, saying, "Banks was a little shaky. But that was the boy's first game in organized ball." Ernie himself wrote, "It wasn't an impressive break-in, to say the least."[15]

Banks did much better in his next game, at St. Louis two days later; he got two hits, drove in two runs, handled six chances flawlessly in the field, and participated in three double plays as the Cubs beat the Cardinals in 12 innings, 5–2. His first major league hit was an RBI single in the seventh inning off lefthander Wilmer (Vinegar Bend) Mizell, a future US Representative from the state of North Carolina. A day later, on September 20, Banks hit the first of his 512 career home runs, off Jerry Staley of the Cardinals. He also had a triple and a single in the game, while driving in three runs. Baker made his MLB debut in the game, striking out as a pinch hitter.

On September 22 Banks and Baker appeared in the starting lineup for the first time. They started each of the last six games together, with Baker smoothly fitting into his new position of second base. When the season ended there were still a few doubts about Baker, who batted .227 in seven games. Wid Matthews indicated that Baker would have to battle Wid's pet, Eddie Miksis, for a starting position in 1954. But there were few doubts about Banks, who had batted .314 with two homers in his 10 September games. The Cubs looked like they had found a star.

◆ ◆ ◆

The Cubs weren't the only major league team to employ their first Black player in 1953. Four days before Banks took the field for the Cubs, 27-year-old former Negro League pitcher Bob Trice became the first Black player for the Philadelphia Athletics. Trice, who had won 21 games in 1953 for Philadelphia's Class AAA Ottawa farm team in the International League, started and lost to the St. Louis Browns, 5–2. He would start twice more in September and win both games. The addition of a Black player to the Athletics roster occurred only after team president Connie Mack, an early opponent of integration, had relinquished control of the team to his sons Roy and Earle. ("You can bet all of the corn in Iowa that the last club in the Major Leagues to sign a sundown star will be Connie Mack's Athletics," Black sportswriter W. Rollo Wilson had written in 1947.)[16] The cash-starved Macks would sell the franchise after the 1954 season to Chicago vending machine magnate Arnold Johnson, who moved the team to Kansas City.

There were slower signs of progress with other teams. While the Detroit Tigers were still five years away from adding a Black player to their major league roster, they were beginning to move forward. In August, one month after the *Detroit Free Press* had run a four-part series that asked the question "Is there a Negro in the Tigers' future?" the Tigers announced the signing of their first Black player. Claude Agee, an 18-year-old outfielder from McKeesport, Pennsylvania, was assigned to Detroit's Class D farm team in Jamestown, New York, beginning in 1954. Agee played for two seasons in the Tigers farm system but never advanced beyond the Class C level.

Even the haughty New York Yankees were beginning to feel the pressure to integrate their team. After signaling that they had reservations about Vic Power, the Yanks began touting the abilities of Ernie Banks's former Monarchs roommate Elston Howard, an outfielder whose serious demeanor figured to make fewer waves than the flamboyant Power. Late in 1953 the *Sporting News* published a glowing feature article about Howard that included a photo of a smiling Howard posing in front of a mirror while trying on a Yankee uniform shirt.[17] The historic occasion of Howard's actually *playing* for the Yankees would conveniently need to wait another year, however: Stating that they wanted to convert Howard into a catcher, a position he had played sporadically in the past, the Yankees sent him to Toronto for the 1954 season.

◆ ◆ ◆

In the minors, three leagues employed their first Black players in 1953: the Longhorn, Piedmont, and South Atlantic (Sally) Leagues. Among the players who integrated the Sally League was 19-year-old Henry Aaron.

The fight to integrate another minor league would wind up in court. Jim and Leander Tugerson were brothers and natives of Florence Villa, Florida; Jim was born 1923, Leander in 1927. Both were pitchers. In 1950 Leander joined the Indianapolis Clowns of the Negro American League, where his teammates included Sam Hairston and future White Sox farmhand Honey Lott. Jim joined the Clowns a year later. Both Tugersons had excellent seasons in 1951—particularly Leander, who was the starting pitcher for the East team in the 1951 East-West All-Star Game at Comiskey Park (he worked three shutout innings). Later that year Leander threw a no-hitter with 16 strikeouts against the Birmingham Black Barons. The White Sox were impressed with Leander's work and signed him to pitch for the Class A Colorado Sky Sox in 1952. He was one of three Black pitchers on the Sky Sox pitching staff at the start of the season, along with Connie Johnson and Gideon Applegate. Leander pitched poorly, however, and rejoined his brother with the Indianapolis Clowns in early May.

In February 1953 the Tugerson brothers signed contracts to pitch for the Hot Springs Bathers of the Cotton States League; they did so on the advice of Brooklyn Dodgers catcher Roy Campanella, a frequent visitor to the area. The Cotton States League, which had four teams in Mississippi, three in Arkansas, and one in Louisiana, was one of about a dozen minor leagues, all in the South, which had never had a Black player. "We know our place in the South because we come from the South," Jim Tugerson said after joining the Bathers. "All we want is an opportunity to prove our ability as baseball players." However, opposition from other league members quickly began to surface. The most outspoken official was former major league pitcher Willis (Ace) Hudlin, who owned the Jackson, Mississippi, Senators. The CSL, said Hudlin, "is hardly ready for Negro players."[18]

Although the Tugersons' contracts had been approved by George Trautman, president of the National Association (the minor leagues' governing body), Mississippi Attorney General J. P. Coleman announced on April 1 that integrated competition would violate the "public policy" of his state. Five days later, the Cotton States league terminated the Hot Springs franchise "as a matter of survival." On April 14 the league readmitted the Bathers with a new majority owner on the condition that the Tugersons be removed from the team's roster. The Bathers accepted the decision and optioned the players to Class D Knoxville prior to the start of the season. But in late May the team recalled Jim Tugerson because of a shortage of pitchers. League president Al Haraway ruled that if Tugerson attempted to play, the game would be forfeited. The Bathers, who were both short of pitchers and suffering from poor attendance, tried to call the league's bluff. They announced that Tugerson would be their starting pitcher at home against the Jackson Senators on May 20, and a big crowd came out for the game. But when Tugerson began to take his warmup pitches, plate umpire Thomas McDermott forfeited the game to Jackson. While the National Association negated the forfeit and ordered the game replayed, Hot Springs sent Tugerson back to Knoxville and did not attempt to recall him again.[19]

Jim Tugerson would not stand for this. He filed suit in federal court against Haraway and the Cotton States League, claiming that he had been denied the right to play in the league on the basis of race. Although he was aware that the process would likely be lengthy and could harm any chance that he could reach the major leagues, Tugerson proceeded. His attorneys argued that the league's "custom of segregation" violated the Fourteenth Amendment to the US Constitution along with five federal civil rights statutes. Meanwhile the Tugerson brothers continued to pitch at Knoxville. Jim had an outstanding year, leading the Mountain States League with

29 wins as the Smokies won the league championship; Leander, who was suffering from a sore arm, posted a 3-5 record before being advised by a physician to rest his arm for the remainder of the season.

Jim Tugerson's suit (*Tugerson v. Haraway*) and the brothers' battle to integrate the Cotton States League received nationwide sympathy and support. But when federal judge John E. Miller, a former US senator and congressman from Arkansas, issued his decision on September 11, he dismissed most of Tugerson's claims. Miller ruled that the Fourteenth Amendment "protects the individual against *state* action but affords no protection against wrongs done by [private] individuals." He also relied on a 1906 Supreme Court decision, *Hodges v. United States*, which had stated that the Constitution did not protect Black Americans from being denied work at a particular occupation solely due to race.[20] Given the history of courts' refusal to tamper with the long tradition of Jim Crow in the South, the decision was not surprising.

Jim Tugerson elected not to appeal Judge Miller's ruling after Hot Springs sold his contract to the Class AA Dallas Eagles of the integrated Texas League. But though unsuccessful, his suit was one of many important cases that fought the legal protection long given to Jim Crow. As Tugerson's legal battle was going on in 1953, the landmark *Brown v. Board of Education of Topeka* case was proceeding before the Supreme Court. Ultimately the court's ruling in the *Brown* case in May 1954, along with the passage of the Civil Rights Act of 1964 and the 1968 reversal of *Hodges v. United States*, would validate most of the arguments made by Tugerson's attorneys in 1953.[21]

Assessing the significance of the Tugerson brothers' fight to integrate the Cotton States League, baseball historian Bruce Adelson wrote,

> Although the brothers were ultimately unsuccessful in breaching one of the South's stiffest color lines, they achieved much, nonetheless. Spurring African Americans to collective action, inspiring black baseball fans in a region where they previously had nothing to cheer about, and undertaking a prescient fight for racial justice in the courts are all part of their legacy. Jim and Leander Tugerson transcended their roles as baseball players, leaving indelible impressions on a small corner of the Deep South.[22]

Jim Tugerson never reached the major leagues, but he continued to pitch in the minors until 1959. He joined the police force in Winter Haven, Florida, in 1957, becoming the city's second Black officer, and coached youth baseball in the area until his death from a heart attack at age 60 in 1983. In recognition of his long service to Winter Haven, the city council

renamed the youth baseball field in Jim's honor.[23] Leander Tugerson ended
his career in white organized baseball after the 1953 season. He died in
Florence at age 37 in 1965 when he was accidentally electrocuted while
trying to move a TV antenna.

◆ ◆ ◆

Although the successful debuts of Gene Baker and (especially) Ernie Banks
would be a feel-good story much as Minnie Miñoso's White Sox debut
had been two years earlier, 1953 was a difficult year for race relations in
Chicago. Harvey Clark was still seeking justice for what happened to his
family when they tried to rent an apartment in Cicero in the summer of
1951—and not finding it. In March the US Court of Appeals reversed the
earlier convictions of police Chief Erwin Konovsky and two Cicero police
officers owing to "prejudicial errors committed during the trial and in
giving instructions to the jury."[24] A new trial was ordered. Meanwhile the
Clarks were among 12 defendants, all of them Black, in a $1 million law-
suit filed by Camille DeRose, the white owner of the apartment building.
DeRose, who at one point during the Cicero trials had walked into court
brandishing a gun, and who had been ordered to spend time in a mental
institution as a result, accused the defendants of conspiring to defraud
her of her property, to send her to prison and to a mental institution, and
to "subject her to peonage and white slavery and illicit concubinage."[25]
DeRose filed the suit coincident with a book she had written about her
experiences, *The Camille DeRose Story.*

In August 1953, a few weeks before Banks and Baker made their Cubs
debuts, rioting broke out at a public housing project in the South Deering neighborhood on the far South Side. The violence began after the
Chicago Housing Authority, which had maintained an unstated policy of
offering rentals only to whites if the project was in a white neighborhood,
"accidentally" integrated the Trumbull Park Homes at 105th Street and
Yates Avenue by renting an apartment to 22-year-old Betty Howard, a fair-
skinned Black woman. After Howard and her husband Donald, a 25-year-
old postal carrier, moved in, the violence began. The attacks accelerated
after the CHA rented units in the Trumbull Park Homes to 10 more Black
families. *Time* wrote:

> In the following weeks, more windows were smashed; sulphur stink
> bombs were hurled into the [Howards'] apartment; effigies of Negroes
> blazed on street corners; two neighborhood stores which sold to Negro
> customers were set afire; scores of fires have been set on the property of
> whites who refused to join the campaign to force the Negroes out; ten

ugly crowds of up to 1,000 people were dispersed by police. As many as 1,000 cops have been on around-the-clock duty in the Trumbull Park area ever since.[26]

Sporadic violence continued for months, extending into the summer of 1955. According to Donald Howard, the police "seemed more intent upon protecting white families from contact with us than in protecting my family from the white mobsters and hoodlums who attacked my home." In May 1954 the Howards moved out of the Trumbull Park Homes. "We just couldn't take it anymore," said Donald.[27]

There was a sad but undeniable link between the Cicero riots, which took place in 1951, the year Black superstar Minnie Miñoso made his triumphant debut with the White Sox, and the Trumbull Park violence, which began in 1953, the year Black superstar Ernie Banks started his immortal career with the Cubs. In his book *Making the Second Ghetto: Race and Housing in Chicago 1940–1960*, Arnold. R. Hirsch wrote, "The people of Trumbull Park frequently pointed to the Cicero riot of 1951 as evidence that violence paid. South Deering residents admired the 'guts' of Cicero's fighters, talked of importing a few of them 'to show us how to get rid of these damn n___,' and openly hoped that Trumbull Park would become 'another Cicero.'"[28]

Those tactics left their mark. "By the 1950s," Hirsch wrote, "it was clear that embittered and frightened whites posed the strongest threat to the city's stability." Rather than risk further uprisings like the ones in Cicero and Trumbull Park, city officials became disinclined to challenge the racial status quo. Although 1953 had been a year of racial progress on Chicago's major league ballfields, the same could not be said for the city overall.[29]

13

Keepin' On

Between November 10, 1948, when he made his first trade as general manager of the White Sox, and January 26, 1953, Frank Lane made 153 player transactions involving a total of 211 players, according to a list compiled by the *Sporting News*.[1] That made basically three deals a month for the man known as Trader Lane. On January 27, Lane made transaction No. 154, and it was a biggie.

It was also bad news for Bob Boyd.

The deal was this: The Sox traded first baseman Eddie Robinson, who had led the team in home runs and RBIs in both 1951 and 1952, along with shortstop Joe DeMaestri and outfielder Ed McGhee, to the Philadelphia Athletics for first baseman Ferris Fain, the American League batting champion in 1951 and 1952, and minor league infielder Bobby Wilson.

The big names, obviously, were Robinson and Fain. Lane was trading a power hitter for a player with a high batting average.[2] The problem for Boyd was that his strengths were very much like Fain's: Both were first basemen with little home run power but with the ability to hit for average and get on base. Boyd was much faster and could steal bases, but Fain had a better reputation as a defensive player. In an era when leading the league in batting average was considered one of the major hallmarks of an elite hitter, landing a two-time American League batting champion was lauded as a major coup for Lane. The *Sporting News* headline about the trade said it all: "Chicago Flag Fever Zooms as Trader Lane Lands Fain." It was a battle that Bob Boyd could not win.

A week after the trade, the White Sox signed Fain to a $35,000 contract, making him the highest-paid player in franchise history. They were paying Bob Boyd $6,000.

♦ ♦ ♦

The 1953 White Sox spring training camp was located in El Centro, California, a city in the southeast part of the state about 10 miles from the Mexican border. The spring camp included three Black players: Minnie Miñoso, Connie Johnson, and Boyd. Both Boyd and Johnson were long shots to make the Opening Day roster, but Boyd helped his cause by hitting three home runs in a four-game span, and Johnson pitched well enough to win one of the final spots on the staff. "I went to spring training with the White Sox just to throw batting practice, and they kept me," he later recalled.[3] Boyd, who was aware that he would be playing very little behind Fain, actually asked Sox manager Paul Richards to option him to the Sox' new Triple-A farm team in Charleston, West Virginia. But with MLB teams allowed to keep three extra players on the roster for the first month of the season, both Boyd and Johnson opened the season with Chicago.

As Boyd had expected, he seldom played once the regular season started, getting only six plate appearances during the first four weeks, all as a pinch hitter. Johnson got a little more work. On April 17 he made his first American League appearance in a relief outing against the St. Louis Browns at Comiskey Park. It was a frigid, 36-degree day, and the game was played in front of only 972 fans, many of whom were probably not around by the time Johnson entered the game in the eighth. Those who stayed witnessed major league history.

In the seventh inning of the game, with the Browns leading 6–2 and the White Sox mounting a threat, St. Louis manager Marty Marion summoned his relief ace, Satchel Paige, who put down the threat. When Johnson entered the game for the White Sox in the next inning, it marked the first time in the white major leagues that two Black pitchers had faced each other. Paige and Johnson knew each other well. They had been teammates for several years with the Kansas City Monarchs, beginning in 1941 when Johnson was only 18 years old and Paige was (by most accountings) 34.

Johnson was impressive in the April 17 game, allowing zero runs and only one hit in his two-inning stint. He even retired Paige himself on a grounder to the mound with one out in the ninth. The White Sox scored solo runs off Paige in the eighth and ninth innings, but Satch finished off the game for his first save of the season.

After working in relief against Detroit six days later—he allowed an inherited run to score but had no runs charged to himself in one and two-thirds innings—Johnson was given his first American League start at Comiskey Park on May 3, in the second game of a Sunday doubleheader against the Philadelphia Athletics. After pitching a scoreless first inning,

Johnson allowed five straight baserunners to start the second (one of them reached first on an error) before being replaced by Fritz Dorish. The A's wound up scoring seven runs in the inning, with five (four of them earned) charged to Johnson. "Johnson just about pitched himself out of the majors," wrote Neil Gazel of the *Daily News*.[4] When the White Sox cut their roster to 25 players on May 14, Johnson and Boyd were optioned to Charleston.

The optioning of Johnson and Boyd left Miñoso as the only Black player on the White Sox for over two months. On July 5, the sixth anniversary of Larry Doby's debut as the American League's first Black player, there were only six Black players in the entire league, four of them with Cleveland (Doby, Luke Easter, Dave Hoskins, and Harry Simpson). The only others were Miñoso and Paige.

♦ ♦ ♦

Hampered by a shoulder injury, Miñoso got off to a slow start in 1953—through Memorial Day, he was batting only .255 with one home run. He found his stroke, however, and finished the year with a .313 average, 15 homers, 104 RBIs, and a league-leading 25 stolen bases. No one in the league could run the bases like Minnie. In the first inning of a game against the Detroit Tigers on May 10, Miñoso reached first on an infield single, driving in a run and advancing another Sox speedster, Jim Rivera, to third base. Sox manager Paul Richards then called for a double steal. The Tigers pitcher, Bill Wight, was so unnerved that he threw a wild pitch that completely eluded Detroit catcher Joe Ginsberg. Rivera trotted home and Miñoso pulled into second—but as Ginsberg scurried to retrieve the ball, Miñoso kept running. When he reached third base, Minnie noticed that no one was covering home plate, so he headed for home without breaking his stride. He slid headfirst across the plate before the Tigers could make a play. He'd scored from first on a stolen base.

"He had an effect on the whole team," Paul Richards said about Miñoso. "I asked Billy Pierce one day who would lead the team in stolen bases, [Jim] Busby or Miñoso."

"Busby," he said.

"Why?" I asked.

"Because Miñoso doesn't stop at first."[5]

In an interview with Donald Honig, Richards would remember Miñoso as one of four players he managed who had the same kind of inner drive possessed by baseball immortal Ty Cobb. The others were Hall of Famers Nellie Fox, George Kell, and Brooks Robinson.

♦ ♦ ♦

While Miñoso was the only Black player on the White Sox roster for much of the 1953 season, almost every Sox farm team had several Black players. The glaring exception was the club's Memphis Chicks farm in the Class AA Southern Association. As more and more minor leagues, even in the South, began to admit Black players, the Southern remained a holdout; apart from a two-game stint by Nat Peeples with the Atlanta Crackers in 1954, the league remained segregated for its entire history, ultimately choosing to go out of business in 1961 rather than admit Blacks. The more promising Black players in the Sox farm system sometimes found themselves in a league that was either above or below their true talent level. That was hardly the most effective way to nurture talented players.

Memphis was still so hostile toward integrated baseball in 1953 that when the White Sox scheduled a spring training game at the Chicks' ballpark as they barnstormed their way back to Chicago, Mayor E. H. "Boss" Crump refused to permit the Sox to use their Black players; he cited Jim Crow laws that prohibited Blacks from playing or associating with whites in public places. Other southern cities such as New Orleans and Atlanta had waived such laws for MLB exhibition games (the increased revenue was good for their pocketbooks), and integrated teams such as the Dodgers, the Giants, and the Indians had long refused to schedule games in southern cities unless they could use their Black players. But Frank Lane acceded to Boss Crump, and the Sox played the game without Miñoso and Johnson.[6]

As for the Black players on the other White Sox farm teams, most seemed to be what Gene Collins had called "window dressing": They were playing, but their careers were not advancing. Collins was still being shunted from team to team, Sam Hairston was still stuck in Colorado Springs, and once-promising players such Gideon Applegate, Mitchell June, Alfredo Ibáñez, and José Bustamante were on their way out of the White Sox system or out of baseball. Bill Powell won 14 games for Triple-A Charleston in 1953 and still hoped to play for the Sox, but never got the chance.

And then there was the strange story of the Black players on the 1953 Danville Dans. Danville, Illinois, is close to the Indiana border, about 125 miles south of Chicago. Its population in 1953 was a little over 35,000, including a substantial Black community. Although many Negro League teams had played in Danville and the city had been home to a Brooklyn Dodgers farm team in the Three-I League from 1946 to 1950, Danville had not welcomed the integration of baseball. In his autobiography, Roy

Campanella wrote that after he had signed with the Dodgers in 1946 and the team attempted to place him with Danville, they were told, "They don't want you."[7] Researcher Gary Fink reports that during the five years that the Danville Dodgers were in operation, the Dodgers farm club never had a Black player.[8]

In 1951 the Dodgers relocated their Three-I League franchise, and Danville joined the Class D Mississippi–Ohio Valley League as the Danville Dans. After operating as an independent team in 1951, the Dans signed a working agreement with the Boston Braves in 1952, and for the first time the team had several Black players. Two of them, pitcher Walter James and infielder-outfielder Orlando Casellas, contributed substantially to the team's first-place finish. So, when the White Sox took over the working relationship from the Braves in 1953, Black players were no longer a novelty.

Class D leagues were at the bottom of the food chain in white organized baseball, and clubs with working agreements had considerable freedom to sign their own players in order to fill out a team's roster along with the players supplied by the parent club. The general manager of the Dans, Hillman Lyons, had been selected as Minor League Executive of the Year (Lower Classification) by the *Sporting News* in 1952 after taking control of the Danville franchise and more than tripling its 1951 attendance. "He amply demonstrated that there is nothing wrong with minor league ball that hustle and promotion will not cure," the paper wrote.[9] Along with promoting the club relentlessly, Lyons was always on the lookout for players. He posted ads in *The Sporting News* ("Catcher and Pitcher WANTED. Veteran or Limited Service. Phone, Wire or Write Hillman Lyons, Gen. Mgr., Danville Baseball Club"). He supervised tryout camps for the White Sox at the Danville ballpark ("Players bring own uniforms, shoes, gloves"). And he seemed happy to add Black players to his roster, as he had shown with the 1952 Danville team. In 1953 he very likely received help from Sox scout and longtime Negro Leaguer John Donaldson.

Lyons, who was 31 years old in 1953, was at the start of a long and successful career as a minor league executive; he would win the *Sporting News* Minor League Executive of the Year award again in 1967. He seemed to know what he was doing. So did player-manager Virl Minnis, who had won the league pennant with the Dans in 1952. But the way the 1953 Dans managed their roster, and in particular, their Black players, seems completely chaotic. The Danville roster featured 37-year-old infielder T. J. Brown, a 12-year Negro League veteran who stood only five feet, four inches tall. It briefly featured outfielder Lloyd Davenport, a 41-year-old outfielder and six-time Negro League All-Star. It featured Willie Hutchinson, a

38-year-old Negro League veteran who had made his debut with the 1939 Kansas City Monarchs, and Willie B. Cunningham, an 18-year-old pitcher whom the Dans obtained from the Mt. Vernon Kings in mid-season. There was a two-month stint for another former Negro League pitcher, 28-year-old Rayford Finch, who had played for the Cleveland Buckeyes. There was a somewhat shorter stint for Lonnie Davis, who started on Opening Day, broke his leg sliding into second base in the third inning—and never again played for Danville.

The aforementioned group included players who may have been too old, too young, too short, too injured, or who simply did not produce. But then there were the cases of Jim Zapp, Alvin Spearman, and Othello Strong. Zapp, who was 29 years old in 1953, was a six-foot, three-inch, 230-pound outfielder who had played for the Negro League Baltimore Elite Giants and Birmingham Black Barons. With the Barons in 1948, Zapp had helped mentor his 17-year-old teammate Willie Mays. "He was like a big brother," Mays wrote about Zapp. "He watched over me. He taught me. He always came when I needed him."[10]

In 1952 Zapp entered white organized baseball with one of the Danville Dans' rivals in the Mississippi–Ohio Valley League, the Paris Lakers. He had an outstanding year, hitting .330 and leading the league with 136 RBIs. After signing with the Dans before the 1953 season, Zapp homered on Opening Day and was hitting .286 in his first 11 games when the Dans abruptly sold him to Lincoln of the Western League. "Here is a fellow who can't run, can't throw and has a hard time hitting when a pitcher can get the ball to his weakness," wrote Howard V. Millard of the *Decatur Daily Review*; he credited Hillman Lyons with "a great bit of salesmanship" in finding a buyer for Zapp, whose high-strung nature may have had something to do with his departure.[11] "Great temperament is not always something I always had," he once admitted. On the other hand, the man could really hit. Zapp played two more years of minor league ball. In 1954, he hit 32 homers in only 90 games for Big Spring in the Class C Longhorn League. In 1955 he hit 37 homers and drove in 119 runs while splitting the year between Big Spring and Port Arthur of the Class B Big State League. When Port Arthur tried to cut his salary, he retired. He died in Nashville at age 92 in 2016. "If I had been a white boy," Zapp said about his baseball career, "ain't nothing would have held me back."[12]

Othello Strong and Alvin Spearman were childhood friends, both born on the South Side of Chicago in 1926. Although they went to different high schools—Spearman to DuSable, Strong to Wendell Phillips—they attended Willard Elementary School together and constantly played ball together at Washington Park. They grew up among Negro League royalty. Othello's older brother Ted was a longtime Negro League star. Blackball legend Ted (Double Duty) Radcliffe, who owned a liquor store in the neighborhood, was a family friend and mentor. Spearman eventually married Double Duty's niece; his wife was also related to Hall of Famer Turkey Stearnes.

Spearman and Strong served in the military during World War II. After the war Othello, who had pitched for the Army team at Fort Warren in Wyoming, spent several years moving from team to team and even sport to sport. "I remember Mr. Strong, Sr. [Othello's father] always talking about how Othello didn't feel he was getting a fair shake," said Sherman Jenkins, who wrote a biography of Ted Strong Jr. "Per Mr. Strong, Sr., Othello jumped from team to team and often went someplace else where he felt that he would be getting a better shake."[13] Between 1947 and 1953 Othello spent a couple of years with Abe Saperstein's Harlem Globetrotters baseball team, played basketball with Saperstein's Kansas City Stars, one of Abe's traveling squads, and had stints with the Negro League Chicago American Giants and the ManDak League Winnipeg Giants. In 1952 and 1953 he was scheduled to enter white organized baseball with the Albuquerque Dukes of the Class C West Texas–New Mexico League, but for some reason did not show up. Instead he and Spearman joined the Galt Terriers, a team in the Intercounty Senior Baseball League in Canada (the team also included former Chicago American Giants pitching star Gentry Jessup). With the Terriers, Strong mostly played the outfield, but when his hitting was disappointing, the team released him.

In early June Othello signed with Danville. Over the course of the next 30 days he appeared in 13 games. As a hitter he batted only .217, but in 23 at-bats he hit a homer and drove in five runs. In one game, he drove in the winning run as a pinch hitter in the 10th inning. As a pitcher, Othello appeared in 10 games, seven as a starter. He had a 3-2 record, pitched a shutout, and allowed only 45 hits in 59 innings. His earned run average was 1.98, which was the second lowest in the MOV League for the 1953 season. But on July 7 the Dans handed Strong his release, with no reason specified. That was the end of Othello Strong's white organized baseball career. He met a woman, got married, and got a job as a truck driver for Careful Cleaners on the South Side.

Othello's friend Alvin Spearman had a much shorter career with Danville—he pitched in three games and was released in early June—but a much longer career in baseball. In 1949, during his time with the Chicago American Giants, Spearman went to spring training with the Cubs' Janesville, Wisconsin, farm team in Carlyle, Illinois. The *Janesville Daily Gazette* said that Spearman was "well liked by all in camp"[14] and described him as "a polished gentleman, very quiet and always wearing a beaming smile."[15] It appeared for a time that Spearman might become the first Black player in Wisconsin State League history, but the team released him in mid-April (Milton Bohannion became the league's first Black player a couple of months later). It was not a happy experience for Spearman, who said, "Downstate Illinois was something like south of the Mason-Dixon line. Some related Southern Illinois as like Mississippi. So it wasn't good." Spearman said the weather was so bad that he never got on the field. After his release, he went back to Chicago.[16]

After being dropped by Danville, Spearman played in independent and semipro leagues until 1955, when he became one of the pioneer American players in Japan. He returned to the American minor leagues in 1956 and had great success, turning in records of 18-3, 17-11, and 20-9 for the next three years. He also pitched in Mexico, and like Othello Strong, in the ManDak League and in an independent league in Canada. In those foreign countries, he said, "I was treated like a celebrity." But in his final year in the minor leagues, with Houston of the Class AAA American Association in 1959, he recalled, "I was treated so shabbily down there that I quit the team and left."[17] Spearman went back to Chicago and got a job as a truck driver and salesman with the 7-Up Bottling Company.

Asked to describe her father, Alvin Spearman's daughter Fabienne Anderson-Johnson said, "He was very competitive. Very determined in his way of thinking, like you had to bring the world down to make him think something different from what he thought was going on. Very outgoing, very outspoken. He could have a bit of a temper. He was fiercely protective. Usually that's when the temper came in. So if he felt like somebody was infringing on his territory or bothering someone he cared about, he could become very fierce." When asked if she felt that her father had not received the opportunities that he deserved, Fabienne said simply, "Most of my relatives felt that way."[18]

◆ ◆ ◆

After spending nearly three months in the minor leagues, Bob Boyd and Connie Johnson were recalled by the White Sox on July 31. Both had begun their 1953 minor league stints with Charleston of the Class AAA American Association, but in early July the Sox had traded Boyd to the Toronto Maple Leafs of the International League, another Triple-A circuit. Boyd remained the property of the White Sox, but it was a strange way to treat a player who was supposed to be one of the team's top prospects. The July 31 recall of Boyd and Johnson was basically forced on the White Sox by a new rule that said that any optioned players not recalled by that date had to finish the year with their minor league team. "We didn't want to call up Connie Johnson and Bob Boyd until later in the season," Lane explained, "but with this new rule in we had to bring them up now or wait until next year. We didn't need them particularly, but it was a hardship on the Charleston club, which did need them."[19] (He apparently forgot that he had traded Boyd to Toronto.)

Maybe the White Sox didn't *need* Johnson and Boyd, but they quickly found both players very helpful. In his first start after being recalled on August 1, Johnson shut out the Washington Senators. He won three more starts between then and the end of the season, finishing the year with a complete-game win over the St. Louis Browns on September 26. His 3.56 earned run average for the season was well below the American League average of 3.99.

Bob Boyd's recall proved a godsend to the White Sox when Ferris Fain, who was batting a disappointing .269, got into a fight in a Maryland bar on the night of August 2. The result was a broken finger that kept Fain out of the lineup for more than three weeks. Boyd got most of the playing time while Fain was out and performed very well, hitting .308 in the month of August. He played less frequently after Fain returned, but still finished the season with a .297 batting average, 41 points higher than Fain. His season highlight came on August 8 at Yankee Stadium, when he doubled with one out in the ninth inning to break up a no-hitter by Yankees starter Bob Kuzava. Boyd was so impressive that during the off-season the White Sox talked about shifting Miñoso from left field to third base in 1954, with either Fain or Boyd taking Minnie's place in the outfield. "Somebody is going to have to be real good to keep him out of the lineup," Sox manager Paul Richards said about Boyd.[20]

◆ ◆ ◆

As White Sox manager, Richards strongly advocated for the team to trade for Orestes Miñoso and made Minnie an everyday player. He also gave significant playing time to Bob Boyd and Connie Johnson; then, after becoming manager and general manager of the Baltimore Orioles in 1955, he traded for both Boyd and Johnson and again made them regulars. Yet Richards's relationships with his Black players were often less than ideal. On one hand, Miñoso wrote of Richards, "I also felt lucky to have Paul Richards as a manager. He was a serious man who nonetheless possessed a dry wit, a man whose practical intelligence enabled him to manage a team with extraordinary success. He knew how to mold players and treated each one of us with kindness and appreciation."[21] On the other hand, Connie Johnson said of Richards, "I don't think he liked blacks too much. He'd hide it in ways you wouldn't notice if you didn't come looking for it." Boyd was grateful to Richards for giving him playing time and helping him during his career, but also said, "He never broke his word . . . but he didn't like blacks. I was in enough team meetings where he would talk about the black players on the team . . . and he wouldn't say very nice things about them." Yet according to Richards biographer Warren Corbett, both Boyd and Johnson called Richards's home to offer condolences after Paul died.[22]

"Boyd and Johnson were really of two minds about him," Corbett said in an interview. "They freely admitted that they probably got a better opportunity in the major leagues because of Richards. But at the same time, they both said he was a racist son of a bitch. The fact that both called his family to offer condolences when he died, indicates to me that they figured they owed him more than they hated him."[23]

"I'm a southerner myself," Corbett continued. "I was born and grew up in the South and lived through the civil rights revolution of the fifties and sixties before I moved to Washington DC. And I think Richards's attitude mirrors that of people of his generation in that they genuinely believe that they were not racist, that they did not hate black people. One of the old sayings about Southern whites was that Southern whites loved black people individually, but despised them as a race. And that's a little bit strong, but that's the general idea."[24]

Sam Lacy, who as a Baltimore writer was able to observe Richards and his Orioles operation firsthand, basically stood up for Paul. "Richards wouldn't be human if he didn't have preference for personalities," Lacy wrote in 1960, "nor would he be human if he didn't nurture prejudices. . . . There are some folk I don't like, and far be it from me to argue that I am free from prejudices. . . . But I am convinced that [neither] Richards nor [Casey] Stengel nor [Al] Lopez nor [Chuck] Dressen permits his dislike for a player to interfere with what he considers to be the most advantageous handling of his team."[25]

Paul Richards was without question a complicated person. In his autobiography *I Had a Hammer*, baseball immortal Hank Aaron was very critical of Richards, who became the Atlanta Braves' general manager while Aaron was still an active player. Aaron was particularly incensed that Richards had traded away Hank's longtime teammate, future Hall of Famer Eddie Mathews, without informing Mathews personally. "To me, that was vintage Richards," Aaron wrote. "He was the kind of guy who'd call you into his office and talk to you as he looked out the window, as if you weren't really there. I couldn't believe it when I saw in the newspaper on New Year's Eve that he'd traded Mathews to Houston. Eddie found out about the deal from a reporter. He was devastated, and so was I." When Richards was replaced by Eddie Robinson, a man who reportedly had refused to shake Larry Doby's hand when Doby joined the Cleveland Indians in 1947, Aaron wrote, "I would have welcomed [segregationist Georgia governor] Lester Maddox if he were replacing Paul Richards."[26]

Like Aaron, Sam Hairston remembered Richards as having a cold personality. "Paul Richards wasn't too friendly," Hairston recalled about his debut with the White Sox in 1951. "But then, he wasn't friendly to anybody." Sportswriter Leonard Koppett noted, "He thought he was smarter than anyone else, which in itself is neither unusual nor necessarily unpleasant. His baseball intelligence was certainly far above average among his peers; but he wielded it with a certain intellectual arrogance."[27]

Baseball executive Bill Giles, who worked with Richards with the Houston Colt .45s, went farther, writing that Richards was "a man of questionable character." Giles, whose father Warren was president of the National League when the Colt .45s were working to sign players for the team's inaugural 1962 season, claimed that Richards asked him to go to his father's office and make copies of the league's secret waiver files, a blatantly illegal act. At the same time, Richards was fearless about signing young Black players for the new team in Houston, which at the time was Major League Baseball's southernmost town. When the Colt .45s showcased their young talent in late 1963 with a starting lineup whose average age was 19, five of the nine players were Black—one of them future Hall of Famer Joe Morgan.[28]

Richards's grandniece Michelle Foster, who produced a documentary about her late uncle, said in an interview, "He certainly kept his distance from his players; he had the belief that a manager shouldn't get too close to his players, because you'll invariably get too close to two or three of them and leave the rest of them out in the cold, and he just did not want to do that. So he was there for them with baseball, but not to go over and have cocktails and dinner." Sox infielder Joe DeMaestri, who was white, described Richards thus: "No conversation. No words of encouragement. Seldom a smile. He never got close to his players. But in a game he was always two, three innings ahead, like he knew what was going to happen."[29]

Richards himself believed that one of the most important traits of a successful manager was restraint. "He must restrain himself when things are tough, when things are not going well," he told Donald Honig. "Restraint under duress is absolutely necessary. And boy, I can tell you, sometimes that's not easy."[30]

Many who knew Richards recalled a man who, along with being highly intelligent, had a great sense of humor. Hall of Famer Goose Gossage played for the last team Richards managed, the 1976 White Sox; the club finished in last place in the American League West with 97 losses, but playing for Richards was a very pleasant experience for Gossage. "I loved Paul," Gossage recalled. "Oh my god, he was a funny guy. He was fun to play for and a very, very smart baseball man." Gossage was the starting pitcher for the White Sox on September 12, 1976, when Miñoso, who was 52 years old (or 53, or 50, depending on the source), got the final hit of his major league career—a single against California Angels' lefthander Sid Monge. "Love him," Gossage said. "Minnie Miñoso. What a fun guy. What a loving guy."[31]

14

Bingo, Bango, and Baseball

As 1954 began, 8 of the 16 major league teams had yet to use a Black player in a game, according to contemporary sources. But the pace of change was finally starting to accelerate. Two teams, the Chicago Cubs and the Philadelphia Athletics, had added their first Black players late in 1953. In January 1954 one of the remaining holdouts, the St. Louis Cardinals, sent four players and cash in excess of $100,000 to the San Diego Padres of the Pacific Coast League for first baseman Tom Alston; the six-foot, five-inch Alston broke the color line for the Redbirds on Opening Day, April 13. That same day second baseman Curt Roberts, who had been Ernie Banks's double-play partner with the Kansas City Monarchs, was recognized as the first Black player in Pittsburgh Pirates history (as previously noted, Puerto Rican outfielder Carlos Bernier, who had debuted with the Pirates in 1953, was not recognized as a Black player at the time). A third National League team, the Cincinnati Reds, broke the color line on April 17 when Nino Escalera and Chuck Harmon appeared as pinch hitters in back-to-back plate appearances. Harmon had been waiting for his major league chance since 1947, when the St. Louis Browns had signed him to a minor league contract. He spent four years in the majors with the Reds, the Cardinals, and the Phillies from 1954 to 1957 but never got a chance to play regularly. "They had guys who couldn't chew gum and run at the same time," Harmon recalled, "and you go two or three weeks without getting an at bat, and you knew you were better."[1]

In the American League, integration continued to move much more slowly. In January the Washington Senators, whose president Clark Griffith had been a staunch foe of MLB integration in the 1940s, announced that his team had invited seven Black players, all natives of Cuba, to its minor league spring training camp in Winter Garden, Florida. One of them, Angel Scull, a speedy outfielder who was said to have beaten Minnie Miñoso in match races, was widely expected to become Washington's first Black player. Things did not go smoothly, however. When the Cuban players arrived in Winter Garden, club officials reported receiving warnings stating, "Have those Negroes out of town by sundown and don't bring them back." The threats were considered credible enough that the FBI sent agents to investigate, and the Cubans refused to return to Winter Garden.[2] Ultimately Scull did not make the team, but on September 6 Cuban outfielder Carlos Paula took the field as the Senators' first Black player. Paula's debut made Washington the 12th of the 16 major league teams to integrate. Six of the 12 had done so in the 12-month period between September 1953 and September 1954.

That left four holdouts: the Boston Red Sox, the Detroit Tigers, the New York Yankees, and the Philadelphia Phillies. The most prominent outlier continued to be the Yankees, who in 1953 had won the World Series for a record fifth consecutive season. In January 1954, Gordon Cobbledick of the *Cleveland Plain Dealer* predicted that not even the Yankees could remain all-white and expect to keep winning.

> The time is fast approaching when no club, not even the Yankees, will dare draw the color line. And it won't be a matter of public relations, nor a play for the support of colored fans, but a simple matter of team strength. The Negro race is producing too many good ball players to make it possible for any club to ignore them.[3]

While the Yankees had traded their most prominent Black prospect, Vic Power, to the Philadelphia A's in December 1953, they had all but announced that Elston Howard, described in a *Sporting News* article as a "quiet, well-behaved young man of 25" who "seems to be what the New York club has wanted in its first Negro player," would soon be breaking the club's color line.[4] Finishing second to Cleveland in 1954 seemed to give the club that final push. In 1955 the Yankees promoted Howard to New York (and returned to the World Series). As things turned out, the 1953 Yankees would be the last team to win, or even reach, the World Series with an all-white roster.

The final three holdouts took several years to add a Black player. The Phillies did not integrate their roster until 1957 (Chico Fernández and John Kennedy), the Tigers, not until 1958 (Ozzie Virgil), and the Red Sox, not until July 21, 1959 (Pumpsie Green). Why did it take these teams—especially American League teams—a decade or more after Jackie Robinson's Dodgers debut to do something that was not only the right thing to do, but which very likely would have helped their team win games? "Years ago, when I was working on my book on Joe Cronin, I asked this central question to John Harrington, who ended up essentially running the Red Sox for the Yawkey Foundation," said author, historian, and Society of American Baseball Research president Mark Armour. "He said something very interesting—that if he could go back in time, he would basically tell them that this is going to come back and make you look really bad. I don't think any of them realized that history was sort of watching them, that it was going to be as incredibly important as it ended up being. I also don't think they realized how good these players were, that there were super-stars that they could sign if they had wished."[5]

Even as the American League slowly began to integrate, it continued to lag behind the National League in the quantity and especially the quality of the Black players who were joining the league. To cite one example, between 1953 and 1956 future baseball immortals Ernie Banks, Henry Aaron, Roberto Clemente, and Frank Robinson all made their debuts with National League teams. Over that time span, the only Black future MVP to debut in the American League was Howard, who won the award in 1963, after years as a part-time player.

Baseball historian Rick Swaine notes that in 1954 there were 19 Black players in the major leagues who could be considered regulars. Only four were in the American League: Larry Doby and Al Smith with the Indians, Minnie Miñoso with the White Sox, and former Yankee prospect Vic Power with the Athletics. The Indians won the American League pennant in 1954 with major help from Doby and Smith, while the White Sox, with Miñoso leading the way, finished a strong third. But most of the Black players who helped the Indians succeed in the early 1950s, like Doby and Smith, had been signed years earlier, when Bill Veeck still owned the franchise. The next Black player signed by Cleveland to have a successful major league career would be pitcher Mudcat Grant, who did not make his MLB debut until 1958. As for the White Sox, they still had Miñoso, as well as several good Black players in the minors. The Sox, however, had notoriously dropped the ball on superstars Mays and Banks, both of whom had been recommended to the team by Black scout John Donaldson, who had quit his job in disgust when the White Sox continued to ignore his advice. "Cleveland and the Chicago White Sox, early leaders in the integration movement," Swaine observed with regard to this period, "seemed to be losing their enthusiasm for recruiting additional black players."[6] They and the rest of the American League seemed to have adopted the attitude of the mighty Yankees: A Black player to two might be able to help us a little, but we can keep on winning with or without them. It was a stance that would leave the American League well behind the National in terms of overall talent level for the next two decades.

Among other things, the National League now had Ernie Banks.

♦ ♦ ♦

When the Cubs reported to spring training in Mesa, Arizona, in March 1954, Banks and Gene Baker were the favorites to win the team's short-stop and second base jobs. Nothing was guaranteed, however. There were no thoughts yet of Banks as a National League superstar; he had played impressively at the end of 1953, but his entire experience in white orga-nized baseball had consisted of those 10 games in September. And Gene Baker was the man the Cubs had kept in Los Angeles for four consecutive seasons.

There were setbacks. In early March intrasquad play Baker twisted his right knee and needed to be removed from the game. A few minutes later Banks, who was not wearing a protective helmet, was hit in the head by a pitch from rookie righthander Don Elston. Banks remained conscious, but he was carried from the field and rushed to the hospital for x-rays, which proved negative. Both players recovered and returned to the lineup after several days.

There were also doubters. The most vocal was Jimmy Dykes, the man-ager who had refused to give a tryout to Jackie Robinson in 1942 and who had welcomed Orestes Miñoso to the White Sox in 1951 with a barrage of racial epithets. Dykes, who was now managing the Baltimore Orioles (the St. Louis Browns had moved to Baltimore after the 1953 season), wagered a Chicago baseball writer two dozen golf balls that Banks wouldn't hit .250 for the Cubs and that he would be out of the National League by mid-season. The Cubs, however, were all in on Ernie. By the time the team had played ten spring training games, Wid Matthews was calling Banks a "cinch .300 hitter" and "the best batter against breaking stuff of any rookie I've ever seen come to the big leagues. And I'm not barring anybody." Cubs catcher Clyde McCullough, who had been in the major leagues since 1940, said, "I've never seen any better wrists on a hitter than Banks has."[7] The Cubs were so impressed with Banks that on March 20 they traded Roy Smalley, the team's primary shortstop since 1948, to the Milwaukee Braves.

Gene Baker's status was less secure, but on March 29 Baker got a break. With the Cubs struggling with a 5-15 record in spring games, Phil Wrigley met with manager Phil Cavarretta, who predicted another losing season, although he did think that Banks and Baker would help. The assessment did not please Wrigley, who fired Cavarretta on the spot. "Phil seems to have developed a defeatist attitude," Wrigley said. "We don't believe he should continue in a job where he doesn't believe success is possible."[8]

Cavarretta's replacement was Stan Hack, who had been Baker's manager with the Los Angeles Angels from 1951 to 1953. Unlike Cavarretta, Hack was an eternal optimist; his nickname was "Smilin' Stan." He was also a manager who believed in putting a player in the lineup and keeping him there every day. And that's what he did with Banks and Baker. The two started on Opening Day and played every 1954 game together except for two brief periods when Baker was out owing to injuries. Banks played in every Cubs game from the start of his career in September 1953 until August 10, 1956—424 consecutive games—when he missed two weeks because of an infected hand. After returning in late August, he played in another 717 consecutive games.

◆ ◆ ◆

For a short while, it appeared that the 1954 Cubs might have a third Black player in their starting lineup. Luis Márquez (Sánchez) was a 28-year-old outfielder and Puerto Rican native who had played in the Negro Leagues with the Homestead Grays and Baltimore Elite Giants from 1946 to 1948. In 1949 the Elite Giants sold Márquez's contract to the New York Yankees, which would have made him the first Black player in the Yankees organization. However, the Grays also claimed ownership of Márquez and arranged to sell him to Bill Veeck's Cleveland Indians. The Yankees and the Indians also both claimed ownership of Negro League infielder Artie Wilson, and the disputes ended up in the hands of Commissioner Happy Chandler; the commissioner awarded Wilson to the Yankees and Márquez to the Indians. Márquez remained in the minors until 1951, when he was claimed by the Boston Braves in the Rule 5 draft of minor league players left unprotected by their MLB team. When he appeared as a pinch runner for the Braves on April 18, 1951, Márquez and New York Giants catcher Ray Noble, a Cuban native who made his white MLB debut in the same game, became the second and third Afro-Latino players to perform in the American or National League; the first had been Orestes Miñoso in 1949.[9]

After batting .197 in 68 games for the Braves in 1951, Márquez returned to the minor leagues. He remained there until December 1953, when he was once again claimed in the Rule 5 draft, this time by the Cubs. Márquez's main assets were his great speed and defensive ability, and the Cubs envisioned him as a potential center fielder covering the ground between aging and immobile sluggers Hank Sauer and Ralph Kiner. Unfortunately,

Márquez reported to Mesa both late and overweight, and he lost the center field battle to Bob Talbot. After going 1-for-12 (.083) in 17 games, Márquez was traded to the Pittsburgh Pirates in June. In 1955 Márquez returned to the minor leagues and remained there until his retirement in 1963. During his 20-year career he won batting titles in the Negro Leagues, minor leagues, and Puerto Rican leagues. In 1988 Márquez died in Puerto Rico at age 62 when he was shot and killed by his son-in-law in a domestic dispute.

◆ ◆ ◆

Along with Banks, Baker, and Márquez on the Opening Day roster, the Cubs had eight Black players in their minor league farm system in 1954. Most were filling out rosters and not considered prospects, but the system included two players of note. The first was Solly Drake, who had been considered one of the team's brightest prospects before spending the 1952 and 1953 seasons in the army. Assigned to Des Moines of the Class A Western League in 1954, Drake batted .282 and was named to the league's all-prospect team at the end of the year. Drake's defensive ability and great speed—his nickname was "Sudden Solly"—intrigued the Cubs; he was invited to spring training in Mesa in 1955 and given a chance to make the Opening Day roster. The Cubs even signed Solly's younger brother Sammy to a minor league contract during the offseason.

And then there was the player known as Superman.

Unlike Solly Drake, who turned 24 in October 1954, Art Pennington was no kid. Born in Memphis in 1923 (he had been given the nickname "Superman" by his mother), Pennington joined the Chicago American Giants at age 18 in 1941 and spent five seasons in the Negro Leagues. In 1946 he was one of many American players, white and Black, who accepted an offer from Jorge Pasquel to play in the Mexican League. He stayed for three years. "The most fun I had was in Mexico," Pennington recalled. "I found I could eat anyplace, and I could go anyplace."[10] He returned to the American Giants in 1949, but early in the season the team sold his contract to the Portland Beavers of the Pacific Coast League. For the next few seasons Pennington played for minor and Negro League teams, as well as in Venezuela. In 1952 he won the Class B Three-I League batting championship, hitting .349 for the Keokuk Kernels. In 1953 Keokuk sold him to the Cedar Rapids Indians, a Cubs farm team. He had an outstanding year for Cedar Rapids in 1954, hitting .345 with 16 homers in 119 games. According to Bill Johnson, who has written extensively about Pennington, he "put on a season-long display that still inspires awe among those few still living who saw him play."[11] But the struggling Cubs weren't interested in Pennington, who was 31 years old in 1955, had been married several times, and was known for speaking his mind.

Like a lot of Black players who were considered too old for white organized baseball, Pennington moved on to the ManDak League in Canada and the Dakotas, and then to the independent South Minnesota League. He finished up playing two seasons with New York Yankees farm teams in 1958–59. Could Pennington have had success in the white major leagues? Almost certainly. His best chance came in 1953, when Bill Veeck, who was running the St. Louis Browns, expressed an interest in purchasing Pennington's contract. Unfortunately, Veeck was on his last legs financially with the Browns and had to sell the franchise at the end of the year. "I know I was cheated," Pennington said in 2007, "but I never think about that."[12]

In his book *Outsider Baseball*, Scott Simkus devoted a chapter to Art Pennington. He wrote,

> Superman hit a home run off an aging Dizzy Dean in an exhibition game, and batted against a young Whitey Ford. He caught fly balls hit by Josh Gibson, Roger Maris, Luis Aparicio, Buck Leonard and Whitey Herzog. He played in two East-West All-Star Games, struck out against Satchel Paige and once topped Harvey Kuenn by nine points, winning a minor league batting championship. . . .
>
> About the only thing Arthur David Pennington never really had an opportunity to do in his life was play in a white major league game. That phone call never came.[13]

♦ ♦ ♦

The Cubs under Smilin' Stan Hack may have shunned Phil Cavarretta's "defeatist attitude," but on the field they performed a lot like the Cubs of Cavarretta . . . and Frankie Frisch . . . and Charlie Grimm. The 1954 Cubs finished in seventh place with a 64-90 record; in 1953 they'd finished seventh with a 65-89 mark. It was the sixth time in seven years that the Cubs had finished seventh or eighth, while winning between 61 and 65 games. Even before Hack had managed a game, Phil Wrigley had said, "I have always felt that jobs in our organization could be, and should be, interchangeable."[14] Wrigley had suggested that Hack and Cavarretta change jobs, with Phil taking over the Los Angeles Angels while Smilin' Stan took the reins of the Cubs. Cavarretta turned down the offer and then got back at the Cubs by signing to play for the White Sox.

The one difference in the Cubs from previous seasons was the rookie double-play combination of Banks and Baker. The duo made a strong impression right from the start. On April 19, six days into the regular season, John Carmichael wrote, "Gene Baker and Ernie Banks could prove to be the best second-short combination to come up as a unit since Lou Boudreau and Ray Mack joined the Indians from Buffalo 15 years ago."[15] Two items of particular note were Baker's smooth transition from shortstop to second base, and the fact that Banks was the first Black player in the American or National League to play regularly at shortstop.

Six weeks into the season, the *Sporting News* published a feature story about the Banks-Baker combo. Cubs beat writer Edgar Munzel, who wrote the piece, observed that the fact that Banks and Baker were the first two Black players to wear a Cubs uniform "may soon be just incidental."

> What will make the date of September 14, 1953, historic is that it meant the merging of a second base combination that that within a short time will be etched into Cub lore alongside such keystone duos as Joe Tinker and Johnny Evers and the two Bills, Jurges and Herman.[16]

The comparison put Banks and Baker in elite company, for the Tinker-Evers and Jurges-Herman duos had been key parts of multiple pennant-winning Cubs teams. Munzel noted that the Banks-Baker combo was already sporting a nickname: "Bingo Bango"; Banks was Bingo, Baker was Bango. "It just seems to fit them, the way they're playing for us," said Joe Garagiola, a teammate of theirs who was in his last year as a player before starting his career as a broadcaster. "They've got rhythm."[17] (When the hulking Steve Bilko was handling first base for the Cubs, double plays could be described as "Bingo to Bango to Bilko.")

For the season Banks and Baker each hit .275, a more than respectable batting average for a middle infielder—especially a rookie. Their power numbers were also impressive. Banks hit 19 home runs while driving in 79 runs; Baker had 13 homers and 61 RBIs. As it turned out, Baker's 1954 numbers in each of the "triple crown" categories would be the best of his career. Banks, who played every inning of every game in 1954, was just getting started. "Ernie Banks didn't look that strong, but he had powerful wrists and a quick bat and Wrigley Field was ideal for him," said Cubs teammate Johnny Klippstein. "Ernie was pretty quiet, but he was very confident. One day a knuckleballer came in to pitch. Nobody liked to hit against a knuckleball. Nobody. Someone told Ernie, 'Watch this guy because he throws a good knuckleball.' He said, 'I love to hit the knuckleball.' He was the only guy I heard say that in my life."[18]

Banks was earning raves for his defense as well as his powerful bat. "In the last six weeks of the season Banks was the greatest shortstop in the league," said Cubs coach Bob Scheffing. "He has learned to play the hitters and gained in confidence." John C. Hoffman wrote that "few will dispute the contention that Banks is the slickest fielding shortstop in the circuit."[19]

After the season Banks finished second in the National League Rookie of the Year voting behind Wally Moon of the Cardinals; Moon received 17 votes, Banks 4, with Gene Conley of the Milwaukee Braves getting 2 votes and Hank Aaron of the Braves 1. In retrospect this looks bad and maybe even racist, but based on Wins Above Replacement (WAR) in 1954, the most deserving National League rookie was Conley, followed by Moon and then Banks.

On the south side of town, White Sox manager Paul Richards was recalling that the Sox had fumbled their opportunity to sign Banks. "Every time I hear that fellow's name I get a headache," said Richards. "A year ago he played with an all-star Negro team in Comiskey park. I was on the road, and asked our scouts to take a look at him. There surely wasn't any carfare or other expenses involved. Here was a guy playing in our home ball park. But somebody goofed on him. I remember asking if Ernie had any power and was told he didn't. I learned, after the Cubs had signed him, that Banks hit one into Comiskey park upper deck in left field!"[20]

◆ ◆ ◆

Although Banks and Baker played for Chicago's North Side team, it went without saying that they would live in a Black neighborhood in the South Side. Banks's first residence was at 72nd Street and Wabash Avenue, an area where he felt comfortable. While Banks and Baker felt accepted by Cubs players, they had little chance to socialize with their white teammates, most of whom lived closer to Wrigley Field. Pitcher Jim Willis recalled that, "with conditions being the way they were, we just didn't see Baker and Banks much after games. I don't know what they did after games." Willis also recalled the casual racism of the time, with white players using the N-word when referring to Black players. "Not to their face, but just when talking about them. It wasn't right, but that's just the way people talked back then."[21]

While the hotels in road cities that the Cubs utilized had all desegregated by 1954—the last holdout, the Chase Hotel in St. Louis, finally allowed Black players to stay there for the first time that year—Banks, Baker, and Márquez had extensive experience with Jim Crow long before the regular season began. In Arizona, the team's Black players were not allowed to stay with the rest of the team at the Maricopa Hotel in Mesa; they had to arrange their own accommodations, usually staying with Black families who lived in the area. Then, the Cubs and Jimmy Dykes's Baltimore Orioles barnstormed their way back to Chicago, playing exhibition games in southern cities along the way. Over an 11-day span the teams played games in Lubbock and Dallas, Texas; Shreveport, Alexandria, Ponchatoula, and New Orleans, Louisiana; Mobile, Alabama; and Hattiesburg, Mississippi. Although Banks and the other Black players were permitted to play in the games (unlike the Black members of the White Sox in Memphis a year earlier), they had to deal with Jim Crow traditions such as separate accommodations, separate dining areas, separate restrooms, and separate drinking fountains.

Banks recalled that in Texas, when he invited a white sportswriter to ride back to the hotel in a "black cab," the driver refused, telling Banks that he could be arrested for taking a white passenger in his taxi.[22] Later, in Mobile, Banks got off the team bus and wandered into the "white" area of the bus station to buy some candy. As he walked in, a group of white people were getting off a bus. Everyone stopped when they saw Ernie, and the owner of the candy stand let loose a string of four-letter words and threatened to call the police unless Banks got out of there fast. These experiences were a shock to Banks, who had grown up in a Black neighborhood and who had had very limited exposure to such treatment. "I didn't understand any of that," Banks recalled. "I didn't understand why people were the way they were. Why people carry hate in their heart and don't know how to release it."[23]

In Chicago, Banks was fortunate to have a group of largely supportive teammates led by veteran stars Ralph Kiner, Hank Sauer, and Frankie Baumholtz. Sauer and Baumholtz, who had lockers close to Ernie's, worked to help Banks feel comfortable. "He was shy, but Hank Sauer and I would talk to him every day after the game," said Baumholtz. "We told him not to change his personality, and he never did." Sauer recalled Banks as "a beautiful person. . . . Once he got used to the other players and came out of his shell, he lightened things up a bit."[24]

Banks also benefited from making his MLB debut along with Baker, who was older than Ernie, outgoing, and much more comfortable in interactions with people (Black or white) than the shy Banks. Ernie recalled,

I was quiet anyway. . . . I didn't say anything, But Gene Baker, he was different. Gene was from Iowa. He played in LA with white players. He had more experience. He was eight years my senior [actually six]. He was more outspoken than I was. He talked more. . . .

He was a very bright guy, the brightest guy I've been around. I really enjoyed him. His comments were more direct. And he allowed me to learn more by my own experience.[25]

"We hung together and actually did everything together on the field," Banks told Art Rust Jr. about Baker. "I kind of followed him, because he had much more experience than I did in baseball. So it was a great, warm, cordial feeling in Chicago."[26]

◆ ◆ ◆

One person who was not having a great, warm, cordial feeling in Chicago was Harvey Clark. In November Federal District Court Judge Joseph Sam Perry dismissed the charges against Cicero police chief Erwin Konovsky and two Cicero police officers for conspiring to allow a mob scene, as well as denying the civil rights of Clark and his family when they tried to move into an apartment in Cicero. The three had been convicted in 1952, but an appeals court had vacated the convictions owing to procedural errors and ordered a new trial. Perry's dismissal of the charges, which had been authorized by United States Attorney General Herbert Brownell, ended that possibility.

In an editorial titled "No One to Blame," the *Chicago Defender* wrote:

When Clark attempted to occupy his apartment, mobs of hooligans sacked the building, doing damage estimated at $50,000. All of Clark's furniture and other possessions were burned.

Police and city officials to whom appeals were made to stop the disorders did nothing. After the disorders had raged for several days Adlai Stevenson, then governor of Illinois, called out the national guard....

Now it seems that no one was responsible for what happened—if anything happened at all. Everyone who was once indicted has been set free.
...

We can't understand it—and we know that Mr. Clark and his family must be baffled, too.[27]

Harvey Clark would not give up. He continued to seek financial damages for the destruction of his property.

15

Stormy Times

In 1954 the White Sox moved their spring headquarters from southern California to Tampa, Florida, where they would be sharing facilities with the Cincinnati Reds. While the team's Black players were no strangers to discrimination, they would now be facing southern-style Jim Crow on a daily basis.

"Generally speaking, the white ballplayers loved it there," former major league player, executive, and broadcaster Bill White wrote about training in Florida. "But for the vast majority of the black major league players . . . Florida was a much different experience":

> If you were a black man and it didn't say COLORED on it, you'd best not go in. For black ballplayers, especially those from the North, it was like suddenly being transported to apartheid South Africa.
>
> And to their shame, for the most part the major league clubs went along with it. Even owners and front office types appalled by the segregationist policies averted their eyes.[1]

The White Sox had five Black players in their spring camp. Minnie Miñoso, Connie Johnson, Bob Boyd, and Willie Pope were Negro League veterans who had often experienced Jim Crow restrictions during their careers. The fifth player, 19-year-old catcher Earl Battey, was a native of Los Angeles starting his second year in white organized baseball; when Jackie Robinson made his debut with the 1947 Dodgers, Battey was 12 years old. Battey had grown up in Whittier, a city in Los Angeles County about 15 miles southeast of downtown Los Angeles, living in a racially mixed neighborhood. "The first kid team I played on in Whittier had an international flavor," he recalled. "It was composed of Mexicans, Chinese,

Negroes and one white American boy." He started as an outfielder, but when the team's only catcher got hurt, Battey went behind the plate and remained a catcher for the rest of his career. He had good coaches. Battey's mother was a catcher on a softball team representing the local Seventh Day Adventist Church. And his "kid team" was coached by Negro League great and future Hall of Fame catcher Biz Mackey.[2]

Battey attended both junior high and high school at Jordan High in Los Angeles. The school had just fielded its first baseball team, and with the junior high and high school squads united, the talented Battey became Jordan's starting catcher as a 13-year-old ninth grader. "That situation gave me six full seasons of team play before I was graduated," said Battey. Though he excelled on the baseball diamond, Battey earned even greater fame on the basketball court. As a sophomore in 1951, Battey was named to the Eastern-Marine League first team; "[Battey] threatens to become the highest scoring basketballer in city prep annals ere he earns his sheep-skin," said the *Hollywood Citizen-News*. As a junior he shared the league's player of the year award with Willie Naulls, who would go on to have a stellar career at UCLA and in the NBA. As a senior he averaged 25 points per game and made the All-City first team, although his eligibility ran out in January.[3]

After graduation Battey was pursued by baseball and basketball scouts, including UCLA basketball coach John Wooden. According to Battey, he received offers from every major league team except the Yankees, the A's, and the Indians. Ultimately White Sox scout Hollis Thurston convinced Battey to sign with the South Siders for a bonus of $3,999 (players who signed for $4,000 or more needed to stay in the major leagues for two years). The Sox assigned Battey to Class A Colorado Springs. With the Sky Sox he played very little, but he was able to watch and learn from the team's top receiver, Sam Hairston. He also encountered racial discrimination to a degree he had never previously experienced. He recalled:

> I was quite a veteran at 18, what with Legion and Municipal League ball as well as with the Junior White Sox in the wintertime. These teams were predominantly white and Mexican. So I never knew what segrega-tion was until I went to Colorado Springs in the Western League in 1953. I'd read about it and thought about it but never thought I'd have to live with it, for I'd played against many white teams, had many white friends, visited their homes and they visited mine. There were three Negroes on the Colorado Springs club, Sam Hairston, Bill Pope, and myself. We were not discriminated against in ball parks, but in Wichita we had to live in a Negro hotel. I thought Kansas was a liberal state, yet not one hotel in Wichita would let a Negro through its front door.[4]

Inviting Battey to spring training in 1954 was a sign of how highly the White Sox regarded him. He missed some time when he was hit on the back of his hand by a bat, but he got into a few games before being assigned to Class B Waterloo of the Three-I League. Battey had an excellent year with the White Hawks, hitting .292 and making the league's All-Star team at age 19. Earl Battey was clearly one of the top prospects in the White Sox farm system.

While Battey wasn't yet ready for the White Sox, Connie Johnson had finished the 1953 season *with* the Sox, and he expected to stay there. Yet Johnson, who was battling several other pitchers for one of the final spots on the roster, did not pitch well in spring training and was optioned to Toronto of the International League on March 19. He had an outstanding year for the pennant-winning Maple Leafs, winning 17 games while usually pitching to the Leafs' number-one catcher, Johnson's former Kansas City Monarchs teammate Elston Howard. Despite his excellent work, the White Sox did not recall Johnson to Chicago in 1954.

As Johnson was struggling in spring training, Bob Boyd was winning raves for playing games in left field as well as his usual position of first base. "Boyd, in fact, has been the hottest performer in camp, both in his outfield assignments and at first base," wrote Ed Burns in the *Sporting News*.[5] In a syndicated article about spring training "bests" and "most improved," Associated Press writer Joe Reichler included Boyd on his lists of "best hitters" and "most improved players."[6]When the White Sox opened the regular season against the Cleveland Indians on April 13, Boyd was in the starting lineup in left field, with Ferris Fain on first base and Minnie Miñoso stationed at third.

◆ ◆ ◆

Like the Cubs and most other major league teams, the White Sox concluded spring training in 1954 barnstorming their way back to Chicago with games in various southern states (Georgia, Alabama, Louisiana, Texas, Arkansas, and Tennessee). Their opponents in all but the last game, which was against the Cubs, were the St. Louis Cardinals. All of these games were in Jim Crow states, but as noted in previous chapters, most southern cities permitted MLB teams to use their Black players—while maintaining segregated seating for the fans, of course. Memphis did not attempt to prohibit the use of Black players in 1954 as it had in 1953; Miñoso, Boyd, Banks, and Baker took the field in Memphis without incident. (Tom Alston of the Cardinals did not play.)

Birmingham was more resistant. After the city had needed a "gentleman's agreement" to prohibit the Detroit Lions of the National Football

League from using Black player Wally Triplett in a 1950 pre-season game, the Birmingham city council passed an ordinance making things clear:

> Sec. 597. Negroes and Whites Not to Play Together
> It shall be unlawful for a negro and a white person to play together or in company with each other in any game of cards, dice, dominoes, checkers, baseball, softball, football, basketball, or similar games.

The ordinance included a fine of $100 and/or imprisonment of up to six months for a violation.[7]

After seeing numerous southern cities bank revenue from games featuring teams with integrated rosters, the Birmingham City Commission voted in January 1954 to repeal the section of the ordinance dealing with baseball and football games. The city then scheduled three spring training games featuring teams with Black players: the White Sox versus the Cardinals on April 1, followed by a two-game series between the Milwaukee Braves and the Brooklyn Dodgers on April 2–3. There were immediate protests from many white residents of the city; one petition that was urging repeal of the exemption for baseball and football asked, "Do you want your children to go to school with negroes? If not, sign here." More than ten thousand signatures were obtained in order to schedule a June referendum on repealing the exemption.[8]

In the meantime, the White Sox–Cardinals and Braves-Dodgers games remained on the schedule. A group called the Preserve Segregation Committee sent telegrams to Cardinals manager Eddie Stanky and White Sox skipper Paul Richards, asking them to bench their Black players in order to "preserve our segregation traditions and customs in the South." Paul Richards promptly replied: "I am very sorry, but that question of racial segregation was settled more than 2,000 years ago on Mount Calvary . . . Christ Jesus died for us all."[9]

The White Sox, the Cardinals, the Braves and the Dodgers all used their Black players in Birmingham. More than twenty-one thousand fans attended the games; although the whites-only grandstands were two-thirds empty, segregated seating was strictly enforced. Describing the rickety "Negro only section," the *Birmingham World* quoted a Black fan as saying, "We feel as if we had stopped at a country store for a sandwich and we had to go around the back of the place and be served from a hole cut in the back wall."[10]

On June 1, 1954, 15 days after the announcement of the *Brown v. Board of Education* decision by the Supreme Court, the residents of Birmingham voted by a nearly three-to-one margin to restore the prohibition against

white and Black athletes competing together. The new law not only prohibited interracial competition involving sports teams including baseball
and football, but also prohibited Blacks and whites mingling at swimming
pools, beaches, lakes, and ponds. Attorney Hugh Locke, leader of the segregation drive, said that the vote "indicates that the people of Birmingham
are not going to take (the breaking down of segregation) lying down. And
it tells that to the people of the United States."[11]

◆ ◆ ◆

Bob Boyd got two hits for the White Sox on Opening Day against the
Cleveland Indians, then started 10 of the team's 14 games in April, all in
left field. Richards generally rested him when the team was facing a left-
handed starter. For the month he batted a respectable .273. But Boyd went
into a slump as Richards began to use him less consistently; he recorded
only one hit in 23 at-bats in his first 11 games during the month of May.
On May 14, Boyd started at first base against left-hander Alex Kellner of
the Philadelphia Athletics. He grounded out in his first at-bat, dropping
his average to .179. When Boyd's turn came up again with two runners on
base in the fifth inning, Richards lifted him for a pinch hitter: Bob Keegan,
a pitcher. (Keegan singled to drive in a run.)

That turned out to be the last game that Boyd would start for the White
Sox. During the next week he appeared in seven games, all as a pinch runner (usually for Ferris Fain). On May 23 Frank Lane sent infielder Grady
Hatton and $100,000 to the Boston Red Sox for third baseman George
Kell, a seven-time All-Star and future Hall of Famer. The addition of Kell
effectively ended the experiment of using Minnie Miñoso at third base
while Boyd played left field. One day later the White Sox signed recently
deposed Cubs player-manager Phil Cavarretta to a contract as a player.
Like Boyd, Cavarretta was a left-handed hitter who played first base and
the outfield. So it was no surprise when, on May 25, the White Sox sold
Boyd to the St. Louis Cardinals, who assigned him to Class AA Houston of
the Texas League. "When they sent me back to Houston, I almost didn't
report," Boyd recalled. "I told them I was going back to the Negro league."[12]
He changed his mind, but he would not return to the major leagues until
1956, when he was acquired by the Baltimore Orioles, a team managed
by Paul Richards. Boyd would finally get the chance to be an everyday
player with Richards's Orioles, and would perform splendidly, with three
solid seasons as a .300 hitter. But by the time he got that chance, he was
36 years old.

◆ ◆ ◆

Entering the 1954 season, Orestes Miñoso was clearly regarded as one of the best players in the American League. In his three seasons with the White Sox Miñoso had been elected *Sporting News* AL Rookie of the Year, finished in the top five in the Most Valuable Player voting in two of the three seasons, and made the AL All-Star team all three years. Big things were expected of Minnie in 1954. "If Miñoso has a good year," said Sox manager Paul Richards, "we can dethrone the Yankees."[13]

Much of the year seemed to be kind of a lovefest for Minnie. In January the *Sporting News* published its annual chart listing writers' selections for the top player on each American League team in categories ranging from Toughest Pitcher for Crucial Game, to Greatest Worrier. For the White Sox, Miñoso was the choice for Most Feared Batter in Clutch, Fastest Runner, Most Box Office Appeal, Has Done Most for Team, Best All-Around Athlete, Happiest, Most Generous, Best Physique, and Wittiest. (Teammate Jim Rivera was the choice for Worst Dressed, Best Pin Ball Player, Seen Most Movies, and Biggest Eater.)[14]

In a March column consisting of random observations, John Carmichael of the *Chicago Daily News* described Miñoso as a "popular fellow . . . whom even the players on other teams label a great guy ([t]hey cluster around him every time he walks onto a field and he has to beg off to take batting practice)."[15]

In June the *Sporting News* published a three-part series in publisher J. G. Taylor Spink's "Looping the Loops" column that told Minnie's life story. "I came from nothing," he told Spink. "I'm still nothing. I play good in Washington today. Tomorrow I have to play good in Philadelphia. Every day I try. In this game you have to produce. When you let publicity go over your head, you're through. Some friends ask you why. I tell reporters I came from the sugar fields. I tell 'em, I can't lie."[16]

In July the *Saturday Evening Post* published a lengthy feature story on Miñoso by Chicago sportswriter William Barry Furlong titled "The White Sox Katzenjammer Kid." The title was based on a long-running comic strip and cartoon series about a pair of precocious German immigrant children who constantly got into scrapes while speaking heavily accented, and often indecipherable, English. Like Spink, Furlong chronicled Minnie's long climb from the sugar cane fields to baseball stardom, with much coverage of his colorful lifestyle. "Miñoso's only excesses are buying clothes and driving too fast," wrote Furlong. "During the season he may buy an average of one or two new suits a week. He changes clothes as many as two or three times a day. His tastes run [to] pastels in blue or grey, snap-brimmed hats and suede shoes. If he tires of a suit, he gives it away." As did most writers of that era, and for many years thereafter, Furlong's quotes from Minnie highlighted Miñoso's stumbles with a second language (just like the Katzenjammer Kids). The following passage quotes Minnie's response to Cleveland Indians general manager Hank Greenburg's question, "What would you do in my position?" after Miñoso had reported to spring training four days late:

> "You mean if you Minnie and me Hank?" asked Miñoso. "Then I say 'Minnie fine fellow. He always in good shape. He all the time hustle. He work hard during winter. I no mind if he come late.'"[17]

In August *Sport* magazine devoted its cover story to Miñoso. Author Furman Bisher focused on Miñoso's exciting play on the field as well as his flamboyant lifestyle off it. "At one time Miñoso had four cars, three of them gifts of adoring fans in Chicago and Cuba," wrote Bisher. "He sold them during the offseason and bought an olive green Cadillac with white sidewall tires and wire spokes. It was the talk of White Sox camp. It is equipped with everything but a kitchen sink." According to Bisher, the car featured police-car aerials, chrome horns, decals showing Miñoso at bat, White Sox emblems, and scenes of Cuba, and a "St. Christopher medal the size of a pancake. . . . The instrument panel has more gadgets than a DC-6."[18]

Bisher, who did a little less than Furlong in quoting Miñoso's "charming" struggles with English, nicely captured the excitement of the Cuban Comet in action:

> As much a part of Miñoso as his ability to run and hit and throw is his electrifying appeal. As soon as he gets on base, which is often, a sort of restless hum sweeps across the stands. He takes his lead in a low crouch, as a cat prowls. He makes his getaway almost with the rustle of a flock of geese taking the air. Merely walking off the field, he is more colorful than most players at their exciting best. He moves in a splayfooted stride, trousers hanging low on his short hips, sunglasses poised above his fuzzy brows, head always erect and eyes sweeping the stands, as if searching for a glimpse of a friendly face. He is a showman, fully conscious of every appealing gesture that is part of him.[19]

In Cuba, where Miñoso was revered as one of the island's greatest and most beloved players, there was a popular song about Minnie: a cha-cha by Enrique Jorrín titled "Miñoso al bate" (Miñoso at bat). The lyrics talked about how the ball "dances the cha-cha-cha" whenever Minnie comes to the plate.[20]

Miñoso responded to the love with arguably the best all-around season of his career. Despite leading the league in hit by pitches for the fourth straight year, he missed only two games. He ranked in the top three in the American League in batting average, on-base percentage, slugging percentage, runs scored, doubles, triples and stolen bases. His 116 RBIs ranked fourth in the league and would be the most of his major league career. And in the all-around category of wins above replacement, he led the American League with 8.2. After the season he finished fourth in the league's voting for Most Valuable Player for the third time in four years. Many thought he should have finished first. "Without Miñoso the White Sox not only aren't a pennant contender, they're not even a first-division club," said manager Paul Richards. "Without him we're right down with the rest of the also-rans."[21]

Yet 1954 was a strange, unsatisfying season for the White Sox, and an extremely controversial year for Miñoso. The Sox won 94 games, the highest win total for the team in 34 years, yet they finished in third place, well behind the pennant-winning Indians (111 wins) and second-place Yankees (103). A seven-game winning streak in June put the Sox in first place with a 35-16 record, but the club could not keep up the pace.

In the third inning of a game against the Philadelphia Athletics on August 27, White Sox infielder Cass Michaels, a popular 28-year-old veteran who had made his major league debut with the Sox at age 17 (he subsequently played with three other teams before returning to Chicago), was struck in the head by a fastball from A's right-hander Marion Fricano. As was true of many players in the days before batting helmets became mandatory, Michaels was wearing a fiberglass liner in his cap that offered little protection to his face and ears. He dropped to the ground, blood leaking from his ears and nose, with a double skull fracture that was nearly fatal. Michaels, who spent three weeks in a Philadelphia hospital after the beaning, never played a professional baseball game again. His injury deeply affected his teammates, including Miñoso, who thought that Fricano may have received advice from Jimmy Dykes to throw at hitters when Dykes was managing the Athletics. "I hope God punishes Marion Fricano slowly so he remembers how he hurt Michaels and his family," Minnie said about the incident.[22]

Then in September, the White Sox lost their manager.

Paul Richards's contract as the club's manager was due to expire at the end of the 1954 season. He wanted a three-year contract; the White Sox would not offer more than two years. When the Baltimore Orioles, who before the 1954 season had failed in an attempt to hire Sox general manager Frank Lane, asked for permission to offer the GM position to Richards, the White Sox said yes. Although the Sox made a belated effort to keep Richards, they did not come close to matching Baltimore's offer. On September 14 the Orioles announced that Richards had agreed to a three-year contract to be both Baltimore's general manager and field manager—for about twice what the White Sox had been paying him.

The new Sox manager was Marty Marion, who had previously managed both the St. Louis Cardinals and the St. Louis Browns before becoming a White Sox coach. As a player with the Cardinals (1940–50), Marion was a slick-fielding shortstop who had won the National League Most Valuable Player Award in 1944. He was one of the team leaders when Jackie Robinson made his major league debut in 1947 and had been accused of taking part in a plan led by Cardinals players to stage a general strike of NL players to force Robinson out of the league. Yet Marion had managed Satchel Paige during his stint with the Browns, and he would manage Miñoso and several other Black players during his White Sox tenure, with no reported difficulties.

Nonetheless, Miñoso had lost the manager who had campaigned for his acquisition by the White Sox and who had given Minnie his first opportunity to play regularly in the formerly all-white major leagues. "Without qualification or reservation, leaving no room for hesitation or ambiguity, I can say that Paul Richards was the best manager I have ever played for," Miñoso wrote. "I wish I could have played my entire career with Richards."[23]

◆ ◆ ◆

Miñoso had more serious problems to deal with in 1954 than the loss of his beloved manager. In May, press reports stated that Barbara Swader, a 22-year-old South Side waitress, had filed a $250,000 breach of promise suit against Miñoso. Swader claimed that Minnie was the father of her daughter Lynette, who had been born in May 1953. She said in the suit that Miñoso had acknowledged that he was the father of the child, that he had contributed $110 per month for the first three months after the baby's birth, and that he had sent Christmas gifts to "My Lynette" in 1953 "with love and a million kisses from your father." She said that her relationship with Miñoso had begun in 1952 and that Minnie had set a wedding date for the spring of 1954. She alleged that Miñoso had "another girl" and two babies in Cuba, with the suit implying that this was his reason for not marrying her.[24] (Miñoso had in fact fathered a son, Orestes Jr., with Julia Pérez in 1952, although the couple was not married.)

In response, Miñoso called the whole matter "a lie." He said that he wanted a blood test. "If a blood test shows I'm the father I will take care

of the child," he said. "If the test shows I'm not, I'll file suit against her."
He denied that he had promised to marry Swader in the spring of 1953 or
that he had played with the child. He did admit to knowing her.[25]

In September Swader said that she and Minnie had been married on
September 8, 1954, by Myles E. Cunat, justice of the peace in Hollywood,
Illinois.[26] Miñoso, whose full name was Saturnino Orestes Armas Miñoso
(Armas was his mother's last name), claimed at first that there was nothing
to the story and that he was not the Saturnino Armas listed on the license.
But the couple had in fact been married in the office of Barbara's attorney,
with Swader agreeing to drop her $250,000 suit. The marriage was brief.
In December, while Minnie was believed to be at home in Cuba, Swader
was granted a divorce from Miñoso in Blue Island City Court on grounds
of cruelty.[27] In the divorce filing, Swader claimed that Miñoso had struck
her five days after the marriage, then repeated the assault six days later.
Judge Maurice J. Schultz ordered Miñoso to pay Barbara $65 per week in
child support and also ordered Swader to quit her waitressing job so that
she could take care of the baby.[28] Swader was not pleased with the judge's
order to quit her job. According to friends, $65 per week hardly matched
what she was earning at the popular Archway Lounge.[29]

In May 1955 Swader wrote an article about her relationship with
Miñoso that was published in *TAN* and summarized in Black newspapers. She wrote that their affair began in 1952, when she was 19, and that
she learned that she was pregnant during the winter, when Minnie was
in Cuba. According to Swader, Miñoso was very fond of the child but
negligent in contributing to her support. She said that his attitude toward
the baby changed when White Sox pitcher Connie Johnson told the dark-
skinned Miñoso in her presence, "You're simple if you think that's your
baby. Nobody your color could have a baby that light." She wrote that
Miñoso stopped taking care of the baby after that, admitting that he did
not think he was the child's father. At that point Swader filed the $250,000
paternity suit. While awaiting court action on the suit, Swader discovered
that Miñoso was living with a woman but not married to her. After she
confronted him about this, she wrote, he agreed to marry her so that the
baby would have a legal name—if she also agreed to divorce him immediately. He also agreed to pay $10 weekly in support, but when the judge
learned that Miñoso was making $27,000 from the White Sox, he increased
the amount to $65.[30]

In July the case returned to court when Swader claimed that Miñoso
owed her $1,950 for nonpayment of support. Miñoso's attorney, Sol R.
Friedman, denied the claim, arguing that the couple had had a prenuptial agreement that there not be any support or alimony demands. At a

subsequent hearing Friedman, who was also a Chicago alderman, quoted from the prenuptial agreement, "where Mrs. Miñoso stated that she was not definitely certain of the paternity of the child."[31] The case was ultimately settled with details not disclosed.

In the second of Miñoso's two autobiographies, *Just Call Me Minnie*, he devoted several pages to the paternity case, leaving out many important, and potentially compromising, details. Miñoso wrote that he had first met Swader (who was never named in the book) in 1952, when he was living at the Wedgewood Hotel at 64th and Woodlawn. He was visiting with teammate Héctor Rodríguez one day when the front desk called and said that a woman wanted to speak with him. When Miñoso went down to the lobby, he recognized the woman as a waitress who worked at a nearby restaurant. When Minnie asked the woman what she wanted, she said that she had no place to stay because her parents were away and she did not have a key. He did not want the woman to stay in his room, so he rented a room in the hotel for her and told the desk clerk that he would take care of the bill. According to Minnie, he did not see the woman again that day or night.

Miñoso wrote that when he subsequently was served with a subpoena claiming his paternity of the child (he wrote that it was for $500,000, double the actual amount), he showed it to White Sox general manager Frank Lane, who turned the matter over to the team lawyer. "Eventually the ugly incident was settled out of court," Miñoso wrote. "It was settled between the lawyers, and I never heard more about it. To this date, I have no idea what the outcome was." He insisted, "I had never been with that young woman. And what happened to me in 1952 could have happened to any man at any time, particularly one who is in the public eye." Miñoso was adamant that there was no way the woman's baby could have been his, because, unlike Minnie, she was light-skinned, as was the baby. That had been Connie Johnson's contention.[32]

Miñoso's account of the events concerning Barbara Swader finished with an incident that occurred in 1976, when Minnie was coaching for the White Sox during Paul Richards's final managerial stint. He was with the team for a game in Anaheim against the California Angels, talking with a man who had followed Minnie during his minor league years in San Diego. The man said he had a message for Miñoso. It was a note from a woman who said she was the mother of Miñoso's child. The woman wanted Minnie to talk to her daughter.

"I took the note and burned it with my lighter," Miñoso wrote. "I don't know if it was another attempt to extort money from me, or whether she was just crazy." He wrote that after the paternity case had settled down, some friends of Minnie's on the police force told him that the woman used to party with white men in the south suburban town of Blue Island and that one of the men was the baby's father. "The incident really hurt me, because the young kids in the neighborhood looked up to me. I would never want to diminish myself in their eyes. The people tended to believe me, but the whole episode never sat well. Things like that never do."[33]

16

Baseball's New Superstar

Nineteen fifty-five would be an important year for race relations in Chicago as well as the United States. As the Cubs and the White Sox were beginning spring training in March, the Cook County Board of Commissioners awarded Harvey Clark and his family a $1,000 damage settlement for the destruction of their property when the Clarks had attempted to move into an apartment in Cicero nearly four years earlier. "Perhaps the one thousand dollars (even after Clark paid attorney's fees, if any) will compensate for the loss of personal property," commented the *Chicago Defender*. "But no doubt, when he glances at the check, Clark will wonder how much it is worth to be free."[1] Meanwhile, Clark continued his battle for justice.

On the far South Side, tension continued at the Trumbull Park Homes, where Black postal worker Donald Howard and his wife had "accidentally" been allowed to move into a previously all-white public housing project two years earlier. In May, Howard filed a $1.7-million-dollar suit against the Chicago Housing Authority and five Chicago newspapers for conspiracy to deprive them of their home. In July, Chicago's newly elected mayor, Richard J. Daley, appointed a 24-man committee to help find a solution to the problem. "We need not only to bring peace and security to Trumbull Park but to insure that no other incidents will arise in other communities," said Daley.[2] One of the city's main solutions, critics would later charge, would be to avoid racial tension by building new public housing units in neighborhoods that were already all-Black and overcrowded.[3]

On August 28, 14-year-old Chicagoan Emmett Till was brutally lynched in Money, Mississippi, where he was visiting relatives. Till's mother Mamie insisted on an open casket during the funeral at Roberts' Temple of God—a mile southeast of Comiskey Park at 4021 South State Street—so that the world could "see what they did to my boy."[4] The viciousness of the murder and the quick acquittal of the killers would help galvanize the civil rights movement.

Finally, in Montgomery, Alabama, on December 1, Rosa Parks refused to surrender her bus seat to a white man. Parks's defiant stance triggered a yearlong bus boycott, one of the first organized, large-scale protests against segregation and Jim Crow laws. The boycott led to a Supreme Court decision ending segregated seating on buses. It also brought one of the leaders of the boycott, Martin Luther King Jr., to national prominence.

◆ ◆ ◆

Although the Cubs had been more than two years behind the White Sox in integrating their major league roster, the success of Ernie Banks and Gene Baker seemed to make them more open to adding Black players. Solly Drake entered the 1955 season with a little over 200 games of minor league experience, none above the Class A level. But his speed and ability to handle center field put him in the running to make the Opening Day roster; when he batted .478 in the spring games in Arizona, he seemed to be on his way to clinching a spot. But as the Cubs were about to break camp on March 30 and begin barnstorming back to Chicago, Drake caught his spikes in the dirt while trying to slide into second base during an intersquad game. The result was a broken leg and a badly dislocated right ankle. Drake missed most of the season and did not make his major league debut until 1956. In 1960 Solly's younger brother Sammy made his MLB debut with the Cubs; the Drakes were the first Black siblings to play in the white major leagues since Fleet and Welday Walker in 1884.

The Cubs' other new Black player was a lot more experienced than Solly Drake. Sam Jones, who would turn 30 in December 1955, was a World War II veteran who had pitched for the Negro League Cleveland Buckeyes in 1947 and 1948 and pitched in 1949 in the South Minnesota League, a strong semipro circuit that was a haven for Black players. He also excelled in winter league action. Jones's work drew the attention of major league scouts, and in 1950 Jones joined the Cleveland Indians farm system. After winning 17 games for Class A Wilkes-Barre in 1950 and 16 for Class AAA San Diego in 1951, Jones made his white major league debut with the Indians on September 22, 1951. Known as "Toothpick Sam" for the toothpicks he chewed on the mound, Jones seemed a cinch for stardom. Hollywood Stars manager Fred Haney, who had managed the St. Louis Browns early in Bob Feller's Cleveland Indians career, said that Jones "throws just like Bob Feller when Bob broke in."[5] The current Indians manager, Al Lopez said, "You'll see a lot of Sam Jones" in 1952.[6]

That did not happen. Between his work for San Diego and San Juan of the Puerto Rican winter league, Jones had pitched more than 400 innings in the 12 months preceding the start of spring training in 1952. He reported to camp with a sore arm, missed much of the season, and was back in the minors in 1953–54. After Jones won 15 games for Class AAA Indianapolis in 1954, the Indians, who were loaded with pitching, dealt him to the Cubs in October 1954 for cash and a player to be named later (future Hall of Famer Ralph Kiner, who was suffering from back problems and close to the end of his career). After Jones turned in another outstanding performance in the Puerto Rican winter league, there was little doubt that he would be part of the Cubs' starting rotation in 1955.

◆ ◆ ◆

A few days after the Cubs completed the deal for Jones, Phil Wrigley demoted the man who had made the trade. In typical Wrigley fashion, Wid Matthews kept his title as director of player personnel, but he would now be reporting to the team's new executive vice president, 76-year-old Clarence (Pants) Rowland. A longtime Wrigley protégé, Rowland had served as a major and minor league manager, a minor league owner and executive, a scout, and even as an umpire during a career that dated back to 1902. Most recently he had served as the president of the Pacific Coast League, which had unsuccessfully attempted to achieve major league status. Rowland's association with Wrigley dated back to the 1930s; Rowland had agreed to try out Black players when he was running Wrigley's Los Angeles Angels farm team during the early 1940s, but then begged off. Yet the PCL had successfully integrated during Rowland's tenure as league president, and he had also added white organized baseball's only Black umpire, Emmett Ashford, to the league's staff in 1954.

Not much was expected from Rowland and the Cubs in 1955. In its April 11 National League preview edition, *Sports Illustrated*—at the time, a fledgling magazine still in its first year of publication—summarized the Cubs' outlook as "Far from bright. Too many weak spots. No better than seventh, possibly the cellar."[7] The issue featured a cover photo of defending World Series champion New York Giants manager Leo Durocher, along with his superstar outfielder, Willie Mays, and Durocher's wife, Hollywood actress Laraine Day. In the photo, Ms. Day was posed standing between Mays and Durocher, with one hand resting on her husband's shoulder, and the other on Mays's. The white actress's hand touching a Black man was a bridge too far for a segment of *Sports Illustrated*'s readership.

"Please cancel my subscription immediately . . . this is an insult to every decent white woman everywhere," wrote a reader from Fort Worth in the April 25 issue of the magazine. Another, from New Orleans, wrote, "Such disgusting racial propaganda is not fit for people trying to build a stronger nation based on racial integrity." A reader from Shreveport, Louisiana, called the photo "the proof . . . that SI is part of the giant plan to flaunt all decency, so long as the conquered of 1865 can be reminded of their eternal defeat." And a reader from Nashville wrote, "To tell you I was shocked would be putting it mildly," and linked the photo with the Supreme Court's recent *Brown v. Board of Education* decision.[8]

In its May 9 issue *Sports Illustrated* reported that, to date, it had received more than 300 letters commenting on its April 25 cover. Twenty-one readers supported the comments of the four writers who were outraged about the photo; 279 readers wrote letters protesting those comments.

◆ ◆ ◆

In baseball, there is a pattern known as the "sophomore jinx": After a solid rookie season, a player often regresses in year two as opposing teams learn the player's weak points and how to exploit them. While the Cubs hoped that Gene Baker and Ernie Banks would improve on their rookie performances, nothing was guaranteed.

For Baker, 1955 proved to be a lot like 1954: His offensive numbers declined a little, but not much, and he was able to stay healthy and play all 154 games. Baker continued to win plaudits for his defense, especially his work with Banks on the double play. Banks, however, improved from promising young player to legitimate superstar in 1955, almost overnight.

An event that was key to Banks's second-year improvement had taken place late in the 1954 season. The Cubs were in New York to play the Giants, and before the game Banks visited with Giants star Monte Irvin, a former Negro League great (and future Hall of Famer) who often served as a mentor to young Black players. At the batting cage Banks picked up one of Irvin's bats, which at 31 ounces was four ounces lighter than the bat Ernie had been using. He liked the feel of the bat and gave it a try during batting practice. The result was both greater bat speed and better ability to handle outside pitches. Most important, the combination of the lighter bat with Ernie's natural wrist action helped greatly increase his power. Former major leaguer Lew Fonseca, one of the first people to analyze players with the use of film, claimed that the lighter bat increased Banks's bat speed by nearly 25 miles per hour.

Banks got off to a slow start in 1955. He hit his first homer in the Cubs' third game on April 14, then hit two more in a 14-inning game at St. Louis two days later. Those were his last home runs in April. But in a 22-game span beginning with the second game of a doubleheader on May 8, he hit nine home runs and drove in 21 runs. Two of the homers came with the bases loaded. On July 1 Banks hit his 19th home run of the year, equaling his total for the entire 1954 season. Two home runs against the Cardinals on July 8 gave him 23 for the year, breaking Glenn Wright's 1930 National League record for most home runs in a season by a shortstop (counting home runs only while in the game at shortstop). He had broken the record in just 83 games. "If I were permitted to take one player out of the National League today, my first choice would be Banks," said White Sox general manager Frank Lane in late June. (Lane did not mention that he had passed on purchasing Banks for the Sox two years earlier).[9]

With Banks leading the way, the Cubs were the surprise of the National League in the first half of the season. Through the games of July 4 the Cubs ranked second in the league with a 44-36 record, though they were a distant 12½ games behind the league-leading Dodgers. The team couldn't maintain the pace and ultimately finished sixth with a 72-81 mark. But Banks continued to shine.

On August 2 against the Pittsburgh Pirates, Ernie's fifth-inning grand slam off left-hander Dick Littlefield gave him four grand slam homers for the season, equaling the major league record held by 10 other players. Although he failed to hit another bases-loaded homer for several weeks, he continued to knock the ball out of the yard. Two days after tying the grand slam record, Banks belted three home runs in a game against the Pirates. On August 11 against the Cincinnati Redlegs, Banks's sixth-inning solo homer off Joe Black gave him 39 for the year, tying the major league record for home runs in a season by a shortstop held by Vern Stephens of the 1949 Boston Red Sox.

Banks was so red-hot that people were starting to consider him a threat to challenge Babe Ruth's single-season home run record of 60. He failed to hit another homer during the remainder of August, however. Number 40, which broke the single-season record for shortstops, finally came on September 2 against the Cardinals, but Banks hit only four more home runs for the remainder of the season. Fatigue was undoubtedly an issue because he played in all 154 games, missing only two innings all year. Banks refused to come out of the lineup even after being hit on the top of his nose by a pitch from Ron Kline of the Pirates on June 25. He lay on the ground without moving for a short time after the beaning, but then picked himself up and headed to first base. When manager Stan Hack asked Banks how he felt, Ernie said, "All right, and you're not going to take me out."[10]

Banks's last great moment of 1955 came on September 19 in St. Louis. Facing 19-year-old rookie right-hander Lindy McDaniel (a future Cubs teammate), Banks homered with the bases full in the seventh inning. The single-season record for grand slams was his at last (it would later be broken by Don Mattingly and Travis Hafner). The home run gave the Cubs a 5–0 lead, but they couldn't hold it; St. Louis came back to win, 6–5. Despite the Cubs' sixth-place finish—the club's 72 wins did mark an eight-game improvement from 1954—Banks's brilliance did not go unnoticed. In the voting for National League Most Valuable Player after the season, Banks got six first-place votes from the 24-voter panel and finished third overall behind Roy Campanella and Duke Snider of the World Series champion Dodgers. And his defensive work continued to draw praise, as did Gene Baker's. A poll of managers and baseball observers solicited by the *Sporting News* during the 1955 season ranked Banks and Baker as the league's top double-play combination.

♦ ♦ ♦

In developing his public persona, Banks emulated a couple of role models. One was his former Kansas City Monarchs manager, Buck O'Neil, whose enthusiasm and constant optimism seemed to rub off on everyone he encountered. The other was Minnie Miñoso. "I followed Minnie Miñoso and tried to pattern myself after him," Banks said in an interview in 2006. "He was nice to people, he signed autographs, he talked to people. He played hard. I admired that."[11]

Like Miñoso, Banks experienced racial prejudice throughout his life, but generally did not get directly involved in the battle for civil rights. "Some people feel that because you are black you will never be treated fairly, that you should voice your opinions, be militant about them. I don't feel this way," he wrote in his 1971 autobiography. "If a man doesn't like me because I'm black, that's fine. I'll just go elsewhere, but I'm not going to let him change my life. I don't think it's up to black athletes to get involved in political or racial issues." He would be criticized for this by more militant Black athletes such as Jackie Robinson and Hank Aaron. It bothered him, but Banks felt that this was not who he was. "He wanted to be in positive situations and environments, not around adversity," said Banks's former wife, Marjorie Lott.[12]

♦ ♦ ♦

The Cubs' other Black player in 1955, Sam Jones, was "an intimidating pitcher," according to his SABR biographer, Rory Costello. "'Toothpick Sam'—he always had one in his mouth—gave no quarter on the mound."[13] Jones threw hard, and his best pitch, a sweeping curveball, could look as if it was coming directly at a right-handed hitter before it broke over the plate. Adding to the intimidation factor was the fact that Jones did not have great control. In four of his first five seasons after joining the Cubs (1955–59), Jones led the National League in walks. Over the same period, only one major league pitcher (Frank Lary) hit more batters. (Jones also led the league in strikeouts in three of those seasons.)

Jones got off to a slow start with the Cubs in 1955; in five games (four starts) during the month of April, his earned run average was 6.31, and he allowed more than a walk per inning. Then on May 12 he took the mound against the Pittsburgh Pirates at Wrigley Field. The start made major league history.

It was not a typical Sam Jones start, at least, not for the first eight innings. Entering the bottom of the ninth, he had allowed only four walks and struck out just three Pirate hitters. He had thrown 107 pitches, not a particularly high total for him. He also had not allowed a hit. No pitcher had thrown a no-hitter at Wrigley Field since May 2, 1917, when, in one of the most famous games in baseball history, both Hippo Vaughn of the Cubs and Fred Toney of the Reds threw nine innings of no-hit ball. (Vaughn allowed two hits and a run in the 10th, but Toney retired the Cubs in order to complete his no-hitter.) On this day there was another element at play: Since the white major leagues had integrated in 1947, no Black pitcher had thrown a no-hitter.

As he took the mound for the bottom of the ninth, Jones seemed in control. The Cubs led, 4–0, and Sam's defense had needed to make only a few difficult plays. But then Jones weakened. He walked Gene Freese on five pitches to open the frame. A wild pitch moved Freese to second, and then Jones walked both Preston Ward and Tom Saffell. The Pirates now had the bases loaded, nobody out, with three outstanding hitters—Dick Groat, Roberto Clemente, and Frank Thomas—due up. Manager Stan Hack went to the mound to talk with Jones, who told him that he felt fine. "I went farther with Jones than I ordinally would have," Hack said after the game. "But had the fourth Pirate reached base, he would have been out of there." Jones got himself together. He retired Groat on three fast curves, none of which Groat swung at. Clemente went down swinging on five pitches, including two foul balls. He threw nothing but curves to Thomas, who took Jones's 136th pitch of the game for strike three to complete the no-hitter.[14]

Afterward Jones said that he had learned his curveball from Satchel Paige when both were in the Negro Leagues. "I watched Paige every chance I got," Sam said. "He taught me how to hold and deliver my curve." He told reporters, "I didn't know it was a no-hitter until the game was over" and said that he had chewed only one toothpick during the game, instead of his usual eight or nine.[15]

The no-hitter was part of a rollercoaster season for Jones. He led the league in strikeouts, but he also led the league in walks, hit batsmen, and losses (20). His 185 walks were the most by a National League pitcher since 1898. He made the All-Star team and pitched in the game, but after getting two outs was removed after loading the bases on two walks and a hit batsman. Along with the no-hitter, he tossed a two-hitter and a three-hitter; he also had five games in which he permitted eight or more walks. He could be mean: "In New York, June 5, Sam Jones of the Cubs low-bridged Giant after Giant, and hit two," reported sportswriter Joe King.[16] Yet teammates and opponents often spoke of him with warmth and affection.

Don Kaiser was a 20-year-old bonus player with the 1955 Cubs who by the rules of the time was required to remain in the majors for his first two years. Veteran players often resented these bonus players, both because teams were giving big money to untried amateurs and because they were taking a veteran's place on the roster. Jones, who had fought for years to get a chance to pitch in the major leagues, had every reason to feel resentful of someone like Kaiser, a white kid who went directly from school to the majors—after pocketing a bonus that was more than twice Sam's salary. Yet Kaiser said, "Sam Jones was one of my best buddies. Hell, he taught me more about pitching than the pitching coach did. I loved Sam Jones." Kaiser also spoke warmly about Banks and Baker. "On the field or off the field, they'd try to help you in any way that they could," he said. "They were people that you could go up and talk to."[17]

Hobie Landrith, a catcher whom the Cubs acquired after the 1955 season, teamed up with Jones in Chicago, St. Louis, and San Francisco, essentially becoming Sam's personal catcher. The two developed a strong working relationship that lasted for years. "Sam claimed that I brought him fame and I claimed he brought me fame," Landrith said about working with Jones.[18] In 1959, with Landrith as his primary catcher, Jones won 21 games, becoming the second Black pitcher to win 20 or more games in an American or National League season (the first was Don Newcombe of the Dodgers in 1955).

◆ ◆ ◆

Four seasons after Minnie Miñoso's White Sox debut, the team's winter roster included only three Black players: Miñoso, Earl Battey, and Connie Johnson. Battey, who was only 20 years old with barely 150 games' experience in white organized baseball, was optioned to Class AAA Charleston on March 21; he would be recalled in September and would make his MLB debut that month. Johnson, who needed a good spring in order to make the Opening Day roster, pitched poorly in the spring training opener and was optioned to Class AAA Toronto on March 29.

That left Miñoso as the team's only Black player, just as he had been for most of 1954. After his outstanding 1954 season, Minnie expected a substantial increase in his $27,000 salary. After denying rumors that he was asking for $40,000 or more, he signed on March 3 for $32,500. That was substantially less than the $40,000 salary of the team's highest-paid player, George Kell, a white veteran who was not nearly as good a player as Miñoso at this point in his career (or probably ever). Kell's main advantage, along with his skin color, was that he had been in the league since 1943, eight years before Minnie received his first real opportunity to play in the white major leagues. Kell had been earning $40,000 or more since 1951. By contrast, Jackie Robinson and Larry Doby, the majors' highest-salaried Black players in 1955, were each making $35,000. Robinson's career high had been $39,750 in 1952.

◆ ◆ ◆

Although the club achieved fewer wins (91) under Marty Marion than with Paul Richards in 1954 (94), the 1955 White Sox stayed in the pennant race all year and held first place as late as September 3. A doubleheader loss to the Cleveland Indians on Sunday, September 4, dropped the Sox to third place, and that's where they finished, five games behind the pennant-winning Yankees.

The Sox likely would have fared better had they not waited until July to recall Connie Johnson from Toronto, where he had posted a 12-2 record. Johnson pitched a complete game to defeat the Kansas City Athletics in his first start after his recall; five days later, he shut out the second-place Indians, 6–0, recording a season-high 12 strikeouts. In his first 11 starts, he posted a 6-1 record with a brilliant 1.97 ERA. Johnson faded a bit in the final five weeks but still finished with a 7-4 record and a fine 3.45 ERA. Between the majors and the minors, Johnson logged 19 wins in 1955.

The biggest blow to the pennant hopes for the White Sox occurred on Wednesday afternoon, May 18, at Yankee Stadium. With two men on base in the top of the first inning, one of Yankee Bob Grim's fastballs went up and in. "It hit me in the head, and I went down in a heap," Miñoso wrote. He was taken to a New York hospital; when x-rays were negative, he was released. But after returning to Chicago, he felt violently ill, and a new set of x-rays revealed a fractured skull.[19]

Miñoso did not return to action until June 4, and when he did, he was obviously feeling the effects of the beaning; in his first 12 games thereafter, he managed only three singles in 38 at-bats, dropping his season average to .226. He recovered and finished the year with a .288 average, but almost all his numbers were well below his usual level. While Minnie claimed that he had recovered from the dizzy spells that bothered him after the beaning, he said that sometimes he lay at night thinking and went two or three days without eating. But he refused to come out of the lineup. "I know you got to hit in this game and catch fly balls and when you don't, they tell you they don't need you any more," Minnie commented.[20]

Miñoso did not feel that Grim was deliberately trying to hit him and wrote that the Yankees pitcher visited him many times while he was recovering. Others weren't so sure. In June 1955 Doc Young wrote an article in *Jet* titled, "Is Dirty Baseball Killing Negro Stars?" Reflecting on Miñoso's comment that his frequent hit-by-pitches were "an accident every time," Young quoted a fan in a Black barber shop who responded, "Getting hit 67 times in four years is a whole lot of accidents." Young also quoted Black infielder Curt Roberts, who had been "nearly killed" by a pitch in a minor league game. "*You* can call it an accident—I say it's dirty baseball!"[21]

Both the White Sox team management and the Chicago press seemed quick to think the worst about an Afro-Latino player who spent most of 1955 recovering from a serious beaning and who a year earlier had seen a teammate, Cass Michaels, nearly killed by a pitched ball. In a September article titled "Marion Fumes as Minnie Flops," John C. Hoffman of the *Chicago Sun-Times* wrote,

> Manager Marion is known to have called Miñoso on the carpet to tell him in no uncertain terms of his displeasure with the outfielder's failure to play his normal game. He told Minnie he had been playing bush league baseball and even hinted he was not so sure the Cuban star was giving it the old college try.[22]

In the same article, Hoffman quoted Sox general manager Frank Lane as saying, "I predicted last spring that he would have a bad season, and I guess I was right"—an apparent accusation that Miñoso had been more concerned about his salary than about playing ball. The harsh words must have been a blow to Miñoso, who referred to Lane as "a surrogate father. Throughout our long association, he always called me 'son,' and he really meant it. In turn, Frank was always my 'Daddy Number Two'."[23]

By season's end "Daddy Number Two" was gone from the White Sox; Lane resigned on September 22, mainly because of increasing friction in his relationship with Chuck Comiskey. Edgar Munzel wrote in the *Sporting News* that the "two most vital moves" that Lane had made in helping the White Sox become contenders were the hiring of Paul Richards as manager and the trade for Minnie Miñoso.[24]

♦ ♦ ♦

By the end of the 1955 season the Cubs and the White Sox had more Black players in prominent roles than ever before. On the North Side, Ernie Banks had become a legitimate superstar. Banks and Gene Baker were regarded by many as the best double-play combination in baseball. And Sam Jones made the All-Star team while becoming the first Black pitcher in the formerly all-white major leagues to throw a no-hitter. On the South Side Minnie Miñoso continued to be an established star, Connie Johnson had won 19 games between the majors and the minors, and Earl Battey was a catcher with a bright future. Shortly after the season ended, the Sox acquired Larry Doby, the American League's first Black player and still an All-Star performer, in a trade with the Cleveland Indians.

Yet Chicago's baseball stars dealt with discrimination and segregated housing just as any Black American did. Racial taunts from fans and opponents were part of the game. Even in the North, they often faced restrictions on where they could sleep or eat. Black players such as Sam Hairston and Willie Pope still toiled in the minor leagues without ever getting a chance to show what they could do with the big club. Major league baseball had no Black coaches or umpires, and the game was still decades away from its first Black manager or executive in an important role. For Black Americans in all walks of life, in Chicago and elsewhere, progress remained painfully slow.

"Baseball is only a pastime, a sport, an entertainment, a way of blowing off steam," wrote Jackie Robinson in 1964. "But it is also the national game, with an appeal to Americans of every race, color, creed, sex or political opinion. It unites Americans in the common cause of rooting for the home team.

"Is it possible that Americans value victory for the home team more than victory in our national life?"[25]

Epilogue

In the decade from 1956 to 1965, the White Sox continued to be a much more successful team than the Cubs. In that period the Sox had a winning record every year, finished in second place five times, never finished lower than fifth place, and won the American League championship in 1959, their first pennant in 40 years. During the same span the Cubs finished as high as fifth only twice and had a winning record just once—in 1963, when they posted an 82-80 mark (and still managed to finish seventh in a 10-team league).

This discrepancy occurred even though the Cubs were becoming much better than the Sox in discovering good Black players. In 1958 Cuban infielder Tony Taylor, essentially Gene Baker's successor as the Cubs' second baseman, began a 19-year career during which he compiled more than two thousand hits (most of them, unfortunately, after he left Chicago). A year later future Hall of Famer Billy Williams made his Cubs debut, appearing in 18 games; he would return for good in 1961 and win the National League Rookie of the Year Award. In 1959 George Altman, a two-time All-Star and one of the last Negro League players to advance to the formerly all-white majors, made his Cubs debut. Late in the 1961 season, future Hall of Famer Lou Brock made his major league debut with the team.

In that same decade the White Sox had far fewer Black players who made a significant impact. When the Sox won the pennant in 1959 their only Black regular was outfielder Al Smith, who had been acquired from Cleveland in a 1957 trade for Miñoso. Of the other Black players who had significant playing time with the White Sox in that time frame apart from Minnie Miñoso—Larry Doby, Don Buford, Tommy McCraw, Juan Pizarro, and Floyd Robinson—only Pizarro made an All-Star team while with the Sox. Meanwhile, three Black players who became Hall of Famers began their major league careers with the Cubs: Banks, Williams, and Brock. A fourth, pitcher Ferguson Jenkins, was acquired in a trade after he had previously played in only eight major league games. Over the same period, zero Black Hall of Famers began their career on the South Side. In fact, the first to reach the Hall who began his career with the White Sox, Harold Baines, did not make his MLB debut until 1980.

One man was largely responsible for the Cubs' success in signing and developing Black players: Buck O'Neil, the longtime Negro League star and Kansas City Monarchs manager. In 1953 O'Neil helped steer Ernie Banks from the Monarchs to the Cubs. He was also George Altman's manager. In 1955 Wid Matthews hired O'Neil as a full-time scout for the North Siders. During his years as a scout, O'Neil signed Brock for the Cubs. He was not responsible for signing Billy Williams, but when a discouraged Williams decided to quit baseball during his minor league career, O'Neil talked him into returning. He also recommended that the Cubs convert Fergie Jenkins from a relief pitcher to a starter. Later in his scouting career, O'Neil was instrumental in signing another future Hall of Famer for the team, relief star Lee Smith; he also signed longtime MLB stars Oscar Gamble and Joe Carter.

In 1962 the Cubs promoted O'Neil to the team's coaching staff, making him the first Black coach in American or National League history. At the time the Cubs were in the midst of a Phil Wrigley experiment called the "College of Coaches" that featured no full-time manager; instead, one of the coaches would take over the managerial job for a short period on a rotating basis. In announcing O'Neil's appointment, Cubs general manager John Holland said that O'Neil "would not be a member of the head coaching rotation," which would have made him the first Black manager in either major league. In his autobiography O'Neil wrote that Holland "vaguely left open the possibility that I would one day become part of the rotation" but that he "soon found out that there was no chance of that happening." He related a story about how, despite his decades of experience as a manager and coach, the Cubs would not even let him coach third base on a day when two other coaches were ejected and he would have been the logical choice to assume the role. "Not going out there that day was one of the few disappointments I've had in over sixty years in baseball," O'Neil wrote. He returned to scouting in 1964.[1]

Why were the White Sox so much more successful in the standings than the Cubs (at least until the late 1960s) when the Cubs did a far better job of finding good Black players? With the Cubs, it was in part bad timing; for instance, Billy Williams began to develop just as Ernie Banks was starting to decline. There was also bad management, such as trading Lou Brock just as he was about to develop into a superstar. As for the White Sox, they were in an American League that, as previously noted, still lagged far behind the National when it came to scouting and developing Black players. Research by Mark Armour of SABR noted that in 1947, the American League and the National League each had one Black future Hall of Famer (Larry Doby and Jackie Robinson, respectively), apart from players who would be honored for their Negro League play. But from then until 1965 the National League added a future Hall of Famer virtually every year, 16 in all, while Miñoso was the only future Hall of Famer to join the AL. Unlike the Cubs, the Sox were competing in a league where *no team* was developing Black superstars.

◆ ◆ ◆

Though not a Hall of Famer, Earl Battey was a talented Black player whom the White let slip through their fingers. Battey played for the Sox in every season from 1955 to 1959, getting limited playing time behind the team's number-one catcher, Sherm Lollar. In April 1960 Bill Veeck, who had purchased the team from the Comiskeys a year earlier, traded the 25-year-old Battey and another young player, first baseman Don Mincher, to the Washington Senators in order to obtain aging slugger Roy Sievers. With the Senators, who became the Minnesota Twins in 1961, Battey quickly developed into a star; he played in five All-Star games (four as a starter), won three Gold Gloves for his defense, and helped lead the Twins to the 1965 World Series.

Hall of Fame pitcher Jim Kaat, who was Battey's teammate from 1960 to 1967, said that Earl was his catcher in almost two hundred games. "When we worked together, I pretty much put my games in Earl's hands," Kaat said in an interview. "He was a gentle soul and such a good influence on me—especially as a young pitcher in stressful times late in the game." Minneapolis sportswriter Patrick Reuss noted that Battey, who spoke Spanish, helped serve as a link between the team's Latin American players and their teammates. "He had the biggest personality on the team," said infielder Frank Quilici. "That was as close a group of players as I've been around, and Earl was probably the main reason."[2]

◆ ◆ ◆

After several frustrating seasons battling for playing time with the White Sox, Bob Boyd and Connie Johnson finally got their chance to show what they could do when Paul Richards acquired them for the Baltimore Orioles.

Boyd spent five seasons with the Orioles (1956–60), reaching his peak in 1957, when he batted .318 in 141 games at age 37. He ended his MLB career as a member of the Milwaukee Braves in 1961. After his professional baseball career ended, Boyd moved to Wichita, got a job with a local bus company, and became a key player for a bus company team called the Dreamliners that competed for the national semipro championship. "The most I ever made in one major league season was $18,500," he recalled. "I was making as much as I had been in the majors between my job driving a bus and playing baseball."[3] Boyd died in Wichita at age 84 in 2004.

Acquired by the Orioles in a 1956 trade with the White Sox, Connie Johnson spent three seasons with Baltimore, winning 14 games in his best year, 1957. After spending 1959–60 in the minor leagues, he briefly returned to Negro League baseball with the barnstorming Philadelphia Stars in the early 1960s. Johnson, who served as an honorary ball player at the 1982 funeral of his old Kansas City Monarchs teammate Satchel Paige, died in Kansas City at age 81 in 2004. "Connie was a good pitcher in the [white] major leagues, but he was a *great* pitcher in the Negro Leagues," recalled Johnson's former manager, Buck O'Neil. "No comparison. He threw hard for the Monarchs. Hard. He had good control. Could have won 20 games in the big leagues. Oh yeah. Could have won 20 games every year. That's Connie Johnson."[4]

◆ ◆ ◆

The White Sox' second Black player, and the first African American, Sam Hairston, played in the club's minor league system until 1960, when he was 40 years old. His career average in 11 seasons of minor league play was .304. He then retired to become a White Sox scout in the Alabama area. One of the few Black scouts in white organized baseball at the time, Hairston also worked as a coach; his ability to speak Spanish was particularly helpful to the organization's Latin players. In 1978 he was the White Sox bullpen coach during Bill Veeck's second stint as the team's owner. He then returned to the minor leagues as a coach for the Birmingham Barons in the Class AA Southern League. In 1994, at age 74, he was a Barons coach during basketball great Michael Jordan's only season in professional baseball.

Hairston was also the patriarch of a baseball dynasty. In 1969 Sam's son John reached the major leagues, playing three games with the Cubs. In 1973 his son Jerry began a 14-year major league career, mainly with the White Sox. In turn Jerry Hairston fathered two MLB players: Jerry Jr. had a 16-year major league career (1998–2013), and Scott Hairston played for 11 seasons (2004–2014). According to Richard Cuicchi, John Hairston's SABR biographer, 10 members of the Hairston family played for or were drafted by professional baseball organizations, and the five Hairstons who played in the white major leagues are tied with the five Delahanty brothers for the most MLB players from one family.[5]

"I've been in professional baseball 55 years, 45 with the White Sox, and I'm still employed," Sam Hairston said in 1995. "That's the way I conduct myself, not so much doing the job, but you've got to conduct yourself as a gentleman in order to go this far. You can do all the things that they want you to do but if you don't conduct yourself as a gentleman, you won't be around."[6] He died in Birmingham at age 77 two years later.

♦ ♦ ♦

Under Paul Richards's leadership, the Baltimore Orioles steadily improved, in large part because of young players whom he nurtured. With the Orioles in third place in the American League race in September 1961, Richards resigned to become general manager of the Houston Colt .45s, a National League expansion team that would begin play in 1962. As he had done in Baltimore, Richards signed and developed a number of excellent players while with Houston, but he was fired after the 1965 season. He then worked as vice president of player personnel with the Atlanta Braves, leading the Braves to a division title in 1969. After being fired by the Braves in 1972, Richards managed the White Sox to a last-place finish in 1976 while working under his old friend Bill Veeck. He then worked as a scout for the White Sox and as a special assistant with the Texas Rangers. He died in his native Waxahachie, Texas, at age 77 in 1986. "Richards' baseball career spanned seven decades, from Ty Cobb and John McGraw to Tony La Russa and Joe Torre," wrote Warren Corbett. "While Richards drilled his players constantly on the fine points of baseball—aggressive base running, throwing to the right base—he also said, 'It's a simple game. You throw the ball. You hit it. You catch it. . . . The simple things in baseball number in the thousands. The esoteric? There is none.'"[7]

♦ ♦ ♦

Frank Lane, who left the White Sox to become general manager of the St. Louis Cardinals late in the 1955 season, lasted two years in St. Louis. His trades improved the team as they had in Chicago: The Cardinals, who finished seventh in the National League in 1955, rose to fourth place in 1956 and then to second in 1957. But Lane often traded younger players for short-term veterans, and even seriously considered trading Cardinals icon Stan Musial, one of several Lane trade proposals that infuriated team owner Gussie Busch. Lane moved on to Cleveland (1958–60), where his deals again improved the team in the short term (the Indians, a sixth-place team in 1957, finished fourth in 1958 and second behind the White Sox in 1959), while often alienating the team's ownership and fans. Lane even traded his manager, sending Joe Gordon to the Tigers for Jimmy Dykes. The kiss of death for Lane was trading the team's most popular player, slugger Rocky Colavito, to Detroit for Harvey Kuenn in April 1960.

Lane spent the rest of his life as a sports vagabond. He lasted a few months as general manager for the volatile Kansas City Athletics owner Charlie Finley, spent two seasons working for future baseball commissioner Bud Selig with the Milwaukee Brewers, scouted for several MLB teams, and even worked as general manager of the Chicago Packers of the National Basketball Association. He never had trouble finding a job. But by the time he died at age 86 in 1981, Lane's early success with the White Sox was all but forgotten—as was his important role in integrating the Sox franchise.

◆ ◆ ◆

In May 1957 the Cubs broke up the "Bingo-Bango" combination by trading Gene Baker to the Pittsburgh Pirates. Baker was a member of the Pirates' National League pennant-winning team in 1960; although he played in only 33 games that year, he was respected as an elder statesman and team leader. ("Gene really helped us," said Baker's Pittsburgh teammate Vern Law.)[8] After his major league playing career ended, Baker made history in 1961 as the first Black manager in white organized baseball, with the Batavia Pirates of the Class D New York–Penn League. As a Pirates coach in 1963 he made more history, albeit unofficially, when he filled in as manager after Danny Murtaugh was ejected from a game (Frank Robinson would officially become the first Black manager of an American or National League team with the 1975 Cleveland Indians). After retiring as a Pirates coach, Baker spent 23 years as the team's chief scout in the Midwest. He died in his hometown of Davenport, Iowa, in 1999 at age 74.

◆ ◆ ◆

After leaving the Cubs, Sam Jones spent two seasons with the Cardinals (1957–58), then three more with Giants (1959–61); in 1959 he led the National League in earned run average, tied for the league leadership in wins, saved five games in relief, and finished second in the Cy Young Award voting to Early Wynn of the White Sox. His major league career ended after the 1964 season. Jones then spent three more seasons in the minors, continuing to pitch after being diagnosed with cancer in his neck. He died of cancer in Morgantown, West Virginia, at age 45 in November 1971. During his last days a constant visitor to Sam's bedside was Johnny

Bushman, a 23-year-old Giants fan whom Jones had befriended, and often visited in the hospital, when Bushman was being treated for polio as a child. "Sam had done so much for me when I was a boy that, in whatever small way I could, I wanted to repay him," Bushman said. "I love Sam as much as my own father."[9]

◆ ◆ ◆

On April 12, 1957, three days before the start of the major league baseball season, the last damage suits filed against the town of Cicero by Harvey Clark and other plaintiffs were finally settled in US District Court. It had been nearly six years since the riots that took place in Cicero when Clark and his family attempted to move into an apartment in the all-white suburb. Camille DeRose, owner of the apartment building, who had filed suit seeking $100,000, was awarded $4,300. Four Black plaintiffs who were seeking a total of $800,000 received $300 each. And the Clarks, who had sued the Cicero town board for $400,000, were awarded $2,400.[10]

In 1970 Harvey and Johnetta Clark's daughter Michele, who had been eight years old when the Cicero riots took place, became a news correspondent for WBBM-TV in Chicago. Two years later she became the first Black female national correspondent for CBS News, earning assignments to the CBS teams covering that year's Republican and Democratic nominating conventions. According to Richard Salant, president of CBS News at the time, Clark was scheduled to join the roster of correspondents on CBS's most powerful and highly rated news show, *60 Minutes*, in the fall of 1973.

On December 8, 1972, 29-year-old Michele Clark was one of 43 people killed when a United Airlines flight crashed while attempting to land at Midway Airport in Chicago. Another of the passengers who died was Dorothy Hunt, wife of Watergate break-in figure Howard Hunt. Watergate conspiracy theorists have posited that Clark was working on a story with Dorothy Hunt that would reveal major secrets about the Watergate scandal. While no specific evidence of sabotage concerning the crash has come to light, James D. Robenalt wrote in the *Washington Post* in December 2022, "Fifty years later, it is still unclear whether there was 'foul play' in the downing of United 553." Robenalt called the crash "a crucial turning point" in the Watergate scandal.[11]

Network correspondent Bill Kurtis termed Michele Clark's death "a terrible blow to CBS News." Joe Peyronnin, a WBBM/CBS producer who worked with Clark, said, "We all thought she could be Walter Cronkite." Richard Salant, president of CBS News, said, "It was as if Ed Murrow had died at a young age."[12] In 1974 Austin High School on Chicago's West Side was renamed Michele Clark Magnet High School in her honor.

Michele's brother Harvey Clark III, who was only six years old when the Cicero riots took place, also went on to a noteworthy career in television news. At the suggestion of Richard Salant, who was impressed with Clark after meeting him at Michele's memorial service, he entered a Columbia University program designed to train minority candidates for careers in journalism (the program, which Michele had also attended, was later renamed in for her). After a stint at WCCO in Minneapolis, Clark became a news correspondent at WCAU-TV in Philadelphia, where he worked from 1978 to 1991. He won two Emmy awards while working at the station and was highly praised for his exhaustive, hands-on reporting during the 1985 MOVE standoff, which culminated in Philadelphia police dropping a bomb on a building occupied by a Black liberation group. The bombing triggered a fire that killed 11, including five children, and the destruction of dozens of homes.

After leaving WCAU, Clark worked on the staffs of Philadelphia mayor Ed Rendell and New Jersey governor Christie Whitman; he also ran for Congress, unsuccessfully, as a Democrat in 1994. Recalling how his family was left homeless after the 1951 Cicero riots, Clark said that the experiences his family endured helped shape his work as a reporter, especially in covering the MOVE bombing. "I know what it's like to lose it all and to start from scratch," he said in 2016. "Eleven people die. Five children. Sixty-one homes were destroyed, and the lives of 200 to 225 people were destroyed. So, a lot more people died out there. They didn't lose their lives, but they lost everything else."[13] Clark died in San Juan, Puerto Rico, at age 76 in 2021.

Harvey and Michele's father, Harvey Clark Jr., died in Swannanoa, North Carolina, in 1998; Johnetta Clark died in Memphis in 2006. In the interim the Justice Department filed suit against the town of Cicero in January 1983 alleging discrimination in housing and employment. "The lawsuit charged that Blacks are excluded from living in the town through harassment and by Cicero's refusal to participate in a program that provides federal money for desegregated housing," reported the *Chicago Defender*. In May 1986, the *Chicago Tribune* reported, "The suburb that supporters of Dr. Martin Luther King Jr. once called 'the Selma, Alabama of the North'" had finally signed a consent decree and "agreed to open its houses and jobs to minorities."[14]

◆ ◆ ◆

As the last few major league teams finally added their first Black players in the late 1950s, the percentage of players of color on MLB rosters continued its steady climb. According to Mark Armour's research, the number of Black players (including African American and Afro-Latino players) reached 10 percent of the total for the first time in 1958; by 1965 the percentage had doubled to 20. By 1986, the 40th season after Jackie Robinson's Brooklyn Dodgers debut, Black players held 28 percent of the roster spots; the figure is over 30 percent today. Armour also noted that their *quality* was disproportionately high. For example, whereas 20 percent of the players in 1965 were Black, they accounted for 38 percent of the players on the All-Star teams.[15]

At the same time, it is important to note that in recent years an ever-increasing share of that total has consisted of players from Latin America; the percentage of African American players (those born in the United States) has steadily declined. The Institute for Diversity and Ethics in Sports (TIDES) at the University of Central Florida began compiling data in 1991. According to TIDES, African American players held 18 percent of the MLB roster spots in 1991; by the start of the 2022 season—the 75th anniversary of Robinson's debut—that figure had dropped to 7.2 percent.[16]

In April 2023 *USA Today* reported the percentage of African American players in MLB at only 6.1 percent. Bob Nightengale wrote that the Chicago teams, representing a city whose Black population was nearly 30 percent of the total, each had only one African American player: Tim Anderson with the White Sox and Marcus Stroman with the Cubs.[17]

◆ ◆ ◆

Ernie Banks generally stayed away from controversy when it came to matters of race. Throughout most of his Cubs career, Banks was happy to live on the South Side: first at 72nd and South Wabash Streets, then at 8123 South Michigan, and finally in a two-story house at 8159 South Rhodes.

In the meantime, he built his legend on the field. In 1956 Banks hit "only" 28 home runs. That was an aberration; from 1957 to 1960, Banks hit 40 or more homers every year, power-hitting numbers that were simply unheard of for a shortstop. He was voted the National League's Most Valuable Player in 1958 and 1959, although the Cubs were a second-division team with losing records. In 1960 Banks won a Gold Glove for his defensive work at shortstop. Along with his stellar play, Ernie's sunny, optimistic personality made him a beloved figure in Chicago and the nation, earning him the nickname "Mr. Cub." Many people close to Banks thought that constantly trying to maintain his bubbly image took its toll on him. "I think a lot of his, 'It's a great day, let's play two,' was a coverup of his sadness," said Ernie's third wife, Marjorie Lott.[18]

While Banks was still a fine player, his performance began to decline after 1960. Injuries forced him to move from shortstop to first base in 1962.

After 1960 he never had another 40-homer season, and only twice did he hit more than 30. Losing took its toll as well. In Ernie's first 14 seasons with the Cubs, the team had a winning record only once. By the time the Cubs finally assembled a team that could contend for a pennant, Banks was in his late 30s and playing for a manager, Leo Durocher, who wanted to trade him. Although Banks continued to be one of the team's top run producers, Durocher wrote in his autobiography that Ernie "couldn't run, he couldn't field; toward the end, he couldn't even hit. . . . But I had to play him. Had to play the man or there would have been a revolution in the street."[19] When the Durocher-led Cubs finally seemed headed toward a pennant in 1969—with Banks ranking second in the club in both home runs (23) and RBIs (106)—they collapsed down the stretch, losing a big lead to the New York Mets. Banks would forever be known as one of the greatest players never to appear in the World Series.

Banks's last great moment as a player came on May 12, 1970, when he hit the 500th home run of his career against Pat Jarvis of the Atlanta Braves. He retired at the end of the 1971 season with 512 career home runs. In 1977 Banks was elected to the Baseball Hall of Fame in his first year of eligibility. In 1982 he became the first player to have his uniform number (14) retired by the Cubs. In 2008 the Cubs unveiled a statue of Banks outside Wrigley Field (although the honor came 10 years after the team had unveiled its first statue, for white broadcaster Harry Caray). And in 2013 Banks was awarded the Presidential Medal of Freedom by President Barack Obama. He died in Chicago on January 23, 2015, eight days before his 84th birthday. When the Cubs finally won the World Series in 2016, the crowds visiting Ernie's grave at Graceland Cemetery, about a half mile north of Wrigley, were so large that police needed to work around the clock in order to control the traffic.

After Banks's death Fred Mitchell, a longtime friend of Ernie's and the first Black sportswriter for the *Chicago Tribune*, wrote that when Banks was playing for the Cubs in the late 1950s, "there were restaurants in America where he was turned away, establishments he could not frequent and houses he could not rent or purchase because of the color of his skin. . . . Yet more than 50 years later, Banks never expressed bitterness or resentment."[20]

◆ ◆ ◆

In 1956 Minnie Miñoso showed that he was fully recovered from his 1955 beaning, hitting .316—28 points higher than in '55—with 21 home runs. But in 1957 the White Sox replaced manager Marty Marion with Al Lopez, who had been the Cleveland Indians' manager when Miñoso was traded to the White Sox in 1951. Despite another good year for Minnie in 1957, the White Sox traded him after the season to Cleveland, whose new general manager was Minnie's "Daddy No. 2," Frank Lane. Miñoso thus missed out on being part of the first White Sox pennant in 40 years.

In 1960 the White Sox, now under the ownership of Bill Veeck, reacquired Miñoso; he celebrated his return by hitting two home runs with six RBI on Opening Day. Veeck, always one of Miñoso's biggest fans, sold the team in 1961; that winter the White Sox traded Minnie to the St. Louis Cardinals. ("I must admit that I never stayed long on a team managed by Al Lopez," Miñoso wrote in one of his autobiographies.)[21] A month into the 1962 season he crashed into the outfield wall at Busch Stadium, sustaining a fractured right wrist and several fractures on the right side of his face. Miñoso missed more than two months while recovering. Two days after his return, he was struck above the eye by a thrown ball during batting practice, affecting his vision. Then, in August, Miñoso's left forearm was fractured when he was hit by a pitch. He missed the rest of the season, finishing the year with a .196 average.

After the 1962 injuries, Miñoso was never again an effective major league hitter. He went to the Mexican League in 1965 and stayed for nine years, hitting above .300 into his late 40s. In 1976, when Veeck purchased control of the White Sox for the second time, he hired Minnie as one of his coaches. In 1976 and 1980 Veeck put Minnie on the active roster late in the year. In 1976 Miñoso, who was 52 years old according to Baseball Reference, got a hit off Angels pitcher Sid Monge; when he played again late in 1980, Minnie became only the second player to perform in the majors in five different decades (Nick Altrock was the first). In 1990 the White Sox considered activating Minnie in order to make him a six-decade man, but commissioner Fay Vincent vetoed the idea. Still, Miñoso played in a game in 1993, and another in 2003, for the independent league St. Paul Saints, a team owned by Bill Veeck's son Mike. Those appearances made Miñoso the only player to perform in professional baseball in seven different decades.

While they underscore Miñoso's longevity, the late-season stunts may have diverted attention from Miñoso's stellar credentials as both a player and a racial pioneer. He was not elected to the National Baseball Hall of Fame until 2022, seven years after his death. (Sadly, Miñoso's induction class also included Buck O'Neil, who had died at age 94 in 2006.) Miñoso did live to see the White Sox retire his jersey number, 9 (in 1983) and the unveiling of a statue in his honor at Guaranteed Rate Field (in 2004). During his lifetime he was inducted into the Cuban Baseball Hall of Fame (1983), the Mexican Professional Baseball Hall of Fame (1996), and the Hispanic Heritage Baseball Museum Hall of Fame (2002).

In an interview, Miñoso's son Charlie called Minnie's posthumous Baseball Hall of Fame induction "very bittersweet, given dad was elected the first time he was eligible since his passing. I just wish he would have been here to experience it, to celebrate it, to feel it even just for a day." Charlie recalled learning from his eldest brother Orestes Jr., who was born in 1952, that Orestes and their dad often had to stay at different hotels from the rest of the team when they were traveling together. "There were so many similar instances; my dad would mention them, but he would never let that define his playing career," said Charlie. "It took quite some time for me to understand the toll it took, because he didn't dwell on negativity. Orestes, Jr. had a front row seat to our dad's career, including playing professionally with him in Mexico, which contributed to dad's induction into the Mexican Baseball Hall of Fame. Orestes, Jr. passing from ALS months before our dad's induction into Cooperstown was another blow—not only was our father deprived of the celebration during his lifetime, but so was his greatest fan."[22]

◆ ◆ ◆

"When something happens that turns out to be so successful, it's seen as inevitable," said Jules Tygiel about the Dodgers' signing of Jackie Robinson. "Nothing surrounding Jackie was inevitable. This was an experiment. And experiments can fail."[23] Robinson's debut was successful by any measure, as was, ultimately, the 1947 debut of Larry Doby, the American League's first Black player. Yet there was no stampede by other white major league teams to tap into this new source of talent. At the start of the 1951 season only two other teams, the New York Giants and the Boston Braves, had Black players on their roster. "Many teams stalwartly resisted desegregation," wrote Tygiel. "Others moved haltingly, bypassing established Negro League stars in favor of young prospects and demanding higher standards of performance from black players than white." There was also a feeling, expressed even by such astute Black sportswriters as Wendell Smith, that there were few Black players qualified to play in the majors.[24]

Then, on April 30, 1951, the White Sox joined the ranks of integrated MLB teams when they traded for Orestes Miñoso. He had such an impact that Washington Senators president Clark Griffith, long a foe of baseball integration, gushed, "That Miñoso is terrific. I wish I had found him. I wonder how my Cuban agents overlooked him. Give me Miñoso and you will see the first Negro on the Senators."[25]

On September 17, 1953, Ernie Banks became the Chicago Cubs' first Black player. By the end of the 1954 season, Banks and his Black double-play partner, Gene Baker, were regarded by many as the best shortstop–second base combination in baseball. At that point, only a few major league teams were holding out against adding Black players to their rosters. The success of the Black players on both of Chicago's MLB teams made it fairly obvious that it was no longer possible for an MLB team to remain segregated and hope to win.

The White Sox were the sixth major league team to integrate; depending on how you count Carlos Bernier with the Pirates, the Cubs were either the eighth or ninth. Given Chicago's large Black population and its long, proud Black baseball history, one has to ask: Why did it take them so long? Until they hired Frank Lane in the late 1940s, the Comiskey family, who owned the White Sox, was stodgy, conservative, and not one to make waves. It took Lane, and especially field manager Paul Richards to finally change things. Phil Wrigley and the Cubs are harder to figure. Wrigley prided himself on being an innovator, and during much of the 1940s, it seemed as though the Cubs were going to be the first MLB team to integrate . . . or the second . . . or the third. But Wrigley could never quite summon the nerve; as much as anything, it was the success of Miñoso and the White Sox that finally convinced the Cubs to cross the line.

It is good that they did, but no real credit should go to the Cubs, or the White Sox, for finally taking a step that was obviously the right thing to do. When they did, both clubs wound up with players so talented and beloved that each team erected statues of them at their ballpark. In a more enlightened world both teams would have integrated decades earlier, and the first statues at their ballparks would have honored Josh Gibson or Satchel Paige or Double Duty Radcliffe or Oscar Charleston. In the same enlightened world, there would also have been more opportunities in baseball, and in life, for the forgotten heroes who never reached the "white" major leagues, such as Charles Pope and Gideon Applegate and Alvin Spearman and Billy Hart.

We did have Minnie and Ernie. Chicago, and the world, are much the better for that.

Notes

Chapter 1. The Comet . . . and the Riot

1. According to a 1968 *Sports Illustrated* article, Lane made a total of 241 deals involving 353 players during his seven-year stint with the White Sox (Mark Kram, "Would You Trade with This Man?" *Sports Illustrated*, August 26, 1968, 30–35).

2. During his major league career and in his 1983 autobiography, Miñoso listed his birth year as 1922. Later in life Miñoso claimed that he was actually born in 1925. The Baseball Hall of Fame, the Society for American Baseball Research, and baseball-reference.com now list his birth year as 1923.

3. Ed McCauley, "Tribe's Minoso Gets Make-Good Chance," *Sporting News*, May 11, 1949, 11.

4. Mitch Angus, "More Padre Duty Looms for Minnie," *San Diego Union*, March 14, 1951, 23.

5. Furman Bisher, "Major League Minnie," *Sport*, August 1954, 5.

6. Gordon Cobbledick, "Plain Dealing," *Cleveland Plain Dealer*, February 15, 1951, 20.

7. Miller, *Whole Different Ball Game*, 39–40.

8. Kram, "Would You Trade?" 32.

9. Davis J. Walsh, "Minoso's Debut Stirs Fans," *Chicago Herald-American*, May 1, 1951, 21.

10. Minnie Miñoso, interviewed by Larry Crowe, June 7, 2002, The HistoryMakers Digital Archive, file A2002.084, tape 3, story 2, https://www.the historymakers.org/biography/minnie-minoso-39.

11. Davis J. Walsh, "Sox Lose, 8–3; Miñoso Homer"; "Miñoso No Rookie—Paige," *Chicago Herald-American*, May 2, 1951, 18.

12. Davis J. Walsh sports column, *Chicago Herald-American*, May 18, 1951, 26.

13. Russ J. Cowans, "Russ' Corner," *Chicago Defender* (national ed.), May 26, 1951, 16.

14. *Cincinnati Enquirer* quoted in Burgos, *Playing America's Game*, 97–98.

15. Bretón and Villegas, *Away Games*, 107.

16. Cepeda and Fagen, *Baby Bull*, 12–13.

17. Author interview with Marcos Bretón, March 25, 2022.

18. Miñoso, Fernandez, and Kleinfelder, *Extra Innings*, 55.

19. Peary, We Played the Game, 207.

20. Miñoso, Fernandez, and Kleinfelder, *Extra Innings*, 66.

21. Edgar Munzel, "Miñoso, as Batting Leader, Also No. 1 Target for Duster," *Sporting News*, June 27, 1951, 10.

22. John C. Hoffman, "Chicago's Minnie Hot-Shot," *Baseball Digest*, October 1951, 50.

23. "Sherif [sic] Defends Negro Family Against Crowd," *Chicago Tribune*, July 11, 1951, 14.

24. "Judge Warns Cicero Officials They Must Guard Negro Family," *Chicago Tribune*, June 27, 1951, 8.

25. Ruth Moore, "How Clarks View the Cicero Riots," *Chicago Sun-Times*, July 15, 1951, 3.

26. N. Moore, *South Side*, 212.

27. Miñoso and Fagen, *Just Call Me Minnie*, 78–79; Branson, *Greatness in the Shadows*, 52. Chicago apartment listings in 2022 described the Del Prado as follows: "Built in 1920, Del Prado was one of the largest of Hyde Park's fashionable apartment hotels and attracted famous visitors, including Amelia Earhart, Babe Ruth, Mickey Mantle, Yogi Berra, and Joe Dimaggio" . . . all white celebrities. www.apartmentlist.com/il/chicago/del-prado.

28. "Six Indicted in Cicero Riot," *Chicago Tribune*, September 19, 1951, 1.

29. "The Cicero Indictments," *Chicago Sun-Times*, September 20, 1941, 33.

30. Ed Burns, "Miñoso, Fox on White Sox 'No Sale' List," *Sporting News*, October 10, 1951, 16.

31. Edgar Munzel, "Rookie Class Led by Mays and Miñoso," *Sporting News*, September 19, 1951, 1.

32. Arch Ward, "In the Wake of the News," *Chicago Tribune*, October 4, 1951, 71.

33. Edgar Munzel, "McDougald Top Rookie," *Chicago Sun-Times*, November 16, 1951, 72.

34. Edgar Munzel, "Change or Scrap Player Awards—Lane," *Sporting News*, November 28, 1951, 1.

Chapter 2. A Long and Winding Road

1. Heaphy, *Black Baseball in Chicago*, 7–17.

2. Hogan, *Shades of Glory*, 77–78.

3. Hogan, *Shades of Glory*, 111–12.

4. Author interview with Leslie Heaphy, April 26, 2022.

5. Tim Odzer, Rube Foster SABR biography, sabr.org/bioproj/person/andrew-rube-foster/#_ednref40.

6. Krist, *City of Scoundrels*, 169–73, 182, 209–11, 236–37.

7. Matt Kelly, "The Negro National League Is Founded," n.d., baseballhall.org/discover-more/stories/inside-pitch/negro-national-league-is-founded.

8. Larry Lester is quoted in Ryan Nilsson, "Founder of the Negro Leagues Was Not Your Average Rube," chicago.suntimes.com/2020/7/12/21317798/negro-leagues-rube-foster-anniversary.

9. John Bauer, "The Chicago American Giants: A History," sabr.org/research/article/the-chicago-american-giants-a-history.

10. Heaphy, *Black Baseball in Chicago*, 20.

11. Wilson, *Let's Play Two*, 5.

12. Profile of Ernie Banks, The HistoryMakers Digital Archive, file A2000.003, tape 2, story 7, https://www.thehistorymakers.org/biography/ernie-banks-40.

13. Profile of Ernie Banks, The HistoryMakers Digital Archive, file A2000.003, tape 1, story 10, https://www.thehistorymakers.org/biography/ernie-banks-40.

14. Lester is quoted in Heaphy, *Black Baseball in Chicago*, 181.

15. Wendell Smith, "Only 10,000 Fans See West Defeat East, 5–1," *New Pittsburgh Courier*, August 22, 1953, 15.

16. Hogan, *Shades of Glory*, 288.

17. Ward and Burns, *Baseball*, 198.

18. Dixon, *Dizzy and Daffy Dean Barnstorming Tour*, 2, 90, 181, 191, 203.

19. Wendell Smith, "Would Be a Mad Scramble for Negro Players if Okayed," *Pittsburgh Courier*, August 12, 1939, 16.

20. Wendell Smith, "Are Negro Ball Players Good Enough to 'Crash' the Majors?" *Pittsburgh Courier*, July 15, 1939, 13.

21. Herman Hill, "Chi White Sox Reject Race Players," *Pittsburgh Courier*, March 21, 1942, 16.

22. A. S. (Doc) Young, "Dedicated Writers and Editors Paved Way for Integration of Major Sports," *Ebony*, October 1970, 61.

23. "Jackie Robertson Stars on Diamond," *Pittsburgh Courier*, March 16, 1940, 16; Herman Hill, "Jackie Tempted by Offers," *Pittsburgh Courier*, March 1, 1941, 16; Hill, "Chi White Sox Reject Race Players."

24. Hill, "Chi White Sox Reject Race Players."

25. Forrest is quoted in William Hageman, "Chicago's 55-Year-Old Secret: Jackie Robinson's Tryout with the White Sox," *Chicago Tribune*, March 26, 1997, 239. Hageman's article, written years before most newspapers became available in digital form, contains a few factual errors but also includes some fascinating speculation from writers and historians about what might have happened had Robinson signed with the White Sox.

26. Joe Cummiskey, "Landis Steps to Bat for Negro Ball Players," *PM*, July

17, 1942, 30. The Durocher quotation is only credited to "a writer" in Cummiskey's article, but Rodney makes clear that it was him, as quoted in Silber, *Press Box Red*, 69–70.

27. Cummiskey, "Landis Steps to Bat."

28. Tom Meany is quoted in Cummiskey, "Landis Steps to Bat."

29. "'I've Seen a Million!'—Leo Durocher," *Pittsburgh Courier*, August 5, 1939, 16.

30. "Judge Landis Decision—Bosh!" *Chicago Defender*, July 25, 1942; "Baseball Season Over: No Big League Tryouts . . . Run-Around Given Negro Ball-Players . . . Lots of Wild Talk, But No Action by Owners or Managers," *Chicago Defender*, October 10, 1942, 24.

31. Author interview with Ed Hartig, January 17, 2022.

32. Dickson, *Bill Veeck*, 74.

33. Fay Young, "Through the Years," *Chicago Defender*, May 30, 1942, 19.

34. Frederick C. Bush, "July 26, 1942: Monarchs' Satchel Paige Garners the Victory on Day in His Honor at Wrigley Field," SABR Baseball Games Project, sabr.org/gamesproj/game/july-26-1942-satchel-paige-garners-the-victory-on-day-in-his-honor; "Kansas City and Memphis Divide Paige Day Games," *Chicago Tribune*, July 27, 1942, 17.

35. Dickson, *Bill Veeck*, 75.

36. "Chicago Cubs' Owner Envisions Major League Doors' Opening to Colored Soon," *Baltimore African-American*, December 26, 1943, 3.

37. "Chicago Cubs' Owner."

38. "Chicago Cubs' Owner."

39. "Chicago Cubs' Owner."

40. Patterson, *Man Who Cried Genocide*, 144.

41. "Coast Owner Refuses Negro Players Tryout," *Pittsburgh Courier*, March 27, 1943, 18.

42. "Negro Pitcher May Get Tryout with Los Angeles Club of Coast League," *Chicago Defender*, December 12, 1942, 21.

43. "Coast Owner Refuses Negro Players Tryout."

44. Holway, *Voices from the Great Black Baseball Leagues*, 12.

45. Lanctot, *Negro League Baseball*, 243–44.

46. Veeck and Linn, *Veeck—As in Wreck*, 171.

47. Dickson, *Bill Veeck*, 79–80.

48. Dickson, *Bill Veeck*, 357–66.

49. Bob Considine, "On the Line," *New York Journal-American*, January 12, 1944.

50. Transcript, BA MSS 105 Joint Major League Meeting, baseballhall.org/discover-more/digital-collection/1389.

51. Fay Young, "Cub Prexy Wrigley to Hire Scout for Race Ball Clubs," *Chicago Defender*, December 25, 1943, 1.

52. Dan Burley, "'Cubs' Might Hire Negroes," *New York Amsterdam News*, January 15, 1944, 1A.

53. Patterson, *Man Who Cried Genocide*, 143.

54. The Major League Baseball statement is quoted in Stanley Frank, "Negroes Receive Wordy 'Brushoff' from Baseball," *New York Post*, December 4, 1943, 22.

55. Frank, "Negroes Receive Wordy 'Brushoff'."

Chapter 3. Not in Our Back Yard

1. Fay Young, "Through the Years," *Chicago Defender*, June 23, 1945.

2. Author interview with Ed Hartig, January 17, 2022.

3. "Need for Commissioner Seen in Rowdyism at Ball Parks," *Philadelphia Tribune*, July 28, 1945, 13.

4. L. S. MacPhail, statement of opinion on "The Negro in Baseball," National Baseball Hall of Fame Library, HOF BA MSS 67, box 1.

5. Sam Lacy, "Looking 'Em Over," *Baltimore Afro-American*, September 29, 1945, 29.

6. Jules Tygiel with John Thorn, "Jackie Robinson's Signing: The Untold Story," in Tygiel, *Extra Bases*, 26.

7. Lowenfish, *Branch Rickey*, 371–72.

8. "Montreal Puts Negro Player on Spot," *Sporting News*, November 1, 1945, 12.

9. Letters to Larry MacPhail from Clark Griffith, Connie Mack, William Benswanger, and Harry Grabiner, National Baseball Hall of Fame Library, HOF BA MSS 67, box 1.

10. "Baseball Democracy," *Chicago Sun*, October 25, 1945, 14; "Robinson Comes to Bat," *Chicago Daily News*, October 25, 1945, 10; John Carmichael, "The Barber Shop," *Chicago Daily News*, October 25, 1945, 33; Gene Kessler, "Negro Clubs Asked for It," *Chicago Daily Times*, October 25, 1945, 38; Associated Press, "Rickey Calls Robinson Top Ball Prospect But Doesn't Think He's Big Leaguer," *Chicago Tribune*, October 25, 1945, 29.

11. Tygiel, *Baseball's Great Experiment*, 82–83.

12. Tygiel, *Jackie Robinson Reader*, 129–33.

13. Si Burick, "Rickey Blasts Magnates in Unfolding Jackie Robinson Story," *Dayton Daily News*, February 17, 1948, 16.

14. Author interview with Doug Wilson, May 8, 2022.

15. David Fleitz, Cap Anson SABR biography, sabr.org/bioproj/person/cap-anson/.

16. David Kauffman, "Did Bud Fowler Almost Break the Major-League Color Line in 1888?" 76–77.

17. Golenbock, *Wrigleyville*, 343.

18. Golenbock, *Wrigleyville*, 343–44.

19. Stanley Woodward, "Views of Sport," *New York Herald Tribune* story reprinted in *Sporting News*, May 21, 1947, 4.

20. Warren Corbett, "The 'Strike' Against Jackie Robinson: Truth or Myth?" *Baseball Research Journal* 46, no. 1 (2017): 88–92.

21. Tygiel, *Baseball's Great Experiment*, 187.

22. Kahn, *Into My Own*, 34.

23. John Nelson, "ESPN Uncovers Evidence of Players' Conspiracy When Robinson Took Field," *Scranton Tribune*, February 28, 1997, 13.

24. Tygiel, *Baseball's Great Experiment*, 188.

25. Golenbock, *Wrigleyville*, 345.

26. "Robinson Makes Dodger Debut; Fans Are Orderly," *Chicago Defender*, May 24, 1947, 20.

27. "Sox to Sign Negro Pitcher?" *Chicago Times*, July 6, 1947, 59.

28. "Cubs to Look Over 2 Negroes," *Chicago Defender*, September 20, 1947, 20.

29. "John Ritchey Ready to Join Cubs Farm in Des Moines," *Chicago Defender*, September 20, 1947, 20.

30. "Negro Backstop Given Chicago Cubs Tryout," *New York Amsterdam News*, September 27, 1947, 12.

31. Hartig interview; Jack Sheehan to J. B. Martin, National Baseball Hall of Fame, Integration Correspondence.

32. Hartig interview.

33. Essington, *Integration of the Pacific Coast League*, 64–65.

34. Hirsch, *Making the Second Ghetto*, 54–55.

Chapter 4. Beginning Their Journey

1. Miñoso and Fagen, *Just Call Me Minnie*, 7–10.

2. Miñoso and Fagen, *Just Call Me Minnie*, 10–17.

3. Miñoso and Fagen, *Just Call Me Minnie*, 25–26.

4. Joe Cummiskey, "Landis Steps to Bat for Negro Ball Players," *PM*, July 17, 1942.

5. Miñoso and Fagen, *Just Call Me Minnie*, 36.

6. Green, *Spinning the Globe*, 203–4, 208–9.

7. Al Vaughn, "Good Ballplayers for Sale," *Chicago Star*, March 13, 1948, 11.

8. Lanctot, *Negro League Baseball*, 336.

9. J. G. Taylor Spink, "Two Ill-Advised Moves," *Sporting News*, July 14, 1948, 8.

10. Veeck and Linn, *Veeck as in Wreck*, 184–85.

11. Ed Burns, "Author Burns Burns up over Chisox' Plight," *Sporting News*, August 25, 1948, 4.

12. William Warren, "White Sox Need Negro Players Like Larry Doby!" *Chicago Defender*, May 8, 1948, 10; "Chicago White Sox Ignore Gold Mine in Negro Talent," *Atlanta Daily World*, May 25, 1948, 5.

13. Gene Kessler, "Veeck to Set All-Time High," *Chicago Sun-Times*, August 12, 1948, 58.

14. Gene Kessler, "Bicycles Built for 150," *Chicago Sun-Times*, September 3, 1948, 58; John C. Hoffman, "Sox Seeking Negro Stars," *Chicago Sun-Times*, August 16, 1948, 54.

15. Harold Burr, "B.R. Offers to Help Cubs—$500,000 for Newcombe!" *Sporting News*, October 27, 1948, 14.

16. Bots Nekola Negro League Scouting Reports, National Baseball Hall of Fame Library, HOF BA MSS 67, box 1.

17. J. Moore, *Larry Doby*, 92.

18. Bots Nekola Negro League Scouting Reports.

19. New York Yankees Negro League Scouting Reports, National Baseball Hall of Fame Library, HOF BA MSS 67, box 1.

20. Miñoso, Fernandez, and Kleinfelder, *Extra Innings*, 37–38.

21. Gordon Cobbledick, "Plain Dealing," *Cleveland Plain Dealer*, October 24, 1948, 24; Miñoso and Fagen, *Just Call Me Minnie*, 37.

22. Miñoso and Fagen, *Just Call Me Minnie*, 39–41.

23. Ernie Banks, interviewed by Julieanna L. Richardson, July 18, 2000, The HistoryMakers Digital Archive, session 1, tape 2, story 9, https://www.the historymakers.org/biography/ernie-banks-40.

24. Rapoport, *Let's Play Two*, 37–38.

Chapter 5. Pioneers

1. Wendell Smith, "Cubs Sign 1st Negro Player," *Chicago Herald-American*, March 24, 1949, 18.

2. "Chicago Cubs Outbid Pirates, Reds for Negro Catcher," *Michigan Chronicle*, April 2, 1949, 12.

3. Royal, Ellinger, and Bradley, *Allensworth*, 41–42.

4. Bob Crawford, "Bobbin' Around," *Visalia (CA) Times-Delta*, May 3, 1949, 8.

5. "Three Visalia Rookies Eye Future Major League Berths," *Pittsburgh Courier*, May 14, 1949, 24.

6. "Visalia Cubs Hand Catcher Charlie Pope Outright Release," *Tulare (CA) Advance-Register*, June 13, 1949, 2.

7. Author interview with Traci Carr, June 12, 2022.

8. Carr interview.

9. Carr interview.

10. Bob Burns family interview posted on Demica Williams's Facebook page, facebook.com/demica.williams.

11. Les Stearns, "Burns Becomes First Negro to Sign Home City Contract," *Springfield (MA) Union*, May 25, 1949, 28; "Cubs Ship Negro Pitcher Bob Burns to Sioux Falls," *Springfield (MA) Union*, July 12, 1949, 18.

12. Quisenberry's remarks are found at cleveland.com/profiles-of-service/2016/02/vietnam_sergeant_accepting_vet.html#:~:text=CLEVELAND%2C%20Ohio%20%2D%2D%20On%20Feb,one%20particular%20man%20in%20mind.

13. Burns family interview.

14. There are several formulas for computing WAR; this book uses the formula as computed by baseball-reference.com.

15. "Angels Sign Booker M'Daniels," *Los Angeles Sentinel*, June 16, 1949, A6.

16. Tommy Kouzmanoff, "Milt Bohanion, Argo Catcher, Unanimous H-A Star Choice," *Chicago Herald-American*, June 11, 1949, 14.

17. Author interview with Sarah Nicholson, November 4, 2021.

18. Ted Talbert, "Opportunity Denied Regrettable All Around," *Detroit Free Press*, March 19, 2003, 38.

19. Ofield Dukes, "Five Negro Leaders Deserve Credit for Detroit Baseball Reformation," *Michigan Chronicle*, June 21, 1958, 14.

20. Merl F. Kleinknecht, "Integration of Baseball After World War II," *1983 Baseball Research Journal*, sabr.org/journal/article/integration-of-baseball-after-world-war-ii.

21. Sammy Gee (as told to Bill Matney), "'I've Been Nervous' Gee Tells Bill Matney," *Michigan Chronicle*, July 12, 1947, 4; Will Robinson, "Gee Has the Jitters in His First Games," *Pittsburgh Courier*, July 19, 1947, 14.

22. "Batting Marks of Gee, Teasley in 'Nose Dive'," *Pittsburgh Courier*, June 5, 1948, 14; Garland, *Bittersweet Memories*, 87.

23. Author interview with Ron Teasley, June 14, 2022.

24. Teasley interview.

25. Jack Saylor, "Black Legends to Honor Greats Holloway, Gee," *Detroit Free Press*, February 17, 1999, 27.

26. Letter to the editor, "Job Prejudice," *Sioux Falls Argus-Leader*, August 11, 1949, 6.

27. Derek Gentile, "The Hart of Williamstown: William F. 'Billy' Hart's Legendary Career Earns Him No. 2 Spot on Eagle's Top 50 Athletes of the 20th Century List," *Berkshire (MA) Eagle*, October 2, 2017.

28. Spence Sandvig, "F-M Twins Snip Canary Winning Streak 8–1," *Sioux Falls Argus-Leader*, August 8, 1949, 13.

29. Author interview with Shelley Arnold, April 6, 2022.

30. "College All Stars Down Holy Cross Senior Five," *North Adams (MA) Transcript*, May 4, 1950, 19. "Offside," *North Adams* (MA) *Transcript*, October 27, 1952, 8.

31. "William 'Billy' Hart, Businessman," *North Adams (MA) Transcript*, March 28, 1995, 2; Gentile, "Hart of Williamstown."

Chapter 6. New Men, Old Ideas

1. Lindberg, *Stealing First in a Two-Team Town*, 119.

2. Lindberg, *Stealing First in a Two-Team Town*, 129.

3. Jack Ryan, "We'd Like You to Meet: The Third Comiskey," *Baseball Digest*, March 1949, 10.

4. Jack Ryan, "Young Comiskey Comes Up Swinging," *Sporting News*, November 24, 1948, 5.

5. "Chicago White Sox Eye Brooklyn Stars," *Atlanta Daily World*, December 15, 1948, 5.

6. "The Future of Negroes in Big League Baseball," *Ebony*, May 1949, 34; Wendell Smith, "Ability, Not Color Sox Test, Lane Says," *Chicago Herald-American*, April 2, 1949, 14.

7. Roger Treat column, *Chicago Herald-American*, February 6, 1949, sec. 2, p. 6.

8. A. S. "Doc" Young, "Sportivanting," *Chicago Defender*, June 19, 1949, 15.

9. "Cubs Sign Negro Scout," *Pittsburgh Courier*, April 2, 1949, 24; Rapoport, *Let's Play Two*, 74; on the Donaldson signing, see Wendell Smith, "Bulletin," *Chicago Herald-American*, June 28, 1949, 14; Comiskey is quoted in "Bulletin," *Chicago Herald-American*, June 28, 1949, 14; Klima is quoted in Bush and Nowlin, *Bittersweet Goodbye*, 401.

10. Jack Ryan, "Sparks Fly Between Jawing Jack and Firecracker Frank," *Sporting News*, June 15, 1949, 9.

11. "Rickey Delays Sale of Jethroe to Major Leagues, Says Frank Lane," *Chicago Defender*, August 277, 1949, 16.

12. Ed Prell, "Sox Spend $250,000 on Rookies!" *Chicago Tribune*, August 18, 1949, 39.

13. Gietschier, *Baseball*, 119–20.

14. Gietschier, *Baseball*, 325.

15. "Bob Feller Sees Few Players Making Grade," *Ebony*, May 1949, 39.

16. "Bob Feller Sees Few Players Making Grade."

17. Sam Lacy, "Indian Star Larry Doby Forced to Live Apart," *Baltimore Afro-American*, March 5, 1949, 15.

18. Sam Lacy, "Indians' Tan Trio Compelled to Walk to Ballpark by Bigoted Texas Taxis," in *Black Writers/Black Baseball*, 30–31.

19. Jim Schlemmer, "Park Packs," *Akron Beacon Journal*, April 17, 149, 37.

20. Oscar Ruhl, "From the Ruhl Book," *Sporting News*, August 10, 1949, 14.

21. Bill Nunn Jr., "Pittsburgh Pirates Manager Slurs Negro Ball Players," *Pittsburgh Courier*, September 17, 1949.

22. Jack Hernon, "Roamin' Around," *Pittsburgh Post-Gazette*, April 2, 1957, 21.

23. Edgar Munzel, "Indians Corner Negro Stars," *Chicago Sun-Times*, March 27, 1949, 70.

24. Ned Cronin, "Señor Cronin Spik with Orestes—Falls Back on an Interpreter," *Sporting News*, June 26, 1949, 23.

25. Miñoso, Fernandez, and Kleinfelder, *Extra Innings*, 44.

26. Randy Galloway, "From Dallas to Cooperstown," *Dallas Morning News*, January 20, 1977, 1.

27. Wilson, *Let's Play Two*, 22.

28. Banks and Enright, *Mr. Cub*, 41.

Chapter 7. At Wid's End

1. Edgar Munzel, "Rickey Dominance Seen in Clip by Cubs," *Sporting News*, October 26, 1949, 1.

2. Edgar Munzel, "'Never Sold Player Worth a Quarter,'" *Sporting News*, November 9, 1949, 5.

3. Gene Kessler, "Wisecracks Backfire," *Chicago Sun-Times*, November 14, 1949, 69.

4. Edgar Munzel, "Cubs Grab Rickey-Trained Matthews as Talent Dealer," *Sporting News*, February 22, 1950, 9; Munzel, "Never Sold Player Worth a Quarter."

5. Lowenfish, *Branch Rickey*, 368; Rapoport, *Let's Play Two*, 78; Klima, *Willie's Boys*, 22–23.

6. Art Daley, "Speed Demon Janes Can Steal Anytime They Wish—Butch," *Green Bay Post-Gazette*, May 20, 1950, 13; "Sports Hash," *Janesville Daily Gazette*, May 26, 1950, 8, and July 31, 1950, 12.

7. Posnanski, *Baseball 100*, 420; Taylor, *Walking Alone*, 76; author interview with Dan Taylor, December 14, 2022.

8. Wendell Smith to Branch Rickey, December 19, 1945, Wendell Smith Papers, BA MSS 1, National Baseball Hall of Fame Library; Roger Birtwell, "Air Duel Looms as Yanks Battle Champion Rams," *Boston Globe*, November 24, 1946, 24.

9. Stanley O. Williford, "Washington's Friends Play Last Respects," *Los Angeles Times*, June 30, 1971, 59.

10. T. Y. Baird Papers, Kenneth Spencer Research Library, University of Kansas.

11. Vic Wall, "Forbes Is Assigned to Cubs by Decatur Squad," *Springfield (MA) Union*, March 31, 1950, 32.

12. Email to author from Joe Black biographer Chuck Schoffner, February 20, 2023; Jeff Angus, Jim Gilliam SABR biography, sabr.org/bioproj/person/jim-gilliam/#_ednref12.

13. Les Stearns, "Bernier's Speed Catches Fancy of Cub Manager," *Springfield (MA) Union*, March 18, 1950, 26.

14. Hogan, *Shades of Glory*, 304.

15. Baird Papers; Fay Young, "Fay Says," *Chicago Defender*, April 29, 1959, 17.

16. "Thurman, in Newark Debut, Hits Homer, Two Singles," *Hackensack Record*, July 30, 1949, 8; Rod Marvin, "For the Record," *Hackensack Record*, August 19, 1949, 12; "Yankees May Call Thurman Next Season," *Pittsburgh Courier*, September 10, 1949.

17. Rick Swaine, Bob Thurman SABR biography, sabr.org/bioproj/person/bob-thurman/.

18. Tony Cooper, "Breaking the PCL Color Barrier," *San Francisco Chronicle*, March 1, 1993.

19. Robert Obojski, "SCD Profiles Former Reds Outfielder Bob Thurman," *Sports Collectors Digest*, October 11, 1991.

20. Cooper, "Breaking the PCL Color Barrier."

21. Baird papers.

22. Les Stearns, "Bernier's Speed Catches Fancy of Cub Manager," *Springfield (MA) Union*, March 18, 1950, 26.

23. Les Stearns, "Cubs Turn Back Kansas City Blues in First Exhibition Contest," *Springfield (MA) Union*, March 20, 1950, 8.

24. Matt Zabitka, "Ferrell Lived a Baseball Dream," *Wilmington Morning News*, August 12, 1975, 25.

25. Wendy Fox, "It Was Habit—Getting Peaches from That Tree," *Wilmington Morning News*, August 12, 1985, 25; Jordan Howell, "The Girl and the Peach Tree" (two-part series), *Delaware Today*, July 22 and September 1, 2020.

26. "Bail Now $130,000, Bailey in Jail," *Wilmington Morning News*, August 12, 1975, 2; Howell, "The Girl and the Peach Tree."

27. Howell, "The Girl and the Peach Tree"; Howard Leroy "Toots" Ferrell Jr. obituary, *Wilmington News Journal*, October 16, 2002, 18. Doug Lesemerises, "Negro Leaguers Work to Keep Memories Alive," *Wilmington News Journal*, June 18, 2003, 23.

28. Dan Burley, "Dan Burley on Sports," *New York Age*, May 6, 1950, 22.

29. "White Sox Are Seeking Colored Ball Players," *Chicago Defender*, July 8, 1950, 18.

30. Brent Kelley interview with Bob Boyd, February 15, 1991, https://sabr.org/interview/bob-boyd-1991/.

31. "Hairston Paces Loop Top Hitters," *Chicago Defender*, August 12, 1950, 16.

32. Wilson, *Let's Play Two*, 25–26.

33. Fred Mitchell, "Banks, Williams Laud Pioneer's Work," *Chicago Tribune*, October 8, 2006, sec. 3, p. 4.

34. Ernie Banks, interviewed by Julieanna L. Richardson, July 18, 2000, The HistoryMakers Digital Archive, session 1, tape 3, story 1, https://www.thehistorymakers.org/biography/ernie-banks-40.

35. Diane Euston with contributing historian Tim Reidy, "Dissecting the Troost Divide and Racial Segregation in Kansas City," martincitytelegraph.com/2020/06/30/dissecting-the-troost-divide-and-racial-segregation-in-kansas-city; Rapoport, *Let's Play Two*, 57.

Chapter 8. Window Dressing

1. Editorial, *California Eagle*, August 1, 1940, 15.

2. Rampersad, *Jackie Robinson*, 31.

3. Williams is quoted in Hudson, *West of Jim Crow*, 1.

4. Edgar Munzel, "Negro First Sacker Gets Chance to Win Berth on White Sox," *Sporting News*, February 21, 1951.

5. Russ J. Cowans, "Russ' Corner," *Chicago Defender*, March 31, 1951, 16.

6. Lane is quoted in Cowans, "Russ' Corner," *Chicago Defender*, March 31, 1951, 16; "Boyd Will Be in Majors in '52, Richards Predicts," *Sporting News*, April 4, 1951, 22.

7. Curley Grieve, "Sports Parade," *San Francisco Examiner*, May 13, 1951, 32.

8. Sam Hairston, Birmingham Black Barons Oral History interviews, June 16, 1995, bplonline.org/virtual/ContentDMSubjectBrowse.aspx?subject=Hairston%2C%20Sam%2C%201920-1997.

9. Associated Press, "Lonesome Rookie Leaves White Sox to Go Home," *Modesto Bee and News-Herald*, March 15, 1951, 21; Associated Press, "Venezuela Rookie Vows 'Never to Return to Chisox'," *Wilmington Morning News*, March 16, 1951, 51.

10. "Smokers Lost Top Star For 2d Half of Season," *Palm Beach Post*, July 6, 1953, 10; Bobby Hicks, "Luis Garcia Recalled by Toronto Club," *Tampa Tribune*, July 5, 1953, 21.

11. Frederick C. Bush and Mark Panuthos, Bill Powell SABR biography, sabr.org/bioproj/person/bill-powell-2/.

12. Kelley, *Negro Leagues Revisited*, 215–16.

13. Kelley, *Negro Leagues Revisited*, 245; "Nine Devils Meet Black Yankees at Local Park Today," *Bradenton Herald*, April 2, 1950, 11.

14. Kelley, *Voices from the Negro Leagues*, 264–65.

15. Kelley, *Voices from the Negro Leagues*, 179–80.

16. Collie J. Nicholson, "White Sox Scout at Grambling," *Jackson (MS) Advocate*, May 5, 1951, 7.

17. Collie J. Nicholson, "Elliott and King May Become First Bonus Players from Negro College to Enter Organized Baseball," Baton Rouge *Weekly Reader*, May 3, 1952, 11.

18. "Crawford Neal," *Oakland Tribune*, May 17, 1983, 32; "Havenscourt's Neal Dies," *Oakland Tribune*, May 18, 1983, 54.

19. Russ J. Cowans, "Monarch Lefty Setting Record Strikeout Pace," *Sporting News*, June 13, 1951, 10.

20. Kelley, *Voices from the Negro Leagues*, 220–21.

21. *Providence Journal* obituary for Gideon Spence Applegate, originally from East Providence and a resident of Vermont, had died peacefully on Dec. 4, GenealogyBank.com www.genealogybank.com/doc/obituaries/obit/16160DC11322D590-16160DC11322D590.

22. Ronald Melcher, "Fetzer Hurls One-Hit Ball in Squad Tilt," *Hartford Courant*, March 28, 1994, 11; Gideon Applegate, William J. Weiss US Baseball Questionnaires, April 21, 1952, Society for American Baseball Research (SABR), San Diego, California, box 555717.

23. "Applegate Is Speaker at East Providence," *Providence Evening Bulletin*, October 15, 1951, 11.

Chapter 9. The Problems We Must Solve

1. Email from Gary Fink to the author, June 8, 2022.

2. Kelley, *Negro Leagues Revisited*, 138. The Stars, the next-to-last last PCL team to integrate, added their first Black player (Roy Welmaker) in May 1951.

3. Kelley, *Negro Leagues Revisited*, 138.

4. George Raubacher, "Cubs Break Camp; Will Arrive in City Tonight," *Janesville Daily Gazette*, April 27, 1951, 12; "Green, Negro Shortstop, Reports to Janesville Cubs," *Janesville Daily Gazette*, June 13, 1951, 18.

5. "'Over-21-Night' at 2B," *Cedar Rapids Gazette*, May 22, 1953, 15.

6. Author interview with Sarah Nicholson, November 4, 2021.

7. Nicholson interview.

8. Nicholson interview.

9. Edgar Munzel, "Frisch Left Fuming by Sudden Dismissal," *Sporting News*, August 1, 1951, 9; Edgar Munzel, "Cavarretta, as Cub Pilot, Seen as Stand-In for Hack," *Sporting News*, August 1, 1951, 9.

10. Golenbock, *Wrigleyville*, 326.

11. Brian Martin, "The Q&A: Chuck Cooper III on the Celtics' Historic Draft of His Father," www.nba.com/news/qa-chuck-cooper-iii.

12. Ron Kroichick, "The 'Jackie Robinson' of the Bears," *San Francisco Chronicle*, November 13, 2005, 33; "Pacific Mourns the Loss of Eddie Macon '53," www.pacificalumni.org/s/749/16/interior.aspx?sid=749&gid=1&pgid=252&cid=5916&ecid=5916&crid=0&calpgid=15&calcid=701.

13. Demas, *Integrating the Gridiron*, 59–60, 872; Bob Spiegel, "Here's How A&M Campus Reacts to Bright Case Now," *Des Moines Tribune*, October 30, 1951, 1.

14. Rob Darcy, "Schmidly Closes Door on Johnny Bright Disgrace," *Daily O'Collegian*, November 14, 2005, www.ocolly.com/schmidly-closes-door-on-johnny-bright-disgrace/article_1a64f87e-2a42-594d-a6f4-3118499c4380.html.

15. "Why Are They Afraid?" *Chicago Defender*, November 10, 1951, 10.

16. Blake Sebring, "Johnny Bright Could Do It All on the Field," *Fort Wayne News-Sentinel*, December 30, 1999, 1s.

17. Darcy, "Schmidly Closes Door."

18. Dave Hanson, "Bright Not Bitter: Blow Helped Clean up Sports," *Des Moines Tribune*, November 13, 1980, 24.

19. Kyle Fredrickson, "Without Rules: The Untold Story of the Johnny Bright Incident," https://www.ocolly.com/sports/football/without-rules-the-untold-story-of-the-johnny-bright-incident/article_1f5c49e2-198d-11e2-9689-001a4bcf6878.html.

20. Al White, "Five Years Later: Negroes in Big League Baseball," *Our World*, October 1950, 53.

21. Joe King, "Mail Threats Spur Jackie to Bat Volley," *Sporting News*, May 30, 1951, 1.

22. Lowenfish, *Branch Rickey*, 525–26.

23. Jacobson, *Carrying Jackie's Torch*, 127–29.

24. Langston Hughes, "The Progress Made in 1951 Spotlights the Problems That Face Us in 1952," *Chicago Defender*, December 29, 1951, 10.

Chapter 10. A Trying Year

1. Miñoso, Fernandez, and Kleinfelder, *Extra Innings*, 73–74.

2. Echevarría, *Pride of Havana*, 287.

3. Howard Roberts, "Lane Back with Hopes High for Sox," *Chicago Daily News*, January 9, 1952, 37.

4. Sam Lacy, "Bob Boyd Optioned to Seattle Club," *Baltimore African-American*, May 25, 1952, 15.

5. "Riot Principal Tells Police Orders," *Chicago Tribune*, March 12, 1952, 16; "Cicero Chief Not Guilty in Rioting, Judge Rules," *Chicago Sun-Times*, March 13, 1952.

6. "Cicero Chief Not Guilty in Rioting"; "Muffing the Cicero Case," *Chicago Sun-Times*, March 14, 1952, 31.

7. Hap Glaudi, "Looking 'Em Over," *New Orleans Item*, April 8, 1952, 16.

8. Howard Roberts, "Greatests," *Chicago Daily News*, April 15, 1952, 26.

9. Warren Brown as quoted in "Wendell Smith's Sports Beat," *Pittsburgh Courier*, April 19, 1952, 15.

10. "Negroes in Game in N.O. Help Boost Race Relations," *Sporting News*, April 16, 1952, 14; Charles J. Doyle, "Si, Senor! Negro Latins Paste 'Beisbol' Against Bucs," *Pittsburgh Sun-Telegraph*, April 8, 1952, 22; "Wendell Smith's Sports Beat," *Pittsburgh Courier*, April 8, 1952.

11. Reisler, *Black Writers/Black Baseball*, 32.

12. Paul Richards as told to Sam Lacy, "Miñoso Has No Fear—Richards," *Baltimore African-American*, April 8, 1952, 15; "Mag Piece Labels Minnie 'Most Exciting Player'," *Baltimore African-American*, May 6, 1952, 15.

13. John Carmichael, "The Barber Shop," *Chicago Daily News*, May 13, 1952, 21.

14. Author interview with Roberto González Echevarría, May 12, 2021.

15. "Clark on Stand, Says Cicero Cop Brandished Gun," *Chicago Tribune*, May 22, 1952, 21; "Mother Tells How Cicero Rioters Forced Family from Home," *Chicago-Sun Times*, May 23, 1952, 5; "Quotes Police on Orders in Cicero Rioting," *Chicago Sun-Times*, May 27, 1952, 12.

16. "Cicero and American Justice," *Chicago Defender*, June 14, 1952, 10.

17. Mark Tierney, "American Association Loaded with Tan Stars," *Pittsburgh Courier*, April 17, 1954, 15; Ed Bouchette, "Memories Golden Here on a Golden Anniversary," *Pittsburgh Post-Gazette*, May 15, 1997, 11.

18. Kelley, *Voices from the Negro Leagues*, 151.

19. "Perez Gains 6th Win as Sox Defeat Giants, 6–3," *Wisconsin Rapids Daily Tribune*, June 9, 1953, 6.

20. Bretón and Villegas, *Away Games*, 38.

21. "Gideon Spence Applegate: E. Providence Native Applegate Was Pioneer Who Battled the Odds," *Providence Journal*, December 17, 2016, www.genealogybank.com/doc/obituaries/obit/16160DC11322D590-16160DC11322 D590.

22. "Gideon Spencer Applegate."

23. "Sky Sox Protest Cards' Conduct," *Council Bluffs Nonpareil*, July 20, 1952, 23.

24. "Omaha's Prexy Answers Charge," *Wichita Eagle*, July 22, 1952, 10.

25. "Sky Sox President Labels Omaha Reply as 'Nebraska Corn,'" *Sioux City Journal*, July 23, 1952, 13.

26. "Movie Clean-up Bill Offered in Senate," *Los Angeles Times*, March 15, 1950, 1.

27. "Western League Boss Apologizes for Conduct of Omaha Players," *Kansas City Times*, August 7, 1952, 23.

28. Rains, *Taking Flight*, Kindle ed., location 111.

29. Frank L. Hayes, "Faith in US Reaffirmed: Riot Victim," *Chicago Daily News*, November 13, 1952, 11.

Chapter 11. The Forgotten One

1. Patrick Joyce, "Edwards' Arm Brings Hope to Troubled Cubs," *Rock Island Argus*, January 10, 1952, 23; John Edwards, *Cubs Journal*, 370; Robert Boyle, "A Shy Man at a Picnic," *Sports Illustrated*, April 14, 1958, 80; Irving Vaughan, "Wrigley Denies He Criticized Wid Matthews," *Chicago Tribune*, January 11, 1952, 36.

2. J. G. Taylor Spink, "Looping the Loops," *Sporting News*, June 11, 1952, 4.

3. "Mason City Team Leads in Champs," *Oelwein (IA) Daily Register*, March 26, 1943, 6A.

4. Frank Finch, "Bronze Beanpole Casts Big Shadow Over Coast," *Sporting News*, September 13, 1950, 21.

5. T. Y. Baird Papers, Kenneth Spencer Research Library, University of Kansas.

6. Jerry Jurgens, "Sport-O-Scope," *Des Moines Tribune*, May 20, 1950, 7.

7. Maury White, "Baker's Speed, Bat Impress D.M. Fans," *Des Moines Tribune*, June 2, 1950, 20.

8. Gordon Gammack column, *Des Moines Tribune*, June 16, 1950, 1.

9. Hudson, *West of Jim Crow*, 188–207.

10. Hadley Meares, "When Nat King Cole Moved In," la.curbed.com/2018/12/20/18140283/nat-king-cole-house-los-angeles-housing-segregation.

11. Rampersad, *Jackie Robinson*, 70–71.

12. J. Johnson, *Black Bruins*, 141–43.

13. John R. Williams, "Wilson, Baker and Austin Top Shortstops in Pacific Coast Loop," *Chicago Defender*, September 16, 1950, 19.

14. Author interview with Artie Harris, January 10, 2023.

15. Frank Finch, "Bronze Beanpole Casts Big Shadow Over Coast," *Sporting News*, September 13, 1950, 21; Gene Kessler column, *Chicago Sun-Times*, October 2, 1950, 48.

16. A. S. "Doc" Young, "Pirates Scout Gene Baker," *Los Angeles Sentinel*, June 7, 1951, B7; A. S. "Doc" Young, "Stars Take on Oaks, Seals; ChiSox Call Sam Hairston," *Los Angeles Sentinel*, July 26, 1951, B2.

17. Oscar Ruhl, "The Ruhl Book," *Sporting News*, June 25, 1952, 14.

18. Bob Hunter, "Bullet-Arm Baker Aims for Cub Job," *Sporting News*, September 24, 1952, 21; Ed Burns, "Cubs Display Early Foot in Roster Race," *Sporting News*, October 22, 1952, 18; "Cubs to Try Angels' Baker; Seventh Club to List Negro," *Sporting News*, November 12, 1952, 23.

19. Ed Burns, "Cubs' Muster-In Shapes up as Old Home Week Affair," *Sporting News*, February 4, 1953, 2 (emphasis added).

20. Rapoport, *Let's Play Two*, 66.

21. Tygiel, *Extra Bases*, 75; Lanctot, *Negro League Baseball*, 387; "Tiger Trade Rumor Has City Buzzing," *Detroit Tribune*, June 21, 1952, 3.

22. Watson Spoelstra, "Hoeft to Get Chance to Win Tiger Stripes," *Sporting News*, February 13, 1952, 25.

23. Luther Webb, "Tigers Would Buy Doby," *Detroit Tribune*, April 19, 1952, 3.

24. "Sports Speaking," *Detroit Tribune*, December 6, 1952, 7.

25. Armour, *Joe Cronin*, 153–55.

26. Tygiel, *Baseball's Great Experiment*, 261–63.

27. Lorenzo "Piper" Davis, "Piper Davis' Own Story as Told to Chic Feldman," *Scranton Tribune*, May 17, 1950, 25.

28. Golenbock, *Fenway*, 225.

29. Dan Daniel, "Majors Must Balance Budget—Weiss," *Sporting News*, July 30, 1952, 1.

30. Kahn, *Era 1947–1957*, 45.

31. Roscoe McGowan, "Jackie off Base in TV Rap, Say Yanks," *Sporting News*, December 10, 1952, 3.

32. McGowan, "Jackie off Base."

33. Dan Daniel, "Jackie off Base in TV Rap, Say Yanks," *Sporting News*, December 10, 1952, 3.

34. John Carmichael, "The Barber Shop," *Chicago Daily News*, December 3, 1952, 55.

35. Wendell Smith, "Wendell Smith's Sports Beat," *Pittsburgh Courier*, December 13, 1952, 13.

Chapter 12. The Arc of History

1. Wendell Smith, "Wendell Smith's Sports Beat," *Pittsburgh Courier*, January 24, 1953, 14.

2. Jerry Mitchell, *New York Post* column excerpted in "Quotes," *Sporting News*, April 1, 1953, 18.

3. Kahn, *Boys of Summer*, 173.

4. Swaine, *Integration of Major League Baseball*, 181.

5. Sam Lacy, "Cubs' Attitude Over Baker Is Baffling," *Baltimore Afro-American*, March 24, 1953, 15.

6. Wendell Smith, "Critics Roast Cubs About Gene Baker," *Pittsburgh Courier*, August 22, 1953, 14.

7. Smith, "Critics Roast Cubs."

8. Wilson, *Let's Play Two*, 37–38.

9. Rapaport, *Let's Play Two*, 70.

10. Rapoport, *Let's Play Two*, 70–71.

11. Wilson, *Let's Play Two*, 49.

12. Rapoport, *Let's Play Two*, 78–81.

13. Ernie Banks interviewed by Julieanna L. Richardson, July 18, 2000, The HistoryMakers Digital Archive, session 1, tape 3, stories 1 and 3, https://www.thehistorymakers.org/biography/ernie-banks-40.

14. Ernie Banks HistoryMakers interview.

15. Ed Prell, "Phils Blast Cubs, 4 Rookies, 16–4," *Chicago Tribune*, September 18, 1953, 51; Neil R. Gazel, "New Cubs Look Just Like Old," *Chicago Daily News*, September 18, 1953, 25; Jack R. Griffin, "Phils, Simmons Crush Cubs, 16–4," *Chicago Sun-Times*, September 18, 1953, 42; Banks and Enright, *Mr. Cub*, 79.

16. "Reports from Courier Sports Experts," *Pittsburgh Courier*, July 19, 1947, 15.

17. Bob Broeg, "Howard, Tapped by Yanks, Proves All-America Boy," *Sporting News*, October 28, 1953, 2.

18. "CSL Negro Players Eyed Cautiously," *Blytheville (AR) Courier News*, March 30, 1953, 17; "Negroes Ask to Be Judged on Abilities," *Northwest Arkansas News*, May 31, 1953, 7.

19. John J. Watkins, "Tugerson v. Haraway: Civil Rights and the Cotton States League," sabr.org/bioproj/topic/tugerson-v-haraway-civil-rights-and-the-cotton-states-league/; Peter Morris, Jim Tugerson SABR biography, sabr.org/bioproj/person/jim-tugerson/.

20. Watkins, "Tugerson vs. Haraway."

21. Watkins, "Tugerson v. Haraway."

22. Adelson, *Brushing Back Jim Crow*, 120.

23. Morris, Jim Tugerson SABR biography.

24. "3 Cicero Cops Win New Trial in '51 Riot Case," *Chicago Tribune*, March 10, 1953, 3.

25. Associated Press, "Dozen Cicero Negroes Sued for $1 Million," *Allentown Morning Call*, March 10, 1953, 1.

26. "Seven Months' War," *Time*, March 1, 1954, time.com/archive/6621820/races-seven-months-war/.

27. "Can't Take It Any Longer," *Chicago Defender*, May 15, 1954, 4.

28. Hirsch, *Making the Second Ghetto*, 246.

29. Hirsch, *Making the Second Ghetto*, 246.

Chapter 13. Keepin' On

1. Edgar Munzel, "A David Harum? A Trader Horn? Lane Makes 'Em Look Like Buns," *Sporting News*, February 18, 1953, 9.

2. In April 1960, when he was running the Cleveland Indians, Lane would make basically the same trade, swapping home-run king Rocky Colavito for batting champion Harvey Kuenn. The trade of Colavito, Cleveland's most popular player, would alienate millions of Indians fans and basically cost Lane his job.

3. Brent Kelley interview with Connie Johnson, February 2, 1990, sabr.org/interview/connie-johnson-1990/.

4. Neil Gazel, "Blue Monday for Chicago," *Chicago Daily News*, Monday, May 4, 1953, 20.

5. Honig, *Man in the Dugout*, 140.

6. Wendell Smith, "Chicago Stars Happy to Be out of South," *Pittsburgh Courier*, April 18, 1953, 14.

7. Campanella, *It's Good to Be Alive*, 120.

8. Gary Fink, email to author, May 16, 2022.

9. Edgar G. Brands, "Awards to Weiss, Stanky, Roberts," *Sporting News*, December 31, 1952, 1.

10. Bush and Nowlin, "Letter from Willie Mays in Commemoration of Jim Zapp," in *Bittersweet Goodbye*, 4–6.

11. Howard V. Millard, "Bait for Bugs," *Decatur Daily Review*, May 27, 1953, 14.

12. Klima, *Willie's Boys*, 58, 97.

13. Author interview with Sherman Jenkins, January 16, 2022.

14. George Raubacher, "Cubs' Opening Drill at Carlyle Cancelled by Rain," *Janesville Daily Gazette*, April 15, 1949, 12.

15. George Raubacher, "Cubs Idle for Second Day Because of Cold," *Janesville Daily Gazette*, April 16, 1949, 10.

16. Alvin Spearman, interviewed by Larry Crowe, January 16, 2003, The HistoryMakers Digital Archive, session 1, tape 4, story 5, https://www.thehistorymakers.org/biography/alvin-spearman-39.

17. Spearman interview, The HistoryMakers.

18. Author interview with Fabienne Anderson-Johnson, February 10, 2022.

19. Oscar Ruhl, "From the Ruhl Book," *Sporting News*, August 19, 1953, 14.

20. "Boyd Seen in Richard's 1954 Plans," *Chicago Defender*, January 23, 1954, 24.

21. Miñoso, Fernández, and Kleinfelder, *Extra Innings*, 58.

22. Corbett, *Wizard of Waxahachie*, 183–84.

23. Author interview with Warren Corbett, October 29, 2021.

24. Corbett interview.

25. Sam Lacy, "Hary Is Scary. . . . $28 per Foot. . . . I'll Take Paul," *Baltimore Afro-American*, August 23, 1960, 10.

26. Aaron and Wheeler, *I Had a Hammer*, 220.

27. Bob Vanderberg, "Though Late, First in Their Fields in Chicago," *Chicago Tribune*, March 31, 1997, 188; Koppett, *Man in the Dugout*, 156.

28. Corbett, *Wizard of Waxahachie*, 266, 283.

29. Author interview with Michelle Foster, March 9, 2022; Zminda, *Go-Go to Glory*, 2.

30. Honig, *Man in the Dugout*, 126.

31. Author interview with Goose Gossage, May 2, 2022.

Chapter 14. Bingo, Bango, and Baseball

1. Jacobson, *Carrying Jackie's Torch*, 105.

2. "Griffith to Move Farm Clubs Unless Negro 'Ban' Is Lifted," *Washington Star*, March 19, 1954, 54.

3. Gordon Cobbledick, "Plain Dealing," *Cleveland Plain Dealer*, January 10, 1954, 51.

4. Dan Daniels, "Ol' Case Earmarks Howard for No. 2 Backstopping Job," *Sporting News*, October 27, 1954, 11.

5. Author interview with Mark Armour, February 17, 2022.

6. Swaine, *Black Stars Who Made Baseball Whole*, 137.

7. Edgar Munzel, "Bang-Up Batting Labels Banks as Cub Rookie Star," *Sporting News*, March 24, 1954, 22.

8. Edgar Munzel, "Cavvy Sealed Fate by Giving P.K. Bare Facts About Bruins," *Sporting News*, April 7, 1954, 9.

9. In the April 18, 1951, game, Noble entered the game as a defensive replacement for the Giants at the start of the ninth inning; Márquez entered the game for the Braves as a pinch runner for the first batter of the inning.

10. Bill Johnson, Art Pennington monograph. Courtesy of Bill Johnson.

11. Bill Johnson, Art Pennington monograph.

12. Bill Johnson, Art Pennington SABR biography, sabr.org/bioproj/person/Art-Pennington/#sdendnote16anc.

13. Simkus, *Outsider Baseball*, 10–11.

14. John Carmichael, "Decides Wid Rates Chance," *Chicago Daily News*, March 30, 1954, 25.

15. John Carmichael, "The Barber Shop," *Chicago Daily News*, April 19, 1954, 13.

16. Edgar Munzel, "Bruins Hit Bingo on Banks-Baker Combo," *Sporting News*, May 26, 1954, 3.

17. Rapoport, *Let's Play Two*, 94.

18. Peary, *We Played the Game*, 250.

19. Edward Prell, "Better Days for the Cubs?" *Chicago Tribune*, April 3, 1955, 116; John C. Hoffman, "Cubs' Regular Infield Okay—But That's It," *Sporting News*, November 17, 1954, 11.

20. Prell, "Better Days for the Cubs?"

21. Wilson, *Let's Play Two*, 60, 58.

22. Banks and Enright, *Mr. Cub*, 82–83.

23. Ernie Banks, interviewed by Julieanna L. Richardson, July 18, 2000, The HistoryMakers Digital Archive, session 1, tape 3, story 2, https://www.the historymakers.org/biography/ernie-banks-40.

24. Peary, *We Played the Game*, 250, 285.

25. Ernie Banks, National Visionary Leadership Project Oral History Archive, https://www.loc.gov/item/2004695153/.

26. Rust, *Get That Nigger off the Field!* 138.

27. "No One to Blame," *Chicago Defender*, December 11, 1954, 9.

Chapter 15. Stormy Times

1. White and Dillow, *Uppity*, 65–66.

2. Charles Dexter, "Battey Up!" *Baseball Digest*, June 1961, 13–14.

3. Dexter, "Battey Up!" 14; Jerry Weiner, "Point Records Tremble as Preps Renew Action," *Hollywood Citizen-News*, January 3, 1951, 15.

4. J. Robinson, *Baseball Has Done It*, 189.

5. Ed Burns, "Boyd Swings Hot Bat While ChiSox Axe-Wielding Starts," *Sporting News*, March 31, 1954, 8.

6. Joe Reichler, "Bosox Called 'Most Improved' Team of Spring Training Play," *Sioux Falls Argus-Leader*, April 4, 1954, 37.

7. Adelson, *Brushing Back Jim Crow*, 121.

8. Adelson, *Brushing Back Jim Crow*, 123.

9. Adelson, *Brushing Back Jim Crow*, 125.

10. Adelson, *Brushing Back Jim Crow*, 126.

11. Martin Waldron, "Segregation Voted for City Sports," *Birmingham Post-Herald*, June 2, 1954, 1.

12. Moffi and Kronstadt, *Crossing the Line*, 54.

13. Wendell Smith, "Chi Fans Busy—Looking," *Pittsburgh Courier*, April 17, 1954, 15.

14. "Lead-Off Men on Writers' A.L. Lists," *Sporting News*, January 6, 1954, 2.

15. John Carmichael, "The Barber Shop," *Chicago Daily News*, March 26, 1954, 31.

16. J. G. Taylor Spink, "Looping the Loops," *Sporting News*, June 23, 1954, 2.

17. William Barry Furlong, "The White Sox Katzenjammer Kid," *Saturday Evening Post*, July 17, 1954, 30.

18. Furman Bisher, "Major-League Minnie," *Sport*, August 1954, 44.

19. Bisher, "Major-League Minnie."

20. Brioso, *Last Seasons in Havana*, 69, "Miñoso al bate" can be heard at www.youtube.com/watch?v=Md9rzKouzZc.

21. Edgar Munzel, "Chisox Just an Also-Ran Without Miñoso—Richards," *Sporting News*, September 1, 1954, 13.

22. Peary, *We Played the Game*, 279. Michaels attempted a comeback in

spring training in 1955, but collapsed during a workout and was advised to retire by his doctors.

23. Miñoso and Fagen, *Just Call Me Minnie*, 54.

24. Associated Press, "Miñoso Accused in Paternity Suit," *Boston Globe*, May 19, 1954, 15; "Miñoso Denies He's Daddy of Waitress' Baby," *Chicago Defender*, May 29, 1954, 1.

25. "Miñoso Denies He's Daddy of Waitress' Baby"; "Miñoso Denies Breach of Promise Charge," *Chicago Daily News*, June 21, 1954, 24.

26. "Does Minnie Take a Wife—or Not?" *Chicago Daily News*, September 23, 1954.

27. "Miñoso's Wife Wins Divorce," *Belleville (IL) News-Democrat*, December 7, 1954.

28. Associated Negro Press, "Judge Says Miñoso's 'Ex' Must Quit Job," *Pittsburgh Courier*, December 18, 1954, 3.

29. Associated Negro Press, "Judge Says Miñoso's 'Ex' Must Quit Job."

30. Barbara Swader, *TAN* article, summarized in *Detroit Tribune*, May 21, 1955, 6.

31. "Barbara Claims Miñoso's in $1,950 Alimony Slump," *Chicago Defender*, July 30, 1955, 1; "Says Ex-Wife Puts Miñoso in Hit Slump," *Chicago Tribune*, August 5, 1955, 47.

32. Miñoso and Fagen, *Just Call Me Minnie*, 85–87.

33. Miñoso and Fagen, *Just Call Me Minnie*, 87.

Chapter 16. Baseball's New Superstar

1. "How Much Is Freedom Worth?" *Chicago Defender*, March 12, 1955, 9.

2. "Group to Study Trumbull Pk Tension," *Chicago Daily News*, July 1, 1955, 3.

3. Hirsch, *Making the Second Ghetto*, 242–43.

4. "Crowds View Body of Kidnaped [*sic*] Boy," *Chicago Daily News*, September 3, 1955, 1.

5. A. S. "Doc" Young, "Padres' Sad Sam Jones Helps Keep San Diego Fans Happy," *Sporting News*, June 20, 1951, 16.

6. Hal Lebovitz, "'You'll See a Lot of Sam Jones in '52,' Says Lopez," *Sporting News*, October 10, 1951, 29.

7. Robert Creamer, "National League Baseball," *Sports Illustrated*, April 11, 1955, 25.

8. "19th Hole: The Readers Take Over," *Sports Illustrated*, April 25, 1955, 74.

9. John P. Carmichael, "The Barber Shop," *Chicago Daily News*, June 27, 1955, 16.

10. "Hit in Face by Pitch, Shows That He Knows About Noses," *Sporting News*, July 20, 1955, 3.

11. Wilson, *Let's Play Two*, 85.

12. Banks and Enright, *Mr. Cub*, 84; Rapoport, *Let's Play Two*, 217.

13. Rory Costello, Sam Jones SABR biography, sabr.org/bioproj/person/sam-jones.

14. Edward Prell, "Story of Cub's No Hitter," "Jones Tells of Fight for Baseball Life," *Chicago Tribune*, May 13, 1955, 1, 45.

15. Edward Prell, "Jones Reveals He Took Page Out of Satch's Book," *Chicago Tribune*, May 14, 1955, 47; "Jones Pitches No-Hit Game for Cubs!" *Chicago American*, May 13, 1955, 14; Marvin Quinn, "Jones Stops Chicago in Its Tracks," *Chicago American*, May 13, 1955, 68.

16. Joe King, "Clouting Him," *Sporting News*, June 22, 1955, 10.

17. Author interview with Don Kaiser, June 23, 2022.

18. Author interview with Hobie Landrith, June 16, 2022.

19. Miñoso, Fernandez, and Kleinfelder, *Extra Innings*, 91–92.

20. "His Son, 2, Doesn't Like Minnie's Hitting Slump," *Chicago Sun-Times*, August 3, 1955, 60.

21. A. S. "Doc" Young, "Is Dirty Baseball Killing Negro Stars?" *Jet*, June 30, 1955, 56.

22. John C. Hoffman, "Marion Fumes as Minnie Flops," *Chicago Sun-Times*, September 16, 1955, 63.

23. Hoffman, "Marion Fumes"; Miñoso and Fagen, *Just Call Me Minnie*, 56.

24. Edgar Munzel, "Lane, as Chisox G.M., Game's Top Trader," *Sporting News*, October 5, 1955, 3.

25. J. Robinson, *Baseball Has Done It*, 24.

Epilogue

1. Richard Dozer, "Cubs Sign Negro Coach," *Chicago Tribune*, May 30, 1962, 47; O'Neil with Wulf and Conrads, *I Was Right on Time*, 213–14.

2. Author interview with Jim Kaat, April 3, 2022; Patrick Reuss, "A Celebration Without a Few Absent Friends," *Minneapolis Star Tribune*, August 19, 2005, C1.

3. Bob Rives, Bob Boyd SABR biography, sabr.org/bioproj/person/Bob-Boyd.

4. Alan Cohen, Connie Johnson SABR biography, sabr.org/bioproj/person/connie-johnson/#_edn42.

5. Richard Cuicchi, John Hairston SABR biography, sabr.org/bioproj/person/john-hairston.

6. Sam Hairston, Birmingham Black Barons Oral History, bplonline.org/virtual/ContentDMSubjectBrowse.aspx?subject=Hairston%2C%20Sam%2C%201920-1997.

7. Warren Corbett, Paul Richards SABR biography, sabr.org/bioproj/person/paul-richards.

8. Author interview with Vern Law, June 27, 2022.

9. Associated Press, "Polio Victim Remembers and Sad Sam Weeps," *Boston Globe*, October 7, 1971, 58.

10. Associated Press, "Cicero Suits Settled," *Chattanooga Daily Times*, April 15, 1957, 9.

11. James D. Robenalt, "A Plane Crashing 50 Years Ago Changed the Course of U.S. History," www.washingtonpost.com/history/2022/12/08/dorothy-hunt-united-crash-watergate.

12. Paul Weingarten, "And Now, the Minority View . . .," *Chicago Tribune*, July 13, 1986, sec. 10, p. 27; author interview with Joe Peyronnin, March 8, 2022.

13. Pioneers of Philadelphia Broadcasting, interview with Harvey Clark, www.youtube.com/watch?v=zl7IEBQWLvwl.

14. Henry Locke, "Calls Cicero Bias Action 'Long Overdue'," *Chicago Defender*, January 24, 1983, 3; Andrew Fegelman, "Cicero Accepts U.S. Plan to Weed out Bias," *Chicago Tribune*, May 14, 1986, 1.

15. Mark Armour, "The Effects of Integration, 1947–1986," *Baseball Research Journal* 36 (2007): 53–54.

16. "MLB Has Lowest Percentage of Black Baseball Players in 3 Decades: Report," www.newsweek.com/mlb-has-lowest-percentage-black-baseball-players-3-decades-report-1708382.

17. Bob Nightengale, "MLB's Percentage of Black Players Is the Lowest Since 1955. What's Baseball Doing to Fix That?" www.usatoday.com/story/sports/mlb/columnist/bob-nightengale/2023/04/14/mlb-percentage-black-players-baseball-jackie-robinson-day/11657961002/.

18. Rapoport, *Let's Play Two*, 149.

19. Durocher and Linn, *Nice Guys Finish Last*, 365–66.

20. Fred Mitchell, "If Racial Bias Hurt, He Never Showed It," *Chicago Tribune*, January 25, 2015, 3–7.

21. Miñoso, Fernandez, and Kleinfelder, *Extra Innings*, 103.

22. Author interviews with Charlie Miñoso, February 21, 2022, and January 11, 2024.

23. Jules Tygiel is quoted in Jacobson, *Carrying Jackie's Torch*, 245.

24. Tygiel, *Baseball's Great Experiment*, 285–86.

25. Dan Daniel, "Nats on Look-out for Negro Stars: 'How Did We Miss Miñoso?'" *Sporting News*, July 4, 1951, 11.

Bibliography

Archives and Manuscripts

Kenneth Spencer Research Library, University of Kansas
  T. Y. Baird Papers
National Baseball Hall of Fame and Museum, Cooperstown, New York
  Integration Correspondence and Clippings
  League and MLB Joint Meeting Transcripts
  Papers of Jules Tygiel
  Wendell Smith Papers

Books

Aaron, Hank, with Lonnie Wheeler. *I Had a Hammer: The Hank Aaron Story*. New York: HarperCollins, 1991.

Adelson, Bruce. *Brushing Back Jim Crow: The Integration of Minor-League Baseball in the American South*. Charlottesville: University of Virginia Press, 1999.

Allen, Lee. *The World Series: A Narrative Account of Baseball's Annual Classic from the First Series to the Present*. New York: Putnam, 1969.

Alou, Felipe, with Peter Kerasotis. *Alou: My Baseball Journey*. Lincoln: University of Nebraska Press, 2018.

Armour, Mark. *Joe Cronin: A Baseball Life*. Lincoln: University of Nebraska Press, 2010.

Banks, Ernie, and Jim Enright. *Mr. Cub*. Chicago: Follett, 1971.

Bjarkman, Peter C. *Baseball with a Latin Beat*. Jefferson, NC: McFarland, 1994.

Boehm, Roy, and Charles W. Sasser. *First Seal*. New York: Pocket Books, 1997.

Bozeka, George. *The 1951 Los Angeles Rams Profiles of the NFL's First West Coast Champions*. Jefferson, NC: McFarland, 2022.

Branson, Douglas M. *Greatness in the Shadows: Larry Doby and the Integration of the American League*. Lincoln: University of Nebraska Press, 2016.

Breton, Marcós, and José Luis Villegas. *Away Games: The Life and Times of a Latin Ball Player*. New York: Simon & Schuster, 1999.

Brioso, César. *Last Seasons in Havana: The Castro Revolution and the End of Professional Baseball in Cuba*. Lincoln: University of Nebraska Press, 2019.

Burgos, Adrian Jr. *Playing America's Game: Baseball, Latinos and the Color Line*. Berkeley: University of California Press, 2007.

Bush, Frederick C., and Bill Nowlin, eds. *Bittersweet Goodbye: The Barons, the Grays and the 1948 Negro League World Series*. Phoenix: Society for American Baseball Research, 2017.

Campanella, Roy. *It's Good to Be Alive*. Boston: Little, Brown, 1959.

Castle, George. *The Million to One Team: Why the Chicago Cubs Haven't Won a Pennant Since 1945*. South Bend, IN: Diamond Communications, 2000.

Cepeda, Orlando, with Herb Fagen. *Baby Bull: From Hardball to Hard Time and Back*. Dallas: Taylor, 1998.

Clark, Dick, and Larry Lester. *The Negro Leagues Book: A Monumental Work from the Negro Leagues Committee of the Society for American Baseball Research*. Cleveland: Society for American Baseball Research, 1994.

Clark, Kristine Setting. *Undefeated, Untied, and Uninvited: A Documentary of the 1951 University of San Francisco Dons Football Team*. Torrance, CA: Griffin, 2002.

Constantino, Rocco. *Beyond Baseball's Color Barrier: The Story of African Americans in Major League Baseball, Past, Present, and Future*. Lanham MD: Rowman & Littlefield, 2021.

Corbett, Warren. *The Wizard of Waxahachie: Paul Richards and the End of Baseball as We Knew It*. Dallas: Southern Methodist University Press, 2009.

Demas, Lane. *Integrating the Gridiron: Black Civil Rights and American College Football*. New Brunswick, NJ: Rutgers University Press, 2010.

DeRose, Camille. *The Camille DeRose Story: The True Story of the Cicero Riots*. Chicago: DeRose Publishing, 1953.

Dickson, Paul. *Bill Veeck: Baseball's Greatest Maverick*. New York: Walker, 2012.

Dixon, Phil S. *The Dizzy and Daffy Dean Barnstorming Tour: Race, Media, and America's National Pastime*. Lanham, MD: Rowman & Littlefield, 2019.

Durocher, Leo, with Ed Linn. *Nice Guys Finish Last*. New York: Simon & Schuster, 1975.

Early, Gerald L. *A Level Playing Field: African American Athletes and the Republic of Sports*. Cambridge, MA: Harvard University Press, 2011.

Echevarría, Roberto González. *The Pride of Havana: A History of Cuban Baseball*. New York: Oxford University Press, 1999.

Epstein, Daniel Mark. *Nat King Cole*. Boston: Northeastern University Press, 1999.

Essington, Amy. *The Integration of the Pacific Coast League: Race and Baseball on the West Coast*. Lincoln: University of Nebraska Press, 2018.

Figueredo, Jorge S. *Who's Who in Cuban Baseball, 1878–1961*. Jefferson, NC: McFarland, 2003.

Forman, Sean, and Cecilia M. Tan, eds. *The Negro Leagues Are Major Leagues: Essays and Research for Overdue Recognition*. Phoenix: Society for American Baseball Research, 2021.

Frick, Ford C. *Games, Asterisks, and People: Memoirs of a Lucky Fan*. New York: Crown, 1973.

Garland, Emily Allen. *Bittersweet Memories: A Memoir*. Bloomington, IN: Authorhouse, 2003.

Gietschier, Steven P. *Baseball: The Turbulent Midcentury Years*. Lincoln: University of Nebraska Press, 2023.

Golenbock, Peter. *Dynasty: The New York Yankees, 1949–1964*. Englewood Cliffs, NJ: Prentice Hall, 1975.

Golenbock, Peter. *Fenway: An Unexpurgated History of the Boston Red Sox*. New York: Putnam's, 1992.

Golenbock, Peter. *Wrigleyville: A Magical History Tour of the Chicago Cubs*. New York: St. Martin's, 1996.

Green, Ben. *Spinning the Globe: The Rise, Fall and Return to Greatness of the Harlem Globetrotters*. New York: Armistad, 2006.

Heaphy, Leslie, ed. *Black Baseball and Chicago: Essays on the Players, Teams and Games*. Jefferson, NC: McFarland, 2006.

Henninger, Thom. *Tony Oliva: The Life and Times of a Minnesota Twins Legend*. Minneapolis: University of Minnesota Press, 2015.

Hirsch, Arnold R. *Making the Second Ghetto: Race and Housing in Chicago, 1940–1960*. Chicago: University of Chicago Press, 2021.

Hogan, Lawrence D. *Shades of Glory: The Negro Leagues and the Story of African-American Baseball*. Washington, DC: National Geographic, 2006.

Holway, John. *Voices from the Great Black Baseball Leagues*, rev. ed. Mineola, NY: Dover, 2010.

Honig, Donald. *The Man in the Dugout: Fifteen Big League Managers Speak Their Minds*. Lincoln: University of Nebraska Press, 1977.

Hudson, Lynn M. *West of Jim Crow: The Fight Against California's Color Line*. Urbana: University of Illinois Press, 2020.

Jacobson, Steve. *Carrying Jackie's Torch: The Players Who Integrated Baseball—and America*. Chicago: Lawrence Hill, 2007.

Jenkins, Sherman L. *Ted Strong Jr.: The Untold Story of an Original Globetrotter and Negro Leagues All-Star*. Lanham, MD: Rowman & Littlefield, 2016.

Johnson, James W. *The Black Bruins: The Remarkable Lives of UCLA's Jackie Robinson, Woody Strode, Tom Bradley, Kenny Washington and Ray Bartlett*. Lincoln: University of Nebraska Press, 2017.

Johnson, Lloyd, and Miles Wolff, eds. *Encyclopedia of Minor League Baseball*, 3rd ed. Durham, NC: Baseball America, 2007.

Kahn, Roger. *The Boys of Summer*. New York: Harper & Row, 1971.

Kahn, Roger. *The Era 1947–1957: When the Yankees, the Giants, and the Dodgers Ruled the World*. Lincoln: University of Nebraska Press, 2002.

Kahn, Roger. *Into My Own: The Remarkable People and Events That Shaped a Life*. New York: Thomas Dunne, 2006.

Kauffman, David. "Did Bud Fowler Almost Break the Major-League Color Line in 1888?" In *The National Pastime—2023 Edition*, edited by Cecilia M. Tan, 76–77. Phoenix: Society of American Baseball Research, 2023.

Kelley, Brent. *Baseball's Biggest Blunder: The Bonus Rule of 1953–1957*. Lanham, MD: Scarecrow, 1997.

Kelley, Brent. *The Negro Leagues Revisited: Conversations with 66 More Baseball Heroes*. Jefferson, NC: McFarland, 2000.

Kelley, Brent. *Voices from the Negro Leagues: Conversations with 52 Baseball Standouts*. Jefferson, NC: McFarland, 1998.

Klima, John. *Willie's Boys: The 1948 Birmingham Black Barons, the Last Negro League World Series, and the Making of a Baseball Legend*. Hoboken, NJ: Wiley, 2009.

Koppett, Leonard. *The Man in the Dugout: Baseball's Top Managers and How They Got That Way*. Philadelphia: Temple University Press, 2000.

Krist, Gary. *City of Scoundrels: The 12 Days of Disaster That Gave Birth to Modern Chicago*. New York: Broadway, 2012.

Lacy, Sam. "Indians' Tan Trio Compelled to Walk to Ballpark by Bigoted Texas Taxis." In *Black Writers/Black Baseball: An Anthology of Articles from Black Sportswriters Who Covered the Negro Leagues*, edited by Jim Reisler. Jefferson, NC: McFarland, 2007.

Lanctot, Neil. *Negro League Baseball: The Rise and Ruin of a Black Institution*. Philadelphia: University of Pennsylvania Press, 2004.

Lester, Larry. *Black Baseball's National Showcase: The East-West All-Star Game, 1933–1962*, expanded ed. Kansas City, MO: NoirTech Research, 2023.

Lindberg, Richard C. *Stealing First in a Two-Team Town: The White Sox from Comiskey to Reinsdorf*. Champaign, IL: Sagamore, 1994.

Lowenfish, Lee. *Branch Rickey: Baseball's Ferocious Gentleman*. Lincoln: University of Nebraska Press, 2009.

Malloy, Jerry, ed. *Sol White's History of Colored Baseball, with Other Documents on the Early Black Game, 1886–1935*. Lincoln: University of Nebraska Press, 1996.

Marshall, William. *Baseball's Pivotal Era: 1945–1951*. Lexington: University of Kentucky Press, 1999.

Miller, Marvin. *A Whole Different Ballgame: The Sport and Business of Baseball*. New York: Birch Lane, 1991.

Miñoso, Minnie, with Ferando Fernández and Robert Kleinfelder. *Extra Innings: My Life in Baseball*. Chicago: Regnery Gateway, 1983.

Miñoso, Minnie, with Herb Fagen. *Just Call Me Minnie: My Six Decades in Baseball*. Champaign, IL: Sagamore, 1994.

Moffi, Larry, and Jonathan Kronstadt. *Crossing the Line: Black Major Leaguers, 1947–1959*. Iowa City: University of Iowa Press, 1994.

Moore, Joseph Thomas. *Larry Doby: The Struggle of the American League's First Black Player*. Mineola, NY: Dover, 1988.

Moore, Natalie Y. *The South Side: A Portrait of Chicago and American Segregation*. New York: St. Martin's, 2016.

Moore, Terence. *The Real Hank Aaron: An Intimate Look at the Life and Legacy of the Home Run King*. Chicago: Triumph, 2022.

Nowlin, Bill. *Tom Yawkey: Patriarch of the Red Sox*. Lincoln: University of Nebraska Press, 2018.

O'Neil, Buck, with Steve Wulf and David Conrads. *I Was Right on Time: My Journey from the Negro Leagues to the Majors*. New York: Simon & Schuster, 1996.

Parker, Reverend Wheeler, Jr., and Christopher Benson. *A Few Days of Trouble: Revelations on the Journey to Justice for My Cousin and Friend, Emmett Till*. New York: One World, 2023.

Patterson, William L. *The Man Who Cried Genocide*. New York: International, 2017.

Peary, Danny, ed. *We Played the Game: 65 Players Remember Baseball's Greatest Era, 1947–1964*. New York: Hyperion, 1994.

Posnanski, Joe. *The Baseball 100*. New York: Avid Reader, 2021.

Rains, Rob. *Taking Flight: The St. Louis Cardinals and the Building of Baseball's Best Franchise*. Chicago: Triumph, 2016.

Rampersad, Arnold. *Jackie Robinson: A Biography*. New York: Knopf, 1997.

Rapoport, Ron. *Let's Play Two: The Legend of Mr. Cub; The Life of Ernie Banks*. New York: Hachette, 2019.

Reisler, Jim, ed. *Black Writers/Black Baseball: An Anthology of Articles from Black Sportswriters Who Covered the Negro Leagues*. Jefferson, NC: McFarland, 2007.

Riley, James A. *The Biographical Encyclopedia of the Negro Leagues*. New York: Carroll & Graf, 1994.

Robinson, Eddie, with C. Paul Rogers III. *Lucky Me: My Sixty-Five Years in Baseball*. Lincoln: University of Nebraska Press, 2011.

Robinson, Jackie. *Baseball Has Done It*. Brooklyn, NY: Ig, 2005.

Robinson, Jackie. *I Never Had It Made: An Autobiography*. New York: HarperCollins, 1995.

Royal, Alice C., with Mickey Ellinger and Scott Bradley. *Allensworth: The Freedom Colony*. Berkeley, CA: Heyday, 2008.

Rust, Art, Jr. *"Get That Nigger off the Field!" An Informal History of the Black Man in Baseball*. New York: Delacorte, 1974.

Seymour, Harold, and Dorothy Seymour. *Baseball: The Golden Age*. New York: Oxford University Press, 1971.

Shelton, Lynn M. *West of Jim Crow: The Fight Against California's Color Line*. Urbana: University of Illinois Press, 2020.

Sickels, John. *Bob Feller: Ace of the Greatest Generation*. Washington, DC: Brassey's, 2004.

Silber, Irwin. *Press Box Red: The Story of Lester Rodney, The Communist Who Helped Break the Color Line in Sports*. Philadelphia: Temple University Press, 2003.

Simkus, Scott. *Outsider Baseball: The Weird World of Hardball on the Fringe,
1876–1950*. Chicago: Chicago Review Press, 2014.

Snyder, John. *Cubs Journal: Year by Year and Day by Day with the Cubs Since
1876*. Cincinnati: Clerisy, 2008.

Snyder, John. *White Sox Journal: Year by Year and Day by Day with the Chicago
White Sox Since 1901*. Cincinnati: Clerisy, 2009.

Spear, Allan H. *Black Chicago: The Making of a Negro Ghetto, 1890–1920*. Chicago: University of Chicago Press, 1967.

Swaine, Rick. *The Black Stars Who Made Baseball Whole: The Jackie Robinson
Generation in the Major Leagues, 1947–1959*. Jefferson, NC: McFarland, 2009.

Swaine, Rick. *The Integration of Major League Baseball*. Jefferson, NC: McFarland, 2006.

Swanton, Barry. *The Mandak League: Haven for Former Negro League Ballplayers, 1950–1957*. Jefferson, NC: McFarland, 2006.

Tan, Cecilia M., ed. *The National Pastime: 2023 Edition*. Phoenix: Society of
American Baseball Research, 2023.

Taylor, Dan. *Walking Alone: The Untold Story of Football Pioneer Kenny Washington*. Lanham, MD: Rowman & Littlefield, 2022.

Thorn, John, Pete Palmer, and Michael Gershman, eds. *Total Baseball: The
Official Encyclopedia of Major League Baseball*, 7th ed. Kingston, NY: Total
Sports, 2001.

Tuttle, William M. Jr. *Race Riot: Chicago in the Summer of 1919*. Urbana: University of Illinois Press, 1996.

Tygiel, Jules. *Baseball's Great Experiment: Jackie Robinson and His Legacy*.
New York: Oxford University Press, 1983.

Tygiel, Jules. *Extra Bases: Reflections on Jackie Robinson, Race, and Baseball
History*. Lincoln: University of Nebraska Press, 2002.

Tygiel, Jules, ed. *The Jackie Robinson Reader: Perspectives on an American
Hero*. New York: Dutton, 1997.

Vanderberg, Bob. *Sox: From Lane and Fain to Zisk and Fisk*. Chicago: Chicago
Review Press, 1994.

Veeck, Bill, with Ed Linn. *Veeck—as in Wreck: The Chaotic Career of Baseball's
Incorrigible Maverick*. New York: Putnam, 1962.

Vincent, David, Lyle Spatz, and David W. Smith. *The Midsummer Classic:
The Complete History of Baseball's All-Star Game*. Lincoln: University of
Nebraska Press, 2001.

Ward, Geoffey C., and Ken Burns. *Baseball: An Illustrated History*. New York:
Knopf, 1994.

White, Bill, with Gordon Dillow. *Uppity: My Untold Story About the Games
People Play*. New York: Grand Central, 2012.

Wilson, Doug. *Let's Play Two: The Life and Times of Ernie Banks*. Lanham,
MD: Rowman & Littlefield, 2019.

Zminda, Don, ed. *Go-Go to Glory: The 1959 Chicago White Sox*. Phoenix: Society
for American Baseball Research, 2019.

Websites

Ancestry.com
Baseball-Reference.com
Geneologybank.com
Newspapers.com
Retrosheet.org
SABR.org
Thehistorymakers.org

Index

DON ZMINDA is a sports historian and the former vice president and director of research at STATS LLC. He is the author of *Double Plays and Double Crosses: The Black Sox and Baseball in 1920* and *The Legendary Harry Caray: Baseball's Greatest Salesman.*

The University of Illinois Press
is a founding member of the
Association of University Presses.

———————————————————

Composed in 10.5/13 Mercury Text
with Gotham display
by Jim Proefrock
at the University of Illinois Press

University of Illinois Press
1325 South Oak Street
Champaign, IL 61820-6903
www.press.uillinois.edu